Real-World LEARNING FRAMEWORK

FOR ELEMENTARY SCHOOLS

Digital Tools and Practical Strategies for Successful Implementation

Marge Maxwell

Rebecca Stobaugh

Janet Lynne Tassell

Solution Tree | Press

a division of
Solution Tree

555 North Morton Street
Bloomington, IN 47404
800.733.6786 (toll free) / 812.336.7700
FAX: 812.336.7790

email: info@SolutionTree.com
SolutionTree.com

Visit **go.SolutionTree.com/instruction** to download the free reproducibles in this book.

Printed in the United States of America

21   20   19   18   17   1   2   3   4   5

Library of Congress Cataloging-in-Publication Data

Names: Maxwell, Marge, author. | Stobaugh, Rebecca, author. | Tassell, Janet
    Lynne, author.

Title: Real-world learning framework for elementary schools : digital tools
    and practical strategies for successful implementation / Marge Maxwell,
    Rebecca Stobaugh, and Janet Lynne Tassell.

Description: Bloomington, IN : Solution Tree Press, [2017] | Includes
    bibliographical references and index.

Identifiers: LCCN 2016052042 | ISBN 9781943874514 (perfect bound)

Subjects: LCSH: Education, Elementary--United States. | Education,
    Elementary--United States--Computer network resources. | Education,
    Elementary--Curricula--United States.

Classification: LCC LA219 .M27 2017 | DDC 372.0973--dc23 LC record available at
https://lccn.loc.gov/2016052042

Solution Tree
Jeffrey C. Jones, CEO
Edmund M. Ackerman, President

Solution Tree Press
President and Publisher: Douglas M. Rife
Editorial Director: Sarah Payne-Mills
Managing Production Editor: Caroline Weiss
Senior Production Editor: Suzanne Kraszewski
Senior Editor: Amy Rubenstein
Copy Editor: Ashante K. Thomas
Proofreader: Jessi Finn
Text Designer: Laura Cox
Cover Designer: Rian Anderson
Editorial Assistants: Jessi Finn and Kendra Slayton

Acknowledgments

We would like to thank the teachers and educators who contributed projects for this book: Ashley Burnette, Hayley Clayton, Tara Cox, Carolyn Crowe, Savannah Denning, Shannon East, Sheriden Edwards, Randa Gary, Angela Gunter, Katelyn Heupel, Cindy Hundley, Rhea Isenberg, Ameliah Leonhardt, Jessica Nissen Bauer, Sam Northern, Andrea Paganelli, Anthony Paganelli, Kelli Ralston, Lydia Renfro, Meghan Rhoads, Stephanie Ross, Morgan Tierney, Gabe VanCappellen, and Lena White.

A special thank-you to Savannah Denning for her keen eye in editing for us internally and for trying out many of the real-world projects and editing the design to final format. We would also like to thank Wesley Waddle and Hart County Schools for the lesson-plan format used in the projects.

Solution Tree Press would like to thank the following reviewers:

Paula Hagan
PBL Coordinator
DeSoto Independent School District
DeSoto, Texas

Beth Johnson
K–12 Technology Instructional Specialist
Broken Arrow Public Schools
Broken Arrow, Oklahoma

Patricia Whitfield-Madison
Instructional Technology Coach
Tulsa Public Schools
Tulsa, Oklahoma

Visit **go.SolutionTree.com/instruction**
to download the free reproducibles in this book.

Table of Contents

Reproducible pages are in italics.

Part II 121

About the Authors

Marge Maxwell, PhD, is a professor of educational technology at Western Kentucky University. She has been helping educators implement technology into teaching and learning for more than thirty years. Her focus is on real-world learning, incorporating critical thinking, high student engagement, and technology.

Marge is the author of several research articles, book chapters, and monographs, and is coeditor of a six-book series, *Explore the Core: Math Problem Solving and Projects*. She has presented numerous research papers at regional, national, and international conferences. Since she began teaching online courses, she has researched and published on the subject of students' sense of community in virtual classes.

Marge earned a bachelor's degree in special education from the University of Georgia as well as a master's degree in exceptional education and a doctorate in curriculum and instruction from the University of North Carolina at Chapel Hill.

Rebecca Stobaugh, PhD, is an associate professor at Western Kentucky University, where she teaches assessment and unit-planning courses in the teacher education program. She also supervises first-year teachers and consults with school districts on critical thinking, instructional strategies, assessment, technology integration, and other topics. Previously, she served as a middle and high school teacher and a middle school principal.

Rebecca has authored several books, including *Assessing Critical Thinking in Middle and High Schools* and *Assessing Critical Thinking in Elementary Schools*. Rebecca regularly serves on accreditation teams and writes grants to support K–12 professional development. She is the executive director and former president of Kentucky ASCD (Association for Supervision and Curriculum Development). Rebecca received the 2004 Social Studies Teacher of the Year Award from the Kentucky Council for the Social Studies.

She earned a bachelor's degree from Georgetown College, a master's degree from the University of Kentucky, and a doctorate in K–12 education leadership from the University of Louisville.

Janet Lynne Tassell, PhD, is an associate professor at Western Kentucky University, where she teaches elementary mathematics methods and directs the Elementary Mathematics Specialist Endorsement program. Janet also teaches identification and current issues courses for the university's gifted and talented master's program. She taught a semester abroad at Harlaxton College in England.

Janet has taught mathematics at the middle school and high school levels. She spent fourteen years as a gifted education coordinator and director of learning and assessment, working with K–12 teachers in curriculum and professional development. She was codirector of the Toyota Math and Technology Leadership Academy and professional development coordinator for the Javits grant Project GEMS (Gifted Education for Math and Science) initiative for grades 3–6 students. She coauthored a chapter on mathematics differentiation menus and techniques. She also led a team of fourteen authors to design and write six books for grades 1–6 students to delve deeper into the Common Core mathematics standards.

Janet received a bachelor's degree in secondary mathematics education, and both a master's degree and a doctorate in curriculum and instruction with a mathematics and gifted education focus from Indiana University.

To book Marge Maxwell, Rebecca Stobaugh, or Janet Lynne Tassell for professional development, contact pd@SolutionTree.com.

Introduction

Gracie walks into her fourth-grade elementary classroom at the beginning of the school year, eager to be progressing to a grade level with more complex and exciting academics. However, she finds that the content is taught through excessive worksheets and old textbooks. Gracie has never had an opportunity to perform a task, do a project, or use hands-on manipulatives to solve real-world problems; she has only solved problems from textbooks. She sees no connection to science, mathematics, and technology that could help the content come to life. Technology is used only for taking quizzes, locating information, and word processing. The teacher uses the interactive whiteboard to show a PowerPoint presentation or asks students to come to the board one at a time to circle an answer. The teacher typically presents the content for the lesson as direct instruction while the students sit in rows listening. Gracie always works alone, never partnering with another student or working in a group on any type of assignment or discussion. When Gracie or another student asks a question, the teacher is always the one to answer, with no discussion. Gracie had hoped to experience the real-world problem solving and interactive classroom discussions and explorations that her friend at another school talks about. She tells her brother that mathematics is just all about memorizing the facts and racing to be the first one finished on a timed multiplication test. She tells her mom that they never get to experience science; they just watch videos or teacher demonstrations.

Students should be excited about learning! They desire assignments with dimensions and substance that make them want to learn more on the topic. They naturally crave meaning when they have the opportunity to be inspired in a school that cultivates a real-world learning environment. Unfortunately, as Neil Postman and Charles Weingartner (1969) assert in *Teaching as a Subversive Activity*, students have been known to enter school as question marks and leave as periods.

Teachers have the power to help students graduate as question marks, with a love of learning as their fuel. While some teachers offer worksheets, others create authentic learning connections for students. In preschool, children ask their parents an average of one hundred questions a day, while questioning decreases through middle school (Bronson & Merryman, 2010). Some teachers are embracing real-world learning to encourage students to ask questions.

Do you want to inspire student inquiry to boost student engagement and authentic learning? If the answer is yes, then ask yourself the following questions.

- Have I given my students the opportunity to show me what interests them? Have I incorporated their interests into my instruction and lesson planning?
- Do I incorporate standards in real-world activities?
- Do I challenge students with provocative questions?
- Are my students working on teacher-directed tasks and projects in isolation?
- Do my students work on technology that does not enrich their learning nor expand on the content?

This book helps you answer these questions and address the concerns they may reveal.

In a real-world environment, creation is not a formulaic set of steps but a messy process. Often, creation of important work involves starting and stopping—revising all the while. If we consider an artist designing a masterpiece, we can envision the artist beginning with personal inspiration, addressing personal questions, working from a blank canvas, and then problem solving to come up with a pathway to brilliance. The masterpiece is the result of the artist's many failures and revisions. The term *create* means bringing something unique into being that did not previously exist and would not evolve on its own. Based on this concept, the instructional framework this book introduces is termed the Create Excellence Framework. With this framework, teachers and students have the opportunity to plan project-based instruction that is comprehensive, pulling from the real world by utilizing cognitive complexity, student engagement, and technology integration.

Teachers must be open to meaningful learning, remembering that the learning will be a messy process, as it is in the complex and often chaotic real-world environment. Students' projects will be personalized and unique. This requires teachers to have flexibility and focus as they plan, keeping in mind the ultimate goal is to support learning that leads to brilliance! As we consider the real world's meaningful impact on education, teachers and students need a tool to help them achieve the best-designed project.

The Create Excellence Framework for Real-World Learning

Researcher Christopher Moersch (2002) developed the H.E.A.T. Framework (higher-order thinking, engaged learning, authentic learning, and technology integration), and we have adapted it to define each component, emphasizing the teacher's need to *create* an experience for the students (Maxwell, Constant, Stobaugh, & Tassell, 2011). The resulting Create Excellence Framework is a research-based, lesson-plan framework that can guide students, parents, and teachers in thinking about learning in a different, yet comprehensive, way (Tassell, Maxwell, & Stobaugh, 2013).

The foundation of the Create Excellence Framework and chapter structure of this book provide readers with a deep understanding of how real-world learning, supported by cognitive complexity, student engagement, and technology integration, can support student learning (see figure I.1). The purpose of this book is to help teachers improve instruction for students by designing instructional tasks that include these four key components. This framework gives us a new lens through which to look at how to plan instruction and balance the demands of rigorous standards. It incorporates the key components necessary to create engaging and meaningful lessons for student learning. The Create Excellence Framework is intended to be a tool to help with enhancing the current curriculum. Throughout the school year, teachers can utilize the framework to design tasks and projects at various levels. In this book, we provide sample tasks and projects to guide the use of the framework.

All the components important for adding depth to learning and planning comprehensive lessons are addressed through this framework. Each component covers the same five levels of increasing complexity to

Real-World Learning		
Students learn from, interact with, and have an impact on the real world.		
Cognitive Complexity	**Student Engagement**	**Technology Integration**
Level of critical thinking required by students for an instructional task or project	Level at which students take responsibility for their own learning, instruction is differentiated, and students partner or collaborate with the teacher, other students, or outside experts to guide their own learning	Level at which students use technology as a research tool, collaborative tool, design tool, and presentation tool; student-directed technology use is seamlessly integrated into real-world content; students' critical thinking with technology use is at Bloom's Analyze, Evaluate, or Create levels

Figure I.1: Structure of Create Excellence Framework and book.

help the teacher target growth in his or her instructional development of tasks and projects: (1) Knowing, (2) Practicing, (3) Investigating, (4) Integrating, and (5) Specializing. The cognitive-complexity component also incorporates the revised Bloom's taxonomy thinking skills: Remember, Understand, Apply, Analyze, Evaluate, and Create. Table I.1 (pages 4–5) highlights this structure, clarifies each component's role, and illustrates how all the framework's pieces fit together. Levels 1–3 involve tasks, while levels 4–5 involve projects. *Tasks* are small classroom activities, while *projects* are more complex and use several instructional strategies, have open-ended solutions, involve more student choice and decision making, and take longer to complete. The lower levels of the framework are teacher directed (levels 1–3), whereas higher levels are more student directed (levels 4–5) with the teacher partnering with students to design projects and assignments (Tassell et al., 2013). The target levels for consistent student learning are levels 3 and 4, which are shaded in tables depicting the framework levels throughout the book. While level 3 is still teacher directed, students are engaging in higher cognitively complex tasks and projects. Students are beginning to take more responsibility for their learning in level 4. Level 5 is attained after consistent learning at levels 3 and 4 and could be accomplished a few times a year.

Real-World Learning

Real-world learning is where the student learns from, interacts with, and has an impact on the real world. The goal is for students to experience real-world, authentic learning by interacting with the real world to complete tasks and solve problems. The real-world learning component is the foundation for the other three components (cognitive complexity, student engagement, and technology integration), as it establishes an authentic context for learning.

Cognitive Complexity

The student's level of thinking with real-world content is vital to creating a quality task. The cognitive-complexity component within the Create Excellence Framework is based on the revised Bloom's taxonomy (Anderson & Krathwohl, 2001). At the teacher-directed level of the framework, students are engaged in learning experiences that the revised Bloom's taxonomy would classify as Remember, Understand, and Apply. Student-directed levels of the Create Excellence Framework embrace Bloom's top three cognitive processes (Analyze, Evaluate, and Create). At these top levels, students, instead of teachers, identify the real-world questions and generate projects while thinking like an expert focused on an open-ended, global-learning emphasis.

Table I.1: Create Excellence Framework

CREATE LEVELS	REAL-WORLD LEARNING	COGNITIVE COMPLEXITY (BLOOM'S COGNITIVE PROCESSES IN PARENTHESES)	STUDENT ENGAGEMENT	TECHNOLOGY INTEGRATION
				Teacher Directed
Level 1: Knowing	• Learning focuses on **nonrelevant** problems using textbooks or worksheets.	• Teacher directs student interaction with content or standard at Bloom's **Remember** level (Recognizing, Recalling).	• **Teacher lectures** or questions and students take notes. OR • **One correct answer** is expected.	(Level 0 for no technology) • **Teacher uses technology** for demonstration or lecture. OR • Students use technology at Bloom's **Remember** level. OR • Technology is a **student option** but is not required or is used for **keyboarding**.
Level 2: Practicing	• Learning provides some application to the real world using **real objects or topics**.	• Teacher directs student interaction with content or standard at Bloom's **Understand** level (Interpreting, Exemplifying, Classifying, Summarizing, Inferring, Comparing, Explaining) and Bloom's **Apply** level (Executing, Implementing).	• Students are engaged in a **task directed by the teacher**. AND • **Multiple solutions** for one task are accepted.	• Students use technology for Bloom's **Understand**- or **Apply**-level thinking tasks. OR • Students use technology for **gathering information**.

Lower Cognitive Complexity

				Student Directed
Level 3: Investigating	Learning **simulates the real world** (such as a class store or assuming the role of a political commentator).	**Teacher directs** student interaction with the content or standard at Bloom's **Analyze** level (Differentiating, Organizing, Attributing), **Evaluate** level (Checking, Critiquing), or **Create** level (Generating, Planning, Producing).	**Students have choice for tasks.** AND **Tasks are differentiated** by content, process, or product (such as addressing learning preferences, interests, or ability levels).	• Technology use appears to be an **add-on** or alternative—not essential for task completion. AND • Students use technology for Bloom's **Analyze-, Evaluate-, or Create-** level thinking tasks.
Level 4: Integrating	• Learning emphasizes and **impacts the classroom, school, or community.** AND • Learning is integrated across subject areas.	• **Students generate** questions or projects with the content or standard at Bloom's **Analyze** level (Differentiating, Organizing, Attributing), **Evaluate** level (Checking, Critiquing), or **Create** level (Generating, Planning, Producing).	• **Students partner with the teacher** to define the content, process, or product. AND • There is a student **inquiry-based** approach. AND • Students **collaborate with other students.**	Student technology use: • Is **embedded in content and essential** to project completion AND • Promotes **collaboration among students and partnership with the teacher** AND • Helps them **solve authentic problems** at Bloom's Analyze, Evaluate, or Create levels
Level 5: Specializing	• Learning has a **positive impact on a national or global** issue or problem. AND • Students **collaborate with experts** in a field or discipline.	• **Students generate** questions or projects with the content or standard at Bloom's **Create** level (Generating, Planning, Producing). AND • Complex **thinking like a content expert** occurs OR there is an open-ended, **global-learning** emphasis.	• **Students initiate their own inquiry**-based learning projects; thorough immersion and full implementation from topic to solution occurs. AND • **Students initiate appropriate collaborations** pertaining to their project.	Student-directed technology use: • Is **seamlessly integrated in content at Bloom's Create** level AND • Has **several technologies** AND • Includes **collaboration with field experts** or **global organizations** to find solutions to an in-depth "real" problem

Higher Cognitive Complexity

Student Engagement

The student-engagement component of the Create Excellence Framework offers guidance in the degree to which learners (1) take responsibility for their own real-world learning; (2) partner or collaborate with the teacher, other students, or outside experts; and (3) use resources such as teachers and experts in the discipline. Teachers can help the students differentiate their interests and make choices in how they approach the task or project. Teachers can also support the students by helping them identify resources and collaboration opportunities.

Technology Integration

Technology integration is relatively new to learning, and it is constantly evolving. However, it is also the component that gives a spark to how real-world learning can be discovered and conveyed. The technology-integration component emphasizes *students* using technology, not teachers using technology. Technology integration is more than just having students go to the computer lab to watch a science video, take an online quiz, locate information on the web, or progress through levels of online mathematics activities or software. The students use technology to display their learning. At the highest level on the Create Excellence Framework, students design projects that are seamlessly integrated in content at the highest level of the revised Bloom's taxonomy, include several technologies, and involve collaboration with field experts or global organizations to find solutions to real, complex problems.

Framework Example

Figure I.2 offers a sample project, highlighting how Gracie's teacher (from the opening scenario) learned to use each component of the Create Excellence Framework.

Education in Today's World: Standards and the Create Excellence Framework

With national and provincial standards now available in the major content areas (mathematics, English language arts, science, and social studies), it is critical to help teachers plan instruction with opportunities for students to learn at higher levels. Furthermore, teachers and students need to make connections to the real world while designing learning.

Many teachers and principals are highly concerned with the acquisition of content knowledge and skills in the standards, and we believe that purposefully designing learning experiences to be unified around real-world concepts and ideas promotes the same knowledge and skills. If teachers use real-world themes and essential or guiding questions to integrate their (otherwise separate) courses and align content standards to the real-world themes, students will have a coherent context for every assignment, classroom activity, fieldwork experience, and project they undertake. Students will also achieve a deeper level of understanding of what they are learning because of the standards' integration in real-world themes and experiences. Students will begin to see that everything is relevant and related (Martinez, 2014).

Standards in the 21st century turn an eye toward authentic-learning opportunities—instruction that must be designed with a unique thread of real-world impact. The standards require a strong attention to appropriate levels of rigor, matching challenge level to the task or project and to the student, and are based on higher-level learning, which is connected to the Create Excellence Framework's cognitive-complexity component. No longer do students work in isolation with the standards. They expect collaboration and mentoring, which incorporates engaged learning techniques. This connects with the framework's student-engagement component. Technology integration is a key element in many standards and is one that students expect and need.

Project Scenario: After learning how to plan a project using the Create Excellence Framework, Gracie's elementary school teacher informs his students that they need to redesign their classroom as they are growing in size by twelve more students. Groups are challenged to develop an optimal classroom design supported with a persuasive rationale that would meet their learning needs and growing size.

	REAL-WORLD LEARNING	COGNITIVE COMPLEXITY	STUDENT ENGAGEMENT	TECHNOLOGY INTEGRATION
Student-Directed Task	The class is told that the classroom redesign groups are in competition for an award. The principal will select the best redesign and work with the winning group to implement its design. The students are excited to influence the design that could actually be chosen and to help, as a class, make the changes for their room. Create Level: 4	In groups, students identify what qualities a classroom should have to meet students' needs. Students then brainstorm various conceptual designs and determine which concept is most likely to meet their needs and is cost-effective. Using their engineering skills, students make calculations of the size of the furniture, cost of materials, and so on. They build a model from supplies the school's PTO provides. Each group develops and evaluates its model; then it restructures and improves the original design. Create Level: 4	Throughout the design process, groups collaborate with the teacher to ensure they are progressing on their solution. Students meet with an interior designer and with a furniture designer to pose questions about their room design and get feedback from the outside experts. Create Level: 4	As groups are formulating their conceptual designs, they use a free online program, Google SketchUp, to develop their interior designs. They create persuasive presentations for the principal in Animoto or PhotoPeach (online presentation programs). The process of designing the prototype also involves technology integration. Create Level: 4

Source: Adapted from Tassell et al., 2013.

Figure I.2: Student-directed project sample to complement the Create Excellence Framework.

Changing Teacher Standards

Teachers face an ever-changing, ever-present challenge of keeping abreast of the best techniques for student learning, while honing their instruction of content standards. Conversation is shifting from the importance of ensuring highly *qualified* teachers in all classrooms to, instead, ensuring highly *effective* teachers for all students. As this conversation grows, many states, like Kentucky and New York, are adopting the research of the Danielson Framework for Teaching (Danielson, 2014) and using this framework's components to develop professional growth systems. Teachers are now looking toward strategies that involve higher-level thinking to boost student learning. Table I.2 illustrates how the Danielson Framework integrates real-world learning, higher-level learning, tools and resources, and differentiation into instruction. In table I.2, we've italicized words to show key phrases in the standards that align to the component.

Other national and international standards also reflect changes in teaching standards. The International Society for Technology in Education (ISTE) standards for teachers (ISTE, 2008) and for students (ISTE, 2016) seek to integrate technology in a meaningful context so the students use technology to create, communicate, collaborate, and think critically. Similarly, the Partnership for 21st Century Learning (P21, formerly the Partnership for 21st Century Skills) emphasizes promoting media literacy with students analyzing media and creating media products while engaging in critical thinking and collaboration. The Partnership for 21st Century Skills (2009) framework states that 21st century teaching "enables innovative learning methods that integrate the use of supportive technologies, inquiry- and problem-based approaches and higher order thinking skills" (p. 8). These expectations indicate that students are to use technology to collaborate as they engage in higher–cognitive learning tasks and projects about real-world topics. This philosophy connects to the Create Excellence Framework as the cognitive-complexity, student-engagement, and technology-integration components all circle around a real-world learning experience.

Changing Content Standards

In content standards for mathematics, English language arts, science, and social studies, one will note a trend calling for students to take more responsibility for their learning. This may play out in the classroom as students generating their own questions, designing projects, facilitating discussions, peer-assessing work, and so on. Teachers will need a tool to help them support the standards' intent. Without a planning framework to help organize and strive for a change in thinking, the fear is that the teachers will not have the structure and tools to make the changes necessary to their planning and, ultimately, instruction. In light of these changes, we, the authors, find it imperative to re-examine how we develop curriculum.

It is no longer acceptable to plan and deliver content in isolation. Teachers must deliver content with context. Teachers are stretched to involve their students at a new and heightened level of involvement in the classroom by applying the content in an interactive and authentic way. The instruction addresses the framework's student-engagement component as students interact in meaningful discussions, collaborate with their classmates, and partner with the classroom teacher in learning. The authentic changes in the standards require students to experience content through the real world. Levels 4–5 of the Create Excellence Framework emphasize the importance of the teacher designing instruction and provide support for teachers making this transition. See table I.3 (page 10) for examples highlighting how the Create Excellence Framework connects to the various student content standards.

Table I.2: Examples of Where Create Excellence Framework Components Connect to Danielson Teacher Standards

DANIELSON FRAMEWORK FOR TEACHING DOMAIN	SAMPLE STANDARD	CONNECTION TO CREATE EXCELLENCE FRAMEWORK COMPONENTS
1: Planning and Preparation	1A: Knowledge of Content and Pedagogy Distinguished: "The teacher displays extensive knowledge of the important concepts in the discipline and *how these relate both to one another and to other disciplines*. The teacher demonstrates understanding of prerequisite relationships among topics and concepts and understands the *link to necessary cognitive structures that ensure student understanding*. The teacher's plans and practice reflect familiarity with a wide range of effective pedagogical approaches in the discipline and the ability to *anticipate student misconceptions*" (Danielson, 2014, p. 9).	Real-world learning
1: Planning and Preparation	1E: Designing Coherent Instruction Distinguished: "The sequence of learning activities follows a coherent sequence, is aligned to instructional goals, and is designed to engage students in *high-level cognitive activity*. These are appropriately differentiated for individual learners. Instructional groups are varied appropriately, with some opportunity for *student choice*" (Danielson, 2014, p. 25). 1E Distinguished Critical Attributes "Learning experiences connect to other disciplines" (Danielson, 2014, p. 25).	Cognitive complexity Student engagement Technology integration Real-world learning
3: Instruction	3B: Using Questioning and Discussion Techniques Distinguished: "The teacher uses a variety or series of questions or prompts to challenge students cognitively, advance high-level thinking and discourse, and promote metacognition. Students formulate many questions, initiate topics, challenge one another's thinking, and make unsolicited contributions. Students themselves ensure that all voices are heard in the discussion" (Danielson, 2014, p. 63).	Cognitive complexity Student engagement
3: Instruction	3C: Engaging Students in Learning Distinguished: "Virtually all students are intellectually engaged in *challenging* content through well-designed learning tasks and activities that require *complex thinking* by students. The teacher provides suitable scaffolding and challenges students to explain their thinking. There is evidence of some *student initiation* of *inquiry* and student contributions to the exploration of important content; students may serve as resources for one another. The lesson has a clearly defined structure, and the pacing of the lesson provides students the time needed not only to intellectually engage with and reflect upon their learning but also to consolidate their understanding" (Danielson, 2014, p. 69).	Cognitive complexity Student engagement

Table I.3: Highlights of How the Create Excellence Framework Connects to Student Content Standards

CONTENT-AREA STANDARDS	SAMPLE STANDARD	CREATE EXCELLENCE FRAMEWORK COMPONENT
Common Core English language arts standards	SL.3.1: "Engage effectively in a range of collaborative discussions (one-on-one, in groups, and teacher-led) with diverse partners on grade 3 topics and texts, building on others' ideas and expressing their own clearly" (National Governors Association Center for Best Practices & Council of Chief State School Officers [NGA & CCSSO], 2010a).	Student engagement
Common Core mathematics standards	Mathematical Practice 4: "Model With Mathematics—Mathematically proficient students can apply the mathematics they know to solve problems arising in everyday life, society, and the workplace. . . . They can analyze those relationships mathematically to draw conclusions. They routinely interpret their mathematical results in the context of the situation and reflect on whether the results make sense, possibly improving the model if it has not served its purpose" (NGA & CCSSO, 2010b).	Real-world learning Student engagement Technology integration Cognitive complexity
Next Generation Science Standards	K–2-ETS1–1: "Ask questions, make observations, and gather information about a situation people want to change to define a simple problem that can be solved through the development of a new or improved object or tool" (Achieve, 2013).	Real-world learning
College, Career, and Civic Life (C3) Framework	D4.3.3–5: "Present a summary of arguments and explanations to others outside the classroom using print and oral technologies (e.g., posters, essays, letters, debates, speeches, and reports) and digital technologies (e.g., Internet, social media, and digital documentary)" (National Council for the Social Studies [NCSS], 2013).	Technology integration

In addition to these connections to standards that professional organizations propose, there are many more notable leaders in the field of education whose works and ideas align to the major components of the Create Excellence Framework. Visit **go.SolutionTree.com/instruction** for a detailed table, "Publications With Elements That Align With the Create Excellence Framework," which illustrates the connection between several scholars' work and our framework.

Structure of This Book

Real-World Learning Framework for Elementary Schools is presented in two parts. In part I, the chapters provide an in-depth look at each component of the Create Excellence Framework, highlighting how to classify levels within the framework and how they align with the standards. We describe each component of the framework in chapters 1–4. Chapter 5 gives guidance for how to use the Create Excellence Framework in your classroom, school, and district. Examples of lessons covering a variety of subjects and framework levels for the elementary grades are interwoven throughout the chapters. Each chapter also includes discussion questions for readers to consider and a Take Action section that provides readers with more in-depth activities and tasks, often including reproducibles.

Part II includes several sample lesson plans from different content areas and spotlights real-world learning, cognitive complexity, student engagement, and technology integration. The projects specify grade levels, but they can be modified for higher or lower grades. Each project description includes the following.

- An assignment overview, including learning objectives, the standards they address, project options, and resources, including technology, needed for the project
- A task or project description and scoring rubric, which teachers can copy and distribute to students to guide their creation of the project
- Sample student work to show how a typical student might complete the project, which the teacher may or may not decide to share with students
- The Create Excellence Framework rating that explains how closely the lesson fulfills the framework's levels, with justification provided for the rating

You may also visit Create Excellence (http://create-excellence.com) to access many additional resources featuring web 2.0 tools and applications highlighted in the projects in this book as well as other resources that we have found to be outstanding in our work with teachers.

Conclusion

At a time when educators are seeking a deeper connection with the content and their students, this book is needed! The Create Excellence Framework is a tool to design instruction with a research base. With the challenging environment of rigorous standards in many content areas requiring engaging and higher-level inquiry, the Create Excellence Framework can help you fill this need. The Danielson Framework for Teaching (Danielson, 2014) also reveals the importance of students driving instruction and making decisions involving their own learning. These manifestations drive and support the timely nature of and need for the Create Excellence Framework—it can provide a guide and a target for student learning, encouraging students such as Gracie, the eager student who is hoping to experience deeper learning. Teachers can use the concepts from the Create Excellence Framework to inspire and reinforce their students' self-directed learning. While advocating for this type of real-world learning in the classroom, teachers can promote a vision for higher levels of cognitive complexity, technology integration, and student engagement. In this type of learning environment, Gracie can realize her dreams and potential.

Discussion Questions

Answer the following five questions to summarize the chapter's concepts.

1. How can the Create Excellence Framework help you plan lessons that tap into real-world and relevant learning?
2. Are there any components of the Create Excellence Framework in your current instruction?
3. How do you see the framework components embedded in the teaching standards at your school?
4. What has been missing from your instructional-planning tools? What struggles have you been having? How would the Create Excellence Framework help you with these struggles?
5. Are the tasks and projects you design more teacher driven or student driven? How does the design difference impact student motivation in your elementary classroom?

Take Action

Consider the following four tasks and activities to help you toward implementing the Create Excellence Framework.

1. Consider a student in your class or school who wants to engage in higher levels of real-world learning than he or she currently has the opportunity to. Have a discussion with the student about aspects of the current curriculum's cognitive complexity, student engagement, and technology integration as related to real-world learning in the Create Excellence Framework. Ask the student to share specific topics or issues that affect him or her that can be explored in class projects.

2. Have your students complete the survey provided in the "Personal Learning Survey" reproducible (page 13 or 14). What did you learn about your class that you did not know before? How can you use this information to design better learning experiences for your students?

3. Examine the content standards for your discipline. Find the elements within the Create Excellence Framework components that you want to develop in your classroom instruction. Discuss this with a colleague who can give you feedback—someone you connect with, someone in a similar position as you, someone on your team, or someone teaching the same content.

4. Meet with a teacher at a level different than yours. How might the Create Excellence Framework impact different levels of elementary classrooms—primary (K–2) versus intermediate (3–5)? What might be some differences? Together, examine an idea one or both of you have, and determine goals for how you can use the framework to enhance your lessons.

Personal Learning Survey—Primary

Name: _____

1. Draw a picture of how you learn best.

2. Draw a picture or give a word or phrase of what you would like to study.

3. Do you prefer working alone, with a partner, or in small groups? (Circle all that apply.)

   a. Alone

   b. With a partner

   c. In small groups

4. What from your life would you like to study? Draw a picture of it, or write it in words.

5. What technology tools would you like to use that support your learning? Explain.

Personal Learning Survey—Intermediate

Name: _____

1. What would designing your own learning look like for you? Would you decide what you learn? Would you determine how it is measured or graded? Explain.

2. If you could have more opportunities to design your own learning, what would you keep the same? What would you change? Explain.

3. Do you prefer working alone, with a partner, or in small groups? Explain.

4. What do you want to study in the current content that connects to something in the real world? Explain.

5. What technology tools would you like to use that support your learning? Explain.

PART I

CHAPTER 1

Real-World Learning

In studying local history, a fifth-grade class walks around the town to view and discuss local monuments and landmarks. One student asks why there is not a monument to commemorate a local army general who was a significant leader in the Korean War. Then another student speaks up, asking why there is not a landmark to honor the woman who founded the first local department store in 1903. As the class walks back to the school, the excited students' discussion focuses on designing and proposing new local landmarks to commemorate other notable persons in the community's history. The students decide to use Draw Island to design the monument or landmark and then create a presentation to convince the town council to build their landmark. The town council is delighted and chooses one of the students' designs. On Saturdays, the students help the people of the town build their landmark.

Real-world learning involves the degree to which a student learns from, interacts with, and has an impact on the actual real world. Real-world learning involves challenging and messy problems. These problems are open to multiple interpretations, multifaceted, and interdisciplinary, and applying an existing algorithm cannot lead to easily solving them. In the course of solving an authentic problem, students will learn skills and curriculum in multiple subjects to augment the real-world application of those skills. For example, students may learn letter-writing skills when they want to write a letter to their city councilperson urging him or her to support a new baseball field in their town. Real-world solutions may not always work, may not always please everyone, and may have consequences beyond the problem or discipline.

Real-world learning is not a new concept. Psychologist Jerome Bruner (1960) discusses constructivism based on the theme that learners construct new ideas or concepts on existing knowledge where learning is an active process. Philosopher and psychologist John Dewey (1938) also believed that learning is a social and interactive process, in which students should experience and interact with the curriculum, and that all students should have the opportunity to take part in their own learning. For instance, apprenticeships have been a primary method of learning a trade for thousands of years and are still popular in the 21st century to learn some skilled trades as well as earn professional credentials. The state of Virginia still has a Law Reader Program whereby under the approved supervision of a licensed lawyer, one can study law, do some of the work of a lawyer, and become a licensed lawyer upon passing the bar exam (Virginia Board of Bar Examiners, 2014).

Real-world applications of knowledge are critical for students to possess deep understandings of content. There are many levels of real-world learning.

Five Levels of Real-World Learning

The following sections describe the five levels of real-world learning.

Knowing

Level 1 tasks focus on problems that are irrelevant to the real world, using textbooks and worksheets. Students are learning foundational knowledge or skills outside a real-world context. Examples of level 1 tasks include reading sight words, filling in multiplication facts on a worksheet, or memorizing historical dates.

Practicing

Level 2 tasks provide some application to the real world, using real objects or topics. For example, students may demonstrate mathematics problems with small rocks they collected or write a paragraph about their state symbols. Another example of a Practicing task would be students comparing local mammals, telling how they are related, and showing the relationships in a Venn diagram.

Investigating

In level 3, learning involves simulation of the real world in a teacher-directed task. Examples include creating and operating a class store or assuming the role of a policeman or firefighter. Teachers can ask students to predict the weather by assuming the role of a weatherperson or to analyze fire evidence data like a fire chief. Having students create a volcano using vinegar and baking soda is another example of an Investigating activity. In this activity, teachers give the students vinegar, baking soda, and a large container and instruct them to use the scientific method to experiment and discover which amounts of vinegar and baking soda make the best volcano. Students write each step of the scientific method during their experiment to answer the question.

Integrating

In level 4, Integrating emphasizes how student actions have a real impact on the classroom, school, or community. Learning is integrated across subject areas, including language arts, mathematics, science, and technology. Learning is student directed as teachers give students the opportunity to decide the direction of their own projects and learning. Students may investigate water costs and document how much water the school is wasting each week. Students may prepare a spreadsheet with their data, create a plan to save water at the school, and give a presentation to the principal and the school-based, decision-making team to persuade them to adopt their plan. Another example of a lesson at this level is students designing and implementing a campaign to preserve the wildlife in their area, with students presenting their findings to and persuading town officials.

Specializing

In level 5, students collaborate with an expert in a field or discipline, and their learning and projects have a positive impact on a national or global issue or problem. For example, See Kids Common Cents' Penny Harvest program (www.seekidsdream.org/parents/penny-harvest) grew from one student's desire to feed the homeless, and students' penny collections have resulted in $8.1 million in matching grants for the homeless (Common Cents New York, 2013). Another example of a level 5 assignment involves your class working with a national or international organization to help stop chemical dumping in the ocean.

Table 1.1 introduces the five levels of real-world learning in the Create Excellence Framework.

Table 1.1: Real-World Learning Levels of the Create Excellence Framework

CREATE LEVEL	DESCRIPTION	SAMPLE TASK OR PROJECT
Level 1: Knowing	• Learning involves problems irrelevant to the real world, using textbooks or worksheets.	Students label the major rainforests of the world on a map.
Level 2: Practicing	• Learning provides some application to the real world, using real objects or topics.	Students create a chart of the world's rainforests and classify them as either tropical or temperate rainforests.
Level 3: Investigating	• Learning simulates the real world (such as a class store or assuming the role of a political commentator).	Students explore the question, How can we save the Sumatran orangutan, one of the species on the world's critically endangered list? They create a digital story from the orangutan's point of view, giving the animal's opinion of why he is critically endangered and what we can do to reverse his fate.
Level 4: Integrating	• Learning emphasizes and impacts the classroom, school, or community. • Learning is integrated across subject areas.	The class has a pen-pal class in Brazil near the Amazon rainforest. The collapse of a mining dam near the pen-pal class causes concern for the students in both classes. The students in the American class decide to begin a fundraiser to help the students in their pen-pal class. The students make small ribbon Brazil flags to sell to others in the school and around their community to show support of Brazil. Some local businesses donate to their cause. This impacts the classroom, school, and community.
Level 5: Specializing	• Learning has a positive impact on a national or global issue or problem. • Collaboration occurs with experts in a field or discipline.	The class has a pen-pal class in Brazil near the Amazon rainforest. Students in the American class contact and begin working with the United Nations Children's Emergency Fund (UNICEF) to assist their pen-pal class that the mining accident affected. They donate their fundraising money as well as organize shoebox donations of basic toiletries for their friends. The students design a website for UNICEF for the Brazil town.

Visit **go.SolutionTree.com/instruction** *for a free reproducible version of this table.*

Beginning instruction with the real world not only grabs students' attention but also engages them much more than traditional lecture and textbook learning. Students need learning to be "real" to them; they need involvement in the real world; and they need to collaborate with other students, the teacher, and outside experts.

Real Versus Relevant

Students prefer real, not just relevant, learning. Relevant means that students can relate to the content you are teaching, connect with it, or apply it to something they know about (for example, sports, music, social networking, movies, or games). The problem with relevance is it does not go far enough to make learning meaningful and engaging. As education innovator Marc Prensky (2010) says, "Real means that there is a continuous perceived connection by the students between what they are learning and their ability to use that learning to do something useful or impact the real world" (p. 72). For students to actively attend to and retain information, it must be relevant to their interests or foreseeable future needs (Sousa, 2006). In fact, traditional learning will usually fall under level 1 or 2, relevant learning under level 2 or 3, and real learning under level 4 or 5, depending on the level of impact. Table 1.2 provides a sample topic to illustrate the differences among traditional, relevant, and real learning.

Table 1.2: Comparison of Traditional, Relevant, and Real Learning

	TRADITIONAL LEARNING	RELEVANT LEARNING	REAL LEARNING
Primary Example	A teacher reads a story about growing a vegetable garden to first graders. The students draw a picture of a vegetable from the story. (This is a level 2 real-world learning task because it involves talking about a real-world topic.)	A teacher tells first graders to pretend that they are farmers and to draw their vegetable gardens for next summer. They will decide what vegetables to grow and be sure to allow the space that each vegetable needs. (This is a level 3 real-world learning task because it is a simulation of the real world.)	A first-grade class plants a small vertical garden outside their classroom. After studying vertical gardens and visiting a local farm, a local greenhouse, and a local farmers' market, the students decide what vegetables to grow, what the plants need to grow, and what prices to ask for their vegetables. When their garden produces vegetables, they harvest the vegetables and take them to the local farmers' market to sell. They plan to use the money to invest in their winter garden and to purchase apps for their class set of iPads. (This is a level 4 real-world learning project because students have an impact on their own class.)
Intermediate Example	A teacher tells the class, "Read this article about healthy eating and write a report about what it means to eat healthy." (This is a level 2 real-world learning task because it involves talking about a real-world topic.)	A teacher tells the class, "We have been studying eating healthy. Assume the role of our school cafeteria director and create a week's worth of food orders and menus for our school. Create a spreadsheet for the food orders and menu." (This is a level 3 real-world learning task because it is a simulation of the real world.)	After studying healthy eating habits, students brainstorm how they can get their own families to eat healthier. Each student decides to record his or her family's meals for one week and analyze the health factors they have been studying. Each student designs an individualized brochure for his or her parents to promote healthy eating for the family. Sixty percent of the students report that it made a difference in their family eating habits. (This is a level 4 real-world learning project because students have an impact on their own families.)

Elements of Real-World Learning

Elements of real-world learning incorporate learning integrated across subject areas, learning as close to the real world as possible, and collaborating with experts in the field or discipline being studied.

Learning Integrated Across Subject Areas

Educators Keith C. Barton and Lynne A. Smith (2000) state that interdisciplinary learning "provide[s] authentic experiences in more than one content area, offer[s] a range of learning experiences for students, and give[s] students choices in the projects they pursue and the ways they demonstrate their learning" (p. 54). Interdisciplinary units enable teachers to use classroom time more efficiently and address content in depth while giving students the opportunity to see the relationship between content areas and engage in authentic tasks and projects.

Students immersed in authentic-learning activities cultivate the kind of portable skills that are applicable in new and different situations, settings, or connections. These skills include judgment to distinguish reliable from unreliable information, patience to follow longer arguments and assignments, the ability to recognize relevant patterns in unfamiliar contexts, and flexibility to work across disciplinary and cultural boundaries to generate innovative solutions (Jenkins, 2009).

In problem-based learning, students work for an extended period of time to investigate and respond to a complex question, problem, or challenge. Problem-based learning is the center of medical students' training as they develop work skills—collaborating, chairing a group, listening, recording, cooperating, respecting colleagues' views, critically evaluating literature, self-directing learning and use of resources, and presenting on and engaging in real medical tasks and projects (Wood, 2003). Within the real-world learning component, this learning would be considered level 3 if they are simulating the medical world; level 4 if they are having an impact on a small scale, such as in their class or school; or level 5 if they collaborate with medical experts and have an impact on a national or international scale. In other words, students are influencing or affecting an issue or problem on a national or international scale.

A level 4 example would be third-, fourth-, and fifth-grade students in your school designing a fundraising campaign and a multimedia presentation to match funds for a new ballpark the town council proposes but expresses concern about its funding. The students in the three grades could meet, brainstorm, and decide how they can work together for fundraising. For example, they could run concessions at after-school ballgames, or they could use a GoFundMe account. They present their ideas to the town council, as well as a plan for parents and other community members to help with the park's construction. Students are making an impact or having an effect on a community level.

Students involved in authentic learning are motivated to persevere despite initial frustration, as long as the project embodies what really counts to them—a social structure they enjoy, topics and activities of personal interest, and a feeling that what they are doing is important and valued (Herrington, Oliver, & Reeves, 2003; Prensky, 2010). By confronting students with uncertainty, ambiguity, and conflicting perspectives, instructors help them develop more mature mental models that coincide with the problem-solving approaches experts use. Be aware that the balance of challenge and uncertainty must be just right so that students are sufficiently engaged but not overwhelmed. Authentic-learning exercises expose the messiness of real-life decision making, where there may not be a right or a wrong answer per se, although one solution may be better or worse than others depending on the particular context or consequences. Such a nuanced understanding involves consider-able reflective judgment, a valuable lifelong skill that goes well beyond content memorization (Keyek-Franssen,

2010). For example, in a yearlong service-learning project, a third-grade class may work with senior citizens at a local assisted-living home. Students might survey residents' needs, make regular visits to read to residents or play music, make a greeting card for a special occasion, and so on. Students can plan a special field trip for themselves and their senior pals at the end of the school year. This project would involve language arts in reading and analyzing passages, mathematics in analyzing the survey data, and social studies in analyzing the issues of senior care. Planning a field trip involves many skills, such as researching trip opportunities, collaborating with the assisted-living staff, making arrangements for the trip, calculating costs and who will pay for what, and evaluating the trip afterward. This would be a level 4 real-world learning project since it is student directed and the students are having an impact on their community.

Learning in the Real World

When a student learns from, interacts with, and has an impact on the real world, higher retention of learning will occur. Real-world learning is organized around complex activities built on multiple themes and academic disciplines and requires multiple steps over an extended duration of time. Students have a real audience for their work. They use real data and learn content through working on projects and real problems that interest them (Schools We Need Project, n.d.). Take, for example, the fifth-grade class featured in the opening vignette of this chapter that decided to design landmarks for local heroes. This would be a level 4 real-world learning project in which learning impacts the school and community. Learning is integrated across subject areas—language arts, mathematics, science, economics, and social studies.

As another example, students may investigate and create projects to solve community issues, such as developing a local walking trail, promoting girls' inclusion in community athletics, or endorsing stricter policies on littering in the community. These would also be level 4 real-world learning projects since they are student directed and the students are having an impact on their community.

Such service projects can be instrumental in promoting real-world learning in many ways, including developing important personal and social skills; fostering stronger ties to the school, the community, and society; exploring various career pathways; and promoting community support for schools (National Service-Learning Clearinghouse, 2007). Parents see service learning as a way to connect students to real-life issues and as a vehicle for better learning (Rasicot, 2006).

Collaborating With Field or Discipline Experts

Real-world problems comprise complex tasks that students investigate over a sustained period of time. Students locate their own resources and are not given a finite list of resources. Collaboration is integral to authentic learning, where teamwork is critical to making decisions, solving problems, creating products, and maneuvering the social aspects of learning with a team. Collaboration between the teacher and students is essential to select the content, design the tasks or projects, and construct the assessment. Finally, authentic learning usually culminates in the creation of a whole product; however, the process is just as valuable to student learning as the product. For example, in a conservation unit, each student may document how much water his or her family uses each week, study personal water use habits, and make recommendations to his or her family about water conservation at home. The process of studying one conservation method at home could lead to other conservation efforts at home. It shows students that they can learn about topics that affect them and make informed decisions about many aspects of their lives.

True collaboration with experts in the field is invaluable in student acquisition of the knowledge, skills, and dispositions necessary to develop discipline, work ethic, and collaboration proficiencies. Collaboration with these experts could occur in person at the school, through a field trip to the expert's work location, or via video conferencing with Skype. Teachers of a specific discipline may find themselves collaborating with other teachers and experts from other disciplines. See table 1.3 for examples of experts whom teachers may engage in various fields and activities that can be applied to those fields. In these examples, experts could perform any of these activities with students.

Table 1.3: Sample Collaboration With Experts

FIELDS	PRACTITIONERS	TYPES OF COLLABORATION ACTIVITIES
Graphic design	• Local graphic designer • Graphic design professor or graduate student	• Teach students drawing principles. • Collaborate and assist pupils in projects. • Judge student projects. • Co-assess projects with the teacher and other pupils.
Technology and game design	• Local software designer • Technology and software design professor or graduate student	• Teach game design principles. • Collaborate and assist students in projects such as GAME:IT Elementary. • Judge student game designs.
Entrepreneurship and business planning	• Successful businessperson • Business professor or graduate student	• Teach students how to design a new charity idea, like making scarves for homeless children in another country. • Judge business ideas. • Guide students in developing a new business idea pitch.
Local food production	• Local farmer • Agriculture professor or graduate student • County farm extension agent	• Teach local farming options and techniques. • Guide students in designing a new farm. • Guide students in developing a real garden at the school or setting up a local farmers' market at the school.
Service learning	• Local nonprofit organization employee • Boy or Girl Scouts leader • Nurse or doctor • Nursing home director	• Teach students about service-learning opportunities. • Arrange volunteer opportunities with a local nursing home or day-care center. • Guide students in making products for nursing home residents, reading to them, or writing letters for them.
Animals	• Local dog or horse trainer • Local veterinarian • Professor of equestrian or veterinary medicine	• Teach students about animal care and training. • Guide students in training an animal or designing a housing or nutrition plan.

Continued →

FIELDS	PRACTITIONERS	TYPES OF COLLABORATION ACTIVITIES
Government	• Local government official • Political science or history professor	• Teach students about government principles and the role of politics. Students should be prepared to ask questions and discuss matters that affect them and their families. • Guide students in writing a letter to a city councilperson about an issue that concerns the students.
Crime scene investigation	• Local police detective • Private detective • University police/crime investigator	• Teach students about crime investigation. In a K–1 class, students could investigate who stole an object in the classroom. Grades 2–5 students could investigate a small crime in the classroom or school. • Guide a crime investigation project.

Table 1.4 provides some sample projects for real-world learning and collaboration with experts.

Table 1.4: Sample Projects for Real-World Learning

PROJECT	LEARNING INTEGRATED ACROSS SUBJECT AREAS	LEARNING IN THE REAL WORLD	COLLABORATION WITH FIELD OR DISCIPLINE EXPERTS
Honeybees are outside a fifth-grade classroom. Students decide they want to move them to a beehive and maintain the bees on the far side of the school property.	**Arts:** Write persuasive letters to the PTA, communicate with a beekeeper, and use research skills **Mathematics and economics:** Calculate the amount of food needed and honey sales **Science:** Research bee anatomy and behavior and beehive maintenance; collaborate with a beekeeper	Bees are indeed in the real world; bees provide an opportunity for pupils to study and make decisions about a real-world problem, collaborate with an expert about bees, and manage this problem by turning it into an entrepreneurial opportunity.	Students in this class can collaborate and learn from a real beekeeper. He or she can help the pupils move the bees, start a new beehive, and maintain it on the school property.
Students in a fifth-grade classroom engage in a waterwheel project at Ferryway School in Malden, Massachusetts (see Edutopia, 2008).	**Language arts:** Complete writing assignments and reflections, describe pictures, and publish writing **Science:** Study simple machines, power tools, and waterwheels **Engineering:** Construct an original waterwheel **Mathematics:** Utilize geometry and measuring concepts **History:** Research the history of waterwheels and related U.S. history **Art:** Design and create historical outfits **Technology:** Conduct research, create a wiki, take digital pictures, publish writing	Students learn how to operate a real waterwheel with engineering concepts and practice.	Students collaborate with a waterwheel operator or university engineering intern.

Teacher's Role in Facilitating Real-World Learning

Instructional methods evoke feelings in students that reinforce, support, or detract from knowledge and skill construction. It is the teacher's responsibility to design appropriate comprehension checks and feedback into the authentic-learning exercise since even the cleverest team of students dealing with complex, sustained investigations may have difficulty making good judgments in the absence of appropriate scaffolding (Lombardi, 2007). For example, students engaged in publishing a peer-reviewed online journal will evaluate each other over the course of the project and may receive additional guidance from the teacher, who assumes the role of publisher or editorial board member. The teacher may provide feedback on writing skills, communication skills, and publishing or reviewing skills. Do not abandon real-world projects if students fail to produce the level of work you expect. If students are not accustomed to real-world projects, they may need coaching and continuous feedback about the process in the beginning. Students need guidance in setting goals and learning strategies. The teacher acts as a partner and facilitator in group discussions. This will assist students in becoming more independent and ready to assume responsibility for their own learning. See chapter 5, page 95, for ideas on monitoring Create Excellence Framework projects.

Teaching Authentic Lessons

Integrated assessment is not merely summative in real-world learning but is woven into the tasks and projects, products, and teamwork. When genuine real-world learning occurs, it is highly unlikely that multiple-choice tests (that seek one right answer) will be adequate as they only capture lower-level knowledge. The embedded assessment in authentic projects analyzes multiple forms of evidence to measure student performance, including student engagement; collaboration with the team, teacher, and outside experts; artifacts produced throughout the task or project (including, for example, students' online journals or blogs); and the final product (Reeves, 2006).

Some teachers may want to teach authentic lessons but are not convinced that they can manage it. John F. Cronin (1993), project director for school transformation for the Loess Hills Area Education Agency, says that teachers do not have to jump in over their heads but can work toward more authenticity through a gradual but steady approach. Over time, a teacher can develop instruction that builds in complexity—for instance, beginning with simulating the real world and later immersing students in the real world. Look for available opportunities for authentic learning. Many textbooks that suggest real-world connections are level 2 or 3 on the Create Excellence Framework. Rarely do textbooks provide activities that are *in* the real world or that could be rated level 4 or 5 on the Create Excellence Framework. A teacher can transform these textbook suggestions into activities that can be immersed in the real world. For example, one second-grade textbook poses the question, "Which leaf shape drips faster?" The textbook activity is to cut different leaf shapes from construction paper. While this activity is about a real-world topic (level 2 of the real-world component in the framework), it may be difficult for some students to make the connection to the real world. The teacher could instead have students bring leaves of different shapes from their home surroundings to class and test which leaf shape drips faster. Better yet, the class could walk into the woods near the school to collect leaf samples for testing right there in the woods. The students' presence in the woods opens the door to so many more topics and discoveries about local plants. For example, a student might comment that her grandmother uses a certain wild herb for healing colds. This could lead to a discussion and further research of healing plants and herbs.

In the same science series, a fourth-grade textbook presents an exploration activity: "How are leaves different from each other?" The textbook's intent is for students to apply the scientific method by making a prediction, testing the prediction, and inferring conclusions. The question for second grade required a higher level of thinking than does the fourth-grade question. Like the second-grade teacher, the fourth-grade teacher could take the class on a walking expedition through the woods close to the school. The students could bring their journals and write observations; they could conduct experiments with different leaf compositions and shapes; they could discuss photosynthesis and leaf color; they could bring a few plant samples back to the classroom to transplant or grow roots from the cuttings. Spontaneous learning within the real world is so much more fun and enriching. Students can come up with their own ideas of ways to experiment and learn in the real world.

Guiding Learning

Teachers' awareness of the classroom composition and their ability to draw on real-life experiences to connect the content to learners' needs improve learning (Lin, 2006). Therefore, the teacher's role is transformed from sole source of information in the classroom to informed guide and expert facilitator of authentic-learning experiences (Renzulli, Gentry, & Reis, 2004). The teacher's role as facilitator is not passive. Yes, the learning is student centered, but a true facilitator must plan, be actively engaged with students as they learn, and have the awareness and finesse to adjust the learning task or project, environment, situation, and so on as needed.

When planning instruction for real-world learning, teachers should reflect on the following critical considerations.

- How close to the real world does learning occur?
  - ◆ If all learning is in the classroom and students are talking about the real world or pretending to be in circumstances or roles from the real world, then it can be classified as a simulation.
  - ◆ If some or most learning occurs in the real world and by interacting with the world outside the classroom, then learning is more authentic.
- Are students having any real impact on or changing something in the classroom, school, community, nation, or world?

Standards and Real-World Learning

Many standards include wording such as *real world* or *authentic learning*. Table 1.5 lists some examples of real-world learning in specific teaching and student content standards. The Create Excellence Framework provides an organized approach to determine levels of student learning that align with the Danielson Framework for Teaching (Danielson, 2014) and curriculum standards like the Common Core State Standards (CCSS); the College, Career, and Civic Life (C3) Framework; and the Next Generation Science Standards.

Table 1.5: Real-World Learning in Standards

SOURCE OF STANDARDS	STANDARD INDICATORS
STUDENT STANDARDS	
English language arts: Common Core English language arts standards	SL.4.1: "*Engage effectively in a range of collaborative discussions* (one-on-one, in groups, and teacher-led) with diverse partners on grade 4 topics and texts, building on others' ideas and expressing their own clearly" (NGA & CCSSO, 2010a).
Mathematics: Common Core mathematics standards	3.MD.D.8: "Solve real world and mathematical problems involving perimeters of polygons, including finding the perimeter given the side lengths, finding an unknown side length, and exhibiting rectangles with the same perimeter and different areas or with the same area and different perimeters" (NGA & CCSSO, 2010b).

Social studies: C3 Framework	D2.Civ.6.3–5: "Describe ways in which people benefit from and are challenged by working together, including through government, workplaces, voluntary organizations, and families" (NCSS, 2013).
Science: Next Generation Science Standards	3-PS2-1: "Plan and conduct an investigation to provide evidence of the effects of balanced and unbalanced forces on the motion of an object" (Achieve, 2013).
TEACHER STANDARDS	
Danielson Framework for Teaching	Domain 1: Planning and Preparation—1f Designing Student Assessments • "Teacher-designed assessments are authentic, with real-world application as appropriate" (Danielson, 2014, p. 29). Domain 3: Instruction—3a Communicating With Students • "The teacher invites students to explain the content to their classmates" (Danielson, 2014, p. 57). • "Students suggest other strategies they might use in approaching a challenge or analysis" (Danielson, 2014, p. 57).

Above and Beyond the Standards

The curriculum's goal should not be just the coverage of content but rather the discovery of content (Kwit, 2012). We do not want students to simply mimic or discuss real-world connections as part of a task. Students are already conditioned to sitting and completing tasks, but students who are busy are not necessarily engaged with the content. Even when the task or project has some connection to the real world, it can still just be that—a task or project *somewhat* related to, relevant to, or connected to the real world. The Create Excellence Framework proposes that standards can be discovered and taught *in* the real world as students solve real (not just relevant) problems.

For example, see the Common Core mathematics geometry standards in table 1.6 (page 28). These standards are much less specific about the topic or what this might look like in the classroom, which leaves them ripe for innovation with real-world application. Ways to apply these standards in imaginative, real-world scenarios are included in the table. Notice the learning progression from elementary to high school using the geometry strand for real-world learning projects.

Here's a word of caution: just because the standard mentions *real world* does not mean that you or students are actually engaging in real-world learning. Just talking about a real-world topic does not make it relevant or real to students. You have to go deeper *in* the real world (such as level 4 or 5), or it is not a high level of real-world learning for students. Student learning should emphasize and impact the classroom, school, or community. The curriculum standards are primarily skills that are best learned while immersed in real-world problems. Because so many new curriculum standards now mention the real world, they give you permission to *do* the real world with your students. Some educators get so excited about the real-world connection that the project takes on a life of its own and the original content connection gets lost. You need to be sure that the content connections are carefully selected, planned, and monitored.

Table 1.6: Real-World Learning With the Common Core Mathematics Geometry Standards

ELEMENTARY SCHOOL	MIDDLE SCHOOL	HIGH SCHOOL
4.GA.1: "Draw points, lines, line segments, rays, angles (right, acute, obtuse), and perpendicular and parallel lines. Identify these in two-dimensional figures" (NGA & CCSSO, 2010b).	6.GA.4: "Solve *real-world* and mathematical problems involving area, surface area, and volume" (NGA & CCSSO, 2010b). 6.GA.1: "Find the area of right triangles, other triangles, special quadrilaterals, and polygons by composing into rectangles or decomposing into triangles and other shapes; apply these techniques in the context of solving *real-world* and mathematical problems" (NGA & CCSSO, 2010b).	HSG.MG.A.3: "Apply geometric methods to *solve design problems* (e.g., designing an object or structure to satisfy physical constraints or minimize cost; working with typographic grid systems based on ratios)" (NGA & CCSSO, 2010b).
Elementary school students are in charge of creating an organic garden at their school. Students can implement their design, grow the vegetables, and sell their products at the local farmers' market. (Level 4 since it has a school and community impact)	**Middle school** students design a new and improved pyramid to be presented to the pharaoh, complete with various antechambers. (Level 3 since it is simulating the real world)	**High school** students are creating a swimming pool that can meet the needs of all people who want to use it—the high school swim team, children taking swimming lessons, or those who have special needs—and at the same time, it meets certain criteria in terms of community building codes, state safety guidelines, standard amounts of water and size, and so on. (Level 4 since it has a school and community impact)

Source: Adapted from Miller, 2011.

Connections of Real-World Learning With Other Components in the Create Excellence Framework

When the real world is the environment, setting, or background for student learning, it naturally merges with or encompasses cognitive complexity, student engagement, and technology integration. The Create Excellence Framework provides a new perspective for planning instruction to balance the needs of rigorous standards while creating engaging and meaningful instruction for student learning. Table 1.7 connects cognitive complexity, student engagement, and technology integration to real-world learning.

Table 1.7: Connection of Real-World Learning With Cognitive Complexity, Student Engagement, and Technology Integration

Real-World Learning
- Real-world learning is where the student learns from, interacts with, and has an impact on the real world.
- Learning is *in* the real world—students impact their class, school, community, nation, or world.
- Learning is integrated across subject areas.
- Students collaborate with field or discipline experts.

Cognitive Complexity
• Real-world problems are complex and messy, making critical thinking essential. They require student involvement and learning at the Analyze, Evaluate, and Create levels of the revised Bloom's taxonomy.
• At the top two levels of Create, the *students*, instead of the teachers, are identifying the real-world questions, tasks, or projects. Students generate projects on the Create level of the framework while thinking like a real-world expert focused on an open-ended, global-learning issue.

Student Engagement
• Engagement is when students take responsibility for their own learning and they partner or collaborate with the teacher, other students, or outside, real-world experts to guide their own learning.
• Twenty-first century jobs or careers require collaboration, inquiry, and solutions beyond the company; a voice and choice in projects; and differentiated assignments or projects according to skills, talents, interests, and individual responsibilities. These same requirements also apply to student learning in a real-world environment—the need for collaboration, inquiry, and solutions beyond the classroom; voice and choice; and differentiated assignments.

Technology Integration
• Technology is such an integral part of the 21st century world that we cannot imagine not using technology for banking, communicating, researching, creating, and so on.
• Students can really *do* real-world work with the availability of information, resources, collaboration and communication tools, project-creation tools, and presentation tools.
• Not only does effective technology integration enable 21st century, real-world learning, but using technology tools is so natural that students are only focused on the content or project, not the technology.

Critical Questions for Real-World Learning

When planning instruction for real-world learning, teachers should reflect on the following critical questions.

- How close to the real world does learning occur in my classroom?
  - If all learning is in the classroom and students are talking about the real world or pretending, using circumstances or roles from the real world, this learning is classified as a simulation. This is level 3, Investigating.
  - If some or most of the learning occurs in the real world and by interacting with the real world (outside the classroom), then learning is more authentic.
- Are my students having any impact on or changing something in the classroom, school, community, nation, or world?

Conclusion

Real-world learning is the cornerstone of the Create Excellence Framework. It focuses on connecting student learning to the real world as much as possible (real learning that is of concern to the student, not just relevant), having an impact on the real world, and working with outside experts. Unlike simply relevant learning, real-world learning doesn't just focus on topics that interest the students; it makes learning meaningful, and therefore more impactful, by also requiring students to collaborate with each other, their teacher, and outside experts. This is not the traditional formula where students work in isolation. Teachers and students can work together to integrate real-world learning across multiple subject areas while also mastering multiple standards in those subject areas. Yes, it does take planning and collaboration, but student learning is much deeper, richer, and longer lasting.

Learning goes deep when teachers and students delve into the complexities of real-world problems and at the same time interweave the appropriate student learning standards. An authentic-learning environment encourages real, substantive conversations with an open sharing of ideas. Teachers and students can begin real-world learning on a smaller scale and expand to more broad-scale, impactful projects as their comfort levels increase.

Discussion Questions

Answer the following five questions to summarize the chapter's concepts.

1.   Why is it important to situate student learning as close to the real world as possible?

2.   How does real-world learning change the way we teach?

3.   How do you distinguish between what is *relevant* and what is *real* in some of your instructional activities?

4.   How might increasing real-world learning to the upper levels of the Create Excellence Framework help student learning beyond the classroom?

5.   How is incorporating the real-world angle different for primary and intermediate grade-level students?

Take Action

Consider the following six tasks and activities to help you toward implementing the Create Excellence Framework.

1.   Identify an assignment you gave last year that you consider to have had an authentic- (or real-world) learning connection. What level would it be on the Create Excellence Framework? Why do you think so? How could you modify your assignment to increase the level of real-world learning?

2.   Complete the reproducible "Analyzing a Task or Project for Real-World Learning."

3.   Explore any technology tool and tell how you and your students can use this tool at level 3 or higher on the real-world learning component of the Create Excellence Framework with your class.

4.   Select one of the Create Excellence Framework projects in part II of this book. How could you modify one of the projects to use it in your classroom? How could you improve one of the projects? Have a conversation with a colleague about implementing the project in your or the colleague's classroom.

5.   Select another Create Excellence Framework project in part II of this book. Use the Create Excellence Framework to rate each component on the framework and justify your ratings. Compare your ratings to the Create Excellence Framework rating table that follows each project's sample student work. Were your ratings and justifications similar to those provided? Why, or why not?

6.   Develop a real-world task or project for your students. Discuss the challenges in creating this task or project. Do you have any concerns about your students' abilities?

Analyzing a Task or Project for Real-World Learning

Examine the scenario in the following table, and answer the questions. Then, compare your answers to the authors' responses.

Scenario: A third-grade class has been learning about the roles and responsibilities of the three branches of the federal government. Divide the class into committees of four or five pupils. In each committee, brainstorm ideas for additional bills to add to the rules in your school or classroom. Each committee will create a new bill and prepare a technology presentation (of its choice) to persuade the class to pass its bill. One committee member will present the bill to the floor (other classmates) using the committee's presentation. The committee will listen to the questions and comments of classmates and revise its bill accordingly. The committee will present it to the floor again after revisions are made. Take a final vote to decide whether the class will adopt the bill. The majority rules! If the bill is accepted, the president (a pupil who was appointed beforehand) immediately signs it into action. The new law is added to the class or school rules.	
Level of Real-World Learning	What is the level of real-world learning of this task? Use the following questions to guide your decision. 1. How close to the real world does learning occur? ⬥ If all learning is in the classroom and students are talking about the real world or pretending circumstances from the real world, then it can be classified as a simulation. This is level 3 (Investigating). ⬥ If some or most of the learning occurs in the real world and through interacting with the real world (outside the classroom), then learning is more authentic. 2. Are students having any impact on or changing something in the classroom, the school, the community, the nation, or the world? Why do you think so?
Ways to Raise the Real-World Learning	What are some ways to increase the level of real-world learning for this task?
New Level of Real-World Learning	What is the new level of real-world learning?

Real-World Learning Framework for Elementary Schools © 2017 Solution Tree Press • SolutionTree.com
Visit **go.SolutionTree.com/instruction** to download this free reproducible.

Authors' Responses

Compare your answers to the authors' responses to the scenario questions.

Level of Real-World Learning

This assignment is at level 3 (Investigating) in the real-world learning component because students are simulating the real world in the classroom.

Ways to Raise the Real-World Learning

The students could form a student government association (SGA) to represent the student body and function as the government for the students. The SGA could assist in forming school rules for all students, receive bill nominations from other students, and so on. The SGA could form a service-learning project for the school to assist with a local nursing home, clean up the local baseball park, or help with town Christmas decorations.

New Level of Real-World Learning

This new level of real-world learning is 4 (Integrating) because student learning emphasizes and impacts the community. This community involvement is interdisciplinary, involving many subject areas.

CHAPTER 2

Cognitive Complexity

Students in Mr. Watt's fifth-grade class are studying recycling. As a culminating project, students are grouped in work teams to identify ways the school could be more environmentally conscious. Teams list possible ways to recycle, and then debate which options will have the strongest environmental impact and be the most feasible to implement. After examining the options and debating the solution, the groups deliver a Prezi presentation to the school principal showcasing their ideas for a new recycling program. The principal selects the best solution to implement in the school.

Twenty-first century classrooms greatly emphasize problem solving and open-ended challenges. Mr. Watt's assignment represents the kind of instructional tasks that engage students in critical thinking while investigating the environmental impact on their school. Cognitive complexity in the Create Excellence Framework is the level of critical thinking required for an instructional task, project, or assessment based on Bloom's (1956) original taxonomy and the revised taxonomy by Lorin W. Anderson and David R. Krathwohl (2001). With the revision of Bloom's original taxonomy, higher-level thinking has been clarified as applying knowledge in new ways and engaging in nonroutine problem solving. This chapter explains the levels in the taxonomy, describes the cognitive-complexity dimension in the Create Excellence Framework, and showcases instructional tasks and projects embedding critical thinking with real-world applications.

Five Levels of Cognitive Complexity

Anderson and Krathwohl's (2001) revisions redefine the levels of Bloom's (1956) original taxonomy as Remember, Understand, Apply, Analyze, Evaluate, and Create. Both the Create Excellence Framework and Bloom's taxonomy are hierarchical, requiring deepening levels of cognitive complexity and student engagement.

Knowing

At the first level of the framework, *Knowing*, teachers engage students in Bloom's basic Remember-level tasks.

Practicing

Advancing to the *Practicing* level of the framework, teachers plan what Bloom's taxonomy classifies as Understand- and Apply-level learning experiences.

Investigating

At *Investigating*, the third framework level, instruction is at the Analyze, Evaluate, or Create level of Bloom's taxonomy. Students complete teacher-directed tasks.

Integrating

The fourth level of the Create Excellence Framework, *Integrating*, embraces the top three cognitive levels from Bloom's taxonomy (Analyze, Evaluate, and Create). A key difference at this level is that the students, instead of the teachers, are using the content standards to identify the questions, tasks, or projects.

Specializing

At the highest level on the Create Excellence Framework—*Specializing*—students generate projects for Bloom's Create level while thinking as an expert or focused on an open-ended, global-learning emphasis. When objectives, activities, and assessments are properly aligned at higher levels of cognitive thinking, not only does instruction improve but student learning has a better chance of improving as well (Raths, 2002).

Table 2.1 provides examples for each level of cognitive complexity in the Create Excellence Framework. At the highest three levels, projects and tasks often have a real-world focus. When real-world elements are interwoven into a task, they deepen the level of complexity as often there are more variables to consider and perhaps multiple correct solutions. As students simulate and perform tasks and projects like professionals in the field, they often naturally engage higher-order thinking skills as they analyze, evaluate, and solve problems just like skilled workers.

Table 2.1: Cognitive-Complexity Levels of the Create Excellence Framework

CREATE LEVEL	DESCRIPTION	SAMPLE TASK OR PROJECT
1: Knowing	• Teacher directs student interaction with the content at Bloom's Remember level (Recognizing, Recalling).	• To reinforce the unit vocabulary terms, play "Scatter, Space Race, Test" on Quizlet and then take the test on these vocabulary words.
2: Practicing	• Teacher directs student interaction with the content at Bloom's Understand level (Interpreting, Exemplifying, Classifying, Summarizing, Inferring, Comparing, Explaining) or Apply level (Executing, Implementing).	• Using Lino, post potential themes of a story. • Create a newspaper headline on Fodey, a website that generates fictional newspaper headlines, to summarize the best aspects of your community. • Create a video presentation using Knovio explaining how to solve a mathematics problem.

3: Investigating	• Teacher directs student interaction with content at Bloom's Analyze level (Differentiating, Organizing, Attributing), Evaluate level (Checking, Critiquing), or Create level (Generating, Planning, Producing).	• Identify which president was the best leader based on his long-term impact on our country. On DecideAlready, move the ratings meter to show which criteria are most important for your decision, and then indicate your choice. • Using MindMeister, a web-mapping tool, design a flowchart showing how critical events in a story changed a character's actions.
4: Integrating	• Students generate questions or projects with content at Bloom's Analyze level (Differentiating, Organizing, Attributing), Evaluate level (Checking, Critiquing), or Create level (Generating, Planning, Producing).	• Students have difficulty assessing websites' quality. Using DebateGraph, the students identify at least five criteria they would use to evaluate a website. Using the technology, they rate each criterion's importance.
5: Specializing	• Students generate questions or projects with content at Bloom's Create level (Generating, Planning, Producing). • Students engage in complex thinking like a content expert or with content that has an open-ended, global-learning emphasis.	• A class begins a unit on the water cycle. Students identify ways they would like to investigate the water cycle in their community. After researching, students identify scientific experiments they could conduct. They conduct an experiment and reflect on the results.

Six Levels of the Revised Bloom's Taxonomy

While many educators know the revised Bloom's taxonomy levels (Remember, Understand, Apply, Analyze, Evaluate, and Create), they might misunderstand the required level of thinking for each level. For example, a teacher might believe that when students *create* a poster, this task is on the Create level. The key is to examine how students are interacting with the content, not the technology. Copying facts about presidents on the poster is a low-level task. To help teachers better understand the taxonomy, the revised version fortunately identifies cognitive processes under each level to clarify the level of thinking. The revised Bloom's taxonomy includes nineteen cognitive processes classified within its six levels (Anderson & Krathwohl, 2001). Table 2.2 (page 36) illustrates where each cognitive process falls within Bloom's levels and how those processes align with the Create levels.

We describe these levels and cognitive processes and provide examples of instructional tasks and projects that align to each cognitive process in the following sections. To show ways to naturally integrate technology and real-world learning, these examples also showcase technology tools and real-world applications of knowledge used to support the critical thinking for each level. (Visit **go.SolutionTree.com/instruction** to access live links to the websites mentioned in the following sections.)

Remember

Remember is the first level of the taxonomy. With Remember, learners must recover information previously memorized. While a low-level thinking process, memorizing information is important for higher-level thinking. For example, knowing the types of rocks can help students analyze problems with rock formations, a higher-level thinking skill. There are two cognitive processes within Bloom's Remember level: recognizing and recalling.

Table 2.2: Alignment of Levels and Cognitive Processes Between the Create Excellence Framework and Bloom's Taxonomy

CREATE EXCELLENCE FRAMEWORK LEVELS	BLOOM'S TAXONOMY LEVELS AND COGNITIVE PROCESSES
Knowing	Remember • Recognizing • Recalling
Practicing	Understand • Interpreting • Exemplifying • Classifying • Summarizing • Inferring • Comparing • Explaining Apply • Executing • Implementing
Investigating Integrating Specializing	Analyze • Differentiating • Organizing • Attributing Evaluate • Checking • Critiquing Create • Generating • Planning • Producing

Recognizing and Recalling

Recognizing involves students selecting the correct memorized answer from answer choices provided, such as in a multiple-choice test. When recalling, students have to bring forth from their memory the correct memorized answer as required in a fill-in-the-blank question. Within the cognitive-complexity component, these tasks would be on level 1 of the Create Excellence Framework, the Knowing level. Following are examples of recognizing and recalling activities.

- Students use flashcards from Study Stack (www.studystack.com) to practice defining words and then checking the answers.
- Students create a set of word cards and definitions based on textbook information on Quizlet (www.quizlet.com) to study terminology.

Understand

While the Remember level is critical for establishing foundational concepts, information that is not processed at deeper levels can be forgotten. In the Understand level, students are establishing new connections with the content. Within the cognitive-complexity component, these tasks would be on level 2 (Practicing) of the Create Excellence Framework. There are seven cognitive processes associated with the Understand level: (1) interpreting, (2) exemplifying, (3) classifying, (4) summarizing, (5) inferring, (6) comparing, and (7) explaining.

Interpreting

When interpreting, students convert information from one form to another, such as changing text into paraphrases, visuals, or music. Following are examples of interpreting activities.

- **Text to paraphrase:** Students paraphrase a reading passage in a Skype (www.skype.com) conversation with a student from another school.
- **Text to visual:** Using the Doodle Buddy app (http://apple.co/1pAVkga), students create a picture that depicts what is happening in the novel or picture book they are reading.
- **Text to music:** Using GarageBand, software designed to create music, students write a song describing one key term they are learning in a curriculum unit.

Exemplifying

With exemplifying, students are asked to provide examples of a concept they are learning. These examples may include connections to other content areas or to prior experiences. Following are examples of exemplifying activities.

- After learning about frogs and their habitats, students play the game "Where Do Frogs Lay Their Eggs?" on ABC Splash (http://splash.abc.net.au/home#!/media/1389147/http&). They search the image for the best habitats for frogs.
- Using a search engine, students find an example of a painting that shows texture.
- Students find a picture showing how wind and water shape the land, and use the app Explain Everything (http://explaineverything.com) to record their explanation of how it represents this concept.

Classifying

When students classify, they categorize information or items based on similar characteristics. Students can group information under headings based on their common attributes. Following are examples of classifying activities.

- In groups, students select ten quotes from a character in a book. Using Padlet (www.padlet.com), an online collaborative board, they create headings to reflect key attributes of the character and post the quotes under the appropriate headings.
- Using an interactive whiteboard, students group mathematics equations into categories based on the basic number properties (for example, the commutative property or the identity property).

Summarizing

When summarizing, students condense information into a succinct statement. The summary could be based on a reading, video clip, or observation of a natural event. Following are examples of summarizing activities.

- Students create a story map using ABC Splash (http://splash.abc.net.au/home#!/home) to summarize a story.

- Students identify three online maps that depict earthquakes and volcanoes. Using Delicious (http://delicious.com), a social bookmarking site, they post links and a summary of how each map shows physical features associated with earthquakes and volcanoes.
- To summarize the group conversation, groups record key ideas using an online collaborative tool called Evernote (https://evernote.com).
- To summarize the water cycle, students create a poster with pictures and text, called a *glog*, using Glogster (www.glogster.com).

Inferring

Inferring uses evidence and reason to make a conclusion. Inferences drawn with limited evidence can be inaccurate. Following are examples of inferring activities.

- On Google Docs (http://docs.google.com), students review a passage and create comment boxes noting logical inferences that can be drawn from sections within the informational text.
- Groups use the Sock Puppets app (http://apple.co/1j3J0CE) to describe their science experiment's results and findings.

Comparing

Comparing involves assessing two ideas or items for similarities and differences. Students can use metaphors or analogies to make their comparisons. Following are examples of comparing activities.

- Using text and pictures with online presentation programs like Animoto (https://animoto.com), students create a metaphor of how decomposers are like another object (for example, a trash can).
- Students complete a comparison diagram of two topics using a website with interactive graphic organizers, such as ReadWriteThink (www.readwritethink.org) or Lucidchart (www.lucidchart.com).

Explaining

Explaining involves understanding cause-and-effect relationships. Following are examples of explaining activities.

- Students use the diagram-drawing website draw.io (www.draw.io) to show an independent variable and the anticipated results on the dependent variable for their science project.
- Students use the online time line generator Tiki-Toki (www.tiki-toki.com) to depict the causes and effects of the major events leading to the Revolutionary War.

Apply

At the Apply level, students execute certain procedures or steps to address a new problem. Within the cognitive-complexity component, all these tasks would be on level 2 (Practicing) of the Create Excellence Framework. There are two cognitive processes in the Apply level: (1) executing and (2) implementing.

Executing

In executing, students are presented with a new problem and must identify which procedure is needed to solve the problem, such as solving for a variable in an algebraic equation or editing a paper for punctuation. Following are examples of executing activities.

- Students play a game called "Warning! Space Boulders! Which Way Can You Direct a Robot?" on ABC Splash (http://splash.abc.net.au/home#!/media/32651/http&) to practice their skills using scales, legends, and directions on a map.

- Students create a Prezi (https://prezi.com) showing how they solved an addition word problem using pictures.
- Students record a video using Screencast (www.screencast.com) that shows how they edited a paragraph for correct subject-verb agreement.

Implementing

Implementing tasks often involve more variables or aspects than executing tasks, and the procedure to complete the task or project is not immediately clear; thus, they are more challenging. Sometimes the problems might have more than one answer. Conceptual and procedural knowledge are needed to answer the problem. Following are examples of implementing activities.

- Students write several lines of music with varying tempos using GarageBand or Soundation (http://soundation.com), music-authoring tools.
- Groups identify the cheapest cereal available at the local store and use Mindomo (www.mindomo.com) to show how they solved the problem.
- Students use what they have learned about acceleration to design a device that can go very fast on the Monster Physics app (https://itunes.apple.com/us/app/monster-physics/id505046678?mt=8).

Analyze

Within the Analyze level, learners use knowledge and understanding to complete higher-level tasks or projects. If a student can search the Internet for the correct answer or give the teacher an answer within a few minutes, the task or project is not at this level. When students complete Analyze-level tasks or projects, they need time to process, sort, examine, and recategorize the information. Analyze provides the basis for higher-level cognitive processes at levels 5 and 6 (Anderson & Krathwohl, 2001). Rebecca Stobaugh (2013) states, "A key component of critical thinking is the process of analyzing and assessing thinking with a view to improving it. Hence, many consider the Analyze level as the beginning of deep thinking processes" (p. 28). In the Analyze level, there are three cognitive processes: (1) differentiating, (2) organizing, and (3) attributing. Depending on whether they are teacher or student directed, these tasks could be at one of the top three levels of the Create Excellence Framework: Investigating, Integrating, and Specializing.

Differentiating

With this cognitive process, students must determine what information is relevant and irrelevant. What makes differentiating a higher-level cognitive process than the comparing cognitive process within the Understand level (Bloom's level 2) is that students must determine how parts fit into the overall structure of the concept. Following are examples of differentiating activities.

- Students read a science report in Microsoft Word and use yellow highlights to note information supporting the hypothesis. With red highlights, they identify information that does not support the hypothesis.
- Students search the web for links to fossils. Using Google Bookmarks, students cite the websites and in the notes section explain how each provides evidence about the types of organisms and environments that existed long ago.
- Students search online for statements that back the idea that democracy is or is not the best type of government. Students create a mind map using Popplet (http://popplet.com), justifying their stance.

Organizing

With organizing, students examine interactions and sequences of events. Students are able to identify connections among relevant information and then design a new arrangement or structure of the information to depict these relationships. To demonstrate their knowledge, students could construct charts, diagrams, outlines, flowcharts, or other graphic organizers to depict the interrelationships of items. Following are examples of organizing activities.

- Using Think Tree (https://itunes.apple.com/US/app/id381528942?mt=8), a mind-mapping application, students diagram consequences of President Lincoln's decision to stop slavery in the Confederate states.
- Using the mapping tool Gliffy (www.gliffy.com), students create a flowchart showing how an invasive plant would impact their environment.
- Students create an infographic on Piktochart (https://piktochart.com) that depicts the interrelationships of two habitats.

Attributing

Attributing involves students identifying biases, assumptions, or points of view in information. Assessing sources' credibility helps students analyze information. Following are examples of attributing activities.

- Using Storybird (https://storybird.com), students create a short story from the perspective of a literary figure, historical figure, or family member.
- Students examine an informational source in a word processing program and add comments when biases, assumptions, or points of view are expressed.

Evaluate

Evaluate is the fifth level of the taxonomy. Typically, the Analyze level (4) and other lower-cognitive processes are employed to engage in the Evaluate level's cognitive processes. With the Evaluate level, students examine informational sources to assess their quality and make decisions based on the identified criteria. There are two cognitive processes in the Evaluate level: (1) checking and (2) critiquing.

Checking

Checking encompasses examining for fallacies or inconsistencies (Anderson & Krathwohl, 2001). Stobaugh (2013) explains, "Students possessing this cognitive ability pursue unsubstantiated claims, question ideas, and demand validation for arguments, interpretations, assumptions, beliefs, or theories" (p. 33). To check a source, the student can examine the author's qualifications, determine whether sufficient and valid evidence is provided, and assess whether reliable sources are used. Following are examples of checking activities.

- On the Edmodo (www.edmodo.com) class website, students address any questionable claims stated in an article posted on the class blog.
- Students complete a multistep mathematics problem and record their explanations on ShowMe Interactive Whiteboard (http://apple.co/QSotX7). They then form pairs and watch their partners' ShowMe presentations and identify any mathematical errors.

Critiquing

Critiquing involves using set criteria to evaluate various options. Students use critiquing to identify reasons each option met or did not meet the criteria. Following are examples of critiquing activities.

- Students identify an interesting field trip that'll help them learn about food webs. They research four options and complete a graphic organizer showing how each option meets the criteria to be interesting and help them learn about food webs. Finally, they vote on the best choice on Polldaddy (http://polldaddy.com), an online voting site.

- Students identify characteristics of a hero. Students then brainstorm several people who possess those characteristics and rank how well each meets the criteria. After selecting the person best meeting the criteria, students write and record a podcast describing the positive attributes of their hero.

Create

Create is the highest level on Bloom's revised taxonomy. It involves organizing information in a new way to design a product. Within this level, students utilize the cognitive processes of the Understand, Analyze, and Evaluate levels to *create* a new product with the content. Students designing a poster or website don't necessarily reach the Create level unless they are engaged in brainstorming new ideas, identifying the best idea, planning a solution, and then implementing an original solution. Authentic tasks and projects are great for planning a Create-level assignment. When students are placed in real-world roles such as journalists or investigators, they can engage in these higher-level processes. See table 2.3 for a creativity rubric to assess assignments on the Create level.

Table 2.3: Creativity Rubric

	IMITATIVE	ORDINARY OR ROUTINE	CREATIVE	VERY CREATIVE
Variety of Ideas and Contexts	Ideas do not represent important concepts.	Ideas represent important concepts from the same or similar contexts or disciplines.	Ideas represent important concepts from different contexts or disciplines.	Ideas represent a startling variety of important concepts from different contexts or disciplines.
Variety of Sources	Created product draws on only one source or on sources that are not trustworthy or appropriate.	Created product draws on a limited set of sources and media.	Created product draws on a variety of sources, including different texts, media, resource persons, or personal experiences.	Created product draws on a wide variety of sources, including different texts, media, resource persons, or personal experiences.
Combining Ideas	Ideas are copied or restated from the sources consulted.	Ideas are combined in ways that are derived from the thinking of others (for example, of the authors in sources consulted).	Ideas are combined in original ways to solve a problem, address an issue, or make something new.	Ideas are combined in original and surprising ways to solve a problem, address an issue, or make something new.
Communicating Something New	Created product does not serve its intended purpose (for example, solving a problem or addressing an issue).	Created product serves its intended purpose (for example, solving a problem or addressing an issue), but is not original or does not effectively solve the problem.	Created product is interesting, new, or helpful, making an original contribution for its intended purpose (for example, solving a problem or addressing an issue).	Created product is interesting, new, or helpful, making an original contribution that includes identifying a previously unknown problem, issue, or purpose.

Source: Adapted from Brookhart, 2013.

There are three Create-level cognitive processes, and they occur sequentially: (1) generating, (2) planning, and (3) producing.

Generating

When students engage in the generating cognitive process, they explore various ideas or solutions to solve an ill-defined problem through hypothesizing and exploring various relevant options. To begin this process, the topic must be researched and thoroughly understood so the ideas generated logically connect to the identified topic. The ideas should also be varied, unique, and detailed (Swartz & Parks, 1994). Following are examples of generating activities.

- After discussing habitats, students select one habitat and brainstorm a new animal that could survive in that habitat. Groups generate a list of all the possible options and then select the best idea.
- After learning about Cinco de Mayo, groups determine the best way to replicate the holiday in their school to promote Mexican culture. Students use DebateGraph (www.debategraph.org) to show their thinking processes as they brainstorm ideas. They present their brainstorming webs, and the class votes on the best plan to implement.
- In groups, students write a new school song using their knowledge of rhymes in poetry.

Planning

Planning is the second step in the creation process. Students will take the best idea they generated and decide on a plan to carry out the project. Often there is more than one way to solve the problem. Also, during the planning process, students often realize they must revise their idea or consider a new idea. Following are examples of planning activities.

- Students take the new animal they developed in the generating process and create a story about the animal living in its habitat.
- Based on the goal from the generating process to educate students about Cinco de Mayo, the class decides how to implement the ideas suggested. Groups are created to plan specific parts of the celebration. Each group creates a table listing actions to be accomplished, individual responsibilities, target dates for completion, and resources needed. Students post the table in Google Docs so all group members can access the file.
- Groups take their best idea for the school song from the generating process and develop a rough draft of their song, writing all the lyrics and deciding on the tune. They also decide how they will produce the song—with instruments or using GarageBand.

Producing

The final step is to follow through with the plan and produce the product. Following are examples of producing activities.

- Using Microsoft Paint, students draw the animal created during the generating and planning processes and import it into Lulu (www.lulu.com) or another book-creation site. Students compose an original story about the new animal.
- Each group follows through with its plan to implement its school Cinco de Mayo celebration created during the generating and planning processes. One group polls the students before and after attending the celebration to measure students' learning about the holiday.
- Using GarageBand, the students develop the new school song they created during the generating and planning processes. Each group's song is video recorded and linked on the school's webpage. Students are encouraged to vote on the best song using the polling website Poll Everywhere (www.polleverywhere.com).

Standards and Cognitive Complexity

The concept of cognitive complexity is embedded in teaching standards as well as performance expectations for each content standard. Most teaching standards indicate that educators should challenge students to think at high levels. In addition, student content standards embrace the concept that students should be engaged in cognitively complex tasks and projects. Standards from the core areas of mathematics, science, social studies, and English language arts all pinpoint the focus on critical thinking while teaching content. Additionally, teaching standards note the importance of cognitively complex instruction. In the standards, words including *critique*, *generate*, and *evaluate* represent the higher-level thinking required in the highest three levels of the Create Excellence Framework and Bloom's taxonomy. See table 2.4 for examples of standards aligned to the cognitive-complexity component. We have italicized key high-level verbs in the standards to emphasize the level of thinking required.

Table 2.4: Alignment of Standards to Cognitive Complexity

SOURCE OF STANDARDS	STANDARD INDICATORS
STUDENT STANDARDS	
Social studies: C3 Framework	D1.4.3–5: "Explain how supporting questions help answer compelling questions in an inquiry" (NCSS, 2013).
	D2.Civ.9.3–5: "Use deliberative processes when making decisions or reaching judgments as a group" (NCSS, 2013).
Science: Next Generation Science Standards	Science Practice 1: Asking Questions and Defining Problems
	• "Define a simple design problem that can be solved through the development of an object, tool, process, or system and includes several criteria for success and constraints on materials, time, or cost" (Achieve, 2013).
	Science Practice 4: Analyzing and Interpreting Data
	• "Analyze and interpret data to make sense of phenomena, using logical reasoning" (Achieve, 2013).
	Science Practice 6: Constructing Explanations and Designing Solutions
	• "Generate and compare multiple solutions to a problem based on how well they meet the criteria and constraints of the design solution" (Achieve, 2013).
Mathematics: Common Core mathematics standards	Mathematical Practice 2: "Reason *abstractly* and quantitatively" (NGA & CCSSO, 2010b).
	Mathematical Practice 3: "*Construct viable arguments and critique* the reasoning of others" (NGA & CCSSO, 2010b).
English language arts: Common Core English language arts standards	RI.2.9: "Compare and contrast the most important points presented by two texts on the same topic" (NGA & CCSSO, 2010a).
	W.4.4: "Produce clear and coherent writing in which the development and organization are appropriate to task, purpose, and audience" (NGA & CCSSO, 2010a).
	W.4.9: "Draw evidence from literary or informational texts to support analysis, reflection, and research" (NGA & CCSSO, 2010a).

Continued →

SOURCE OF STANDARDS	STANDARD INDICATORS
TEACHER STANDARDS	
Danielson Framework for Teaching	Domain 1: Planning and Preparation—1C Setting Instructional Outcomes • Distinguished level: "All outcomes represent high-level learning in the discipline" (Danielson, 2014, p. 17). Domain 1: Planning and Preparation—1E Designing Coherent Instruction • Distinguished level: "The sequence of learning activities follows a coherent sequence, is aligned to instructional goals, and is designed to engage students in high-level cognitive activity" (Danielson, 2014, p. 17).

Critical Questions for Cognitive Complexity

When planning instruction for cognitive complexity, teachers should reflect on the following critical questions.

- What is the Bloom's level of student thinking in the task?
- Will the student work produce this level of thinking?
- Is the project standards based and part of the curriculum?
- Is the project teacher directed (level 3) or student directed (level 4)?
- Do students have opportunities to generate open-ended, high-level thinking questions (level 5)?

Conclusion

Cognitive complexity is one dimension in the Create Excellence Framework for real-world learning. Bloom's revised taxonomy identifies a hierarchy of six thinking levels and nineteen cognitive processes. The Create Excellence Framework builds on this taxonomy by defining five levels of integration of cognitive complexity. Teachers can draw from the examples of student activities found in this chapter to design critical-thinking tasks and projects to improve student learning in their classrooms.

Discussion Questions

Answer the following six questions to summarize the chapter's concepts.

1. Why do elementary students need to have critical-thinking skills?
2. How does embedding critical-thinking activities into your instruction change the way you teach?
3. How might increasing the level of cognitive complexity in your class help students beyond the classroom?
4. How would teaching critical thinking be different in a primary versus intermediate elementary classroom?
5. Identify a critical-thinking task you assigned, and determine where it fits into Bloom's taxonomy. Then, apply the Create Excellence Framework to raise the level of critical thinking.
6. Which instructional task or project in this chapter could you adapt to use in your classroom?

Take Action

Consider the following seven tasks and activities to help you toward implementing the Create Excellence Framework.

1. Fill in the "Critical-Thinking Dispositions Evaluation Form for Teachers" reproducible (page 46), and ask your students to complete the form as well (page 47). Use the results to engage in a discussion about critical thinking.

2. Complete the reproducible "Revised Bloom's Taxonomy Quiz" (page 48), and check your answers with the answer key. Alternatively, take the online quiz on Quizlet (http://quizlet.com/389701/test).

3. Examine the scenario in the reproducible "Analyzing a Task or Project for Cognitive Complexity" (page 50), and complete the questions. Review and compare your answers to the authors' responses provided in the reproducible.

4. Read *Designing Instruction Using Revised Bloom's Taxonomy* (Maxwell, 2012) about the cognitive-complexity dimension of the Create Excellence Framework. Visit http://goo.gl/PAUFr0 to access the book.

5. Examine the rubrics on page 52 and page 53. How can you use these tools in your classroom?

6. Select one of the Create Excellence Framework projects in part II of this book. How could you modify the project to use in your classroom? How could you improve one of the projects? Have a conversation with a colleague about implementing the project.

7. Select another project in part II. Rate each component of the project based on the framework levels. Compare your ratings to the rating table following the project description. How could you increase the ratings for each Create Excellence Framework component?

Critical-Thinking Dispositions Evaluation Form for Teachers

Read each of the following statements. For each statement, mark if it is something you do seldom, occasionally, or frequently. Complete the open-ended questions after the survey, and then discuss your weaknesses and strengths.

CRITICAL-THINKING DISPOSITIONS	SELDOM	OCCASIONALLY	FREQUENTLY
Seeks a clear statement of the thesis or question			
Seeks reasons			
Uses and mentions credible sources			
Takes into account the total situation			
Tries to remain relevant to the main point			
Keeps in mind the original or basic concern			
Looks for alternatives			
Is open-minded			
Takes a position (and changes a position) when the evidence and reasons are sufficient to do so			
Seeks as much precision as the subject permits			
Deals in an orderly manner with the parts of a complex whole			

Source: Adapted from Ennis, 1987.

1. Which is the critical-thinking disposition that is the most challenging, and which is the easiest for you?

2. What do you need to do to improve on the area you struggle with?

Critical-Thinking Dispositions Evaluation Form for Students

Read each of the following statements. For each statement, mark if it is something you do none of the time, some of the time, or always. Then, discuss your weaknesses and strengths with a partner.

CRITICAL-THINKING DISPOSITIONS	NONE	SOME	ALWAYS
I try to solve problems.			
I reflect on what I'm learning and doing.			
I try to do my best work.			
I ask good questions.			
I take responsibility for my own learning.			
I listen and consider others' ideas.			

1. Circle which of the statements is the most challenging for you.

2. How can you improve your most challenging area?

3. Put a check mark by the statement that is easiest for you.

4. Why is this easy for you?

Revised Bloom's Taxonomy Quiz

Directions: Identify the cognitive process under each revised Bloom's taxonomy level, and use the answer key that follows to check your answers.

Remember	
	1. Identify the parts of an ecosystem using the word bank provided.
	2. Define the meaning of an acronym as stated in class.
Understand	
	3. Design a symbol to represent the purpose of one of the technology tools.
	4. Contrast two characters in the story.
	5. Group objects into living or nonliving categories.
	6. What mathematical mistake was in each of the three problems?
	7. Compose a tweet that explains the point of today's lesson.
	8. In what ways is your family democratic?
	9. In your experiment, what caused the water to turn green?
Apply	
	10. Read and write numbers to one thousand using base-ten numerals, number names, and expanded form.
	11. Use the formula to write a five-paragraph essay.
Analyze	
	12. Determine the point of view in the story.
	13. Select three editorials, and, based on their sources, determine the differences between various political parties.
	14. Construct a flowchart showing how colonial rebellion led to the Revolutionary War.
Evaluate	
	15. Read the scientific lab report, and examine if the conclusions are appropriate.
	16. Determine which of Dr. Seuss's poems represents his best work.
Create	
	17. Develop a list of the webpages and what content will be on each page.
	18. Design the webpage.
	19. Brainstorm all possible web layouts for our school webpage to best meet parent, teacher, and student needs.

Answer Key

Remember

1. Recognizing

2. Recalling

Understand

3. Interpreting

4. Comparing

5. Classifying

6. Inferring

7. Summarizing

8. Exemplifying

9. Explaining

Apply

10. Implementing

11. Executing

Analyze

12. Attributing

13. Differentiating

14. Organizing

Evaluate

15. Checking

16. Critiquing

Create

17. Planning

18. Producing

19. Generating

Analyzing a Task or Project for Cognitive Complexity

Examine the scenario in the following table, and answer the questions. Then, compare your answers to the authors' responses.

Scenario: Students will group pictures of prehistoric animals based on similar characteristics.	
Level of Cognitive Complexity	What is this task's level of cognitive complexity?
Ways to Raise the Cognitive Complexity	What are some ways to increase the level of thinking for this task?
New Level of Cognitive Complexity	What is the new level of cognitive complexity?

Authors' Responses

Compare your answers to the authors' responses to the scenario questions.

Level of Cognitive Complexity

This assignment is on the Understand level of the revised Bloom's taxonomy using the classifying cognitive process.

Ways to Raise the Cognitive Complexity

To challenge students toward deeper learning:

- Students could brainstorm a new animal that could have survived along with the other prehistoric animals. They would need to consider the habitat and survival characteristics.
- Students could then use an online or software paint program to draw their animal and then import that picture into a presentation program like Prezi.
- Students then could record themselves explaining how their animal could best survive among the other animals making a PreziCast with the help of a screen-capturing program like Screencast-O-Matic (www.screencast-o-matic.com) or ScreenFlow (www.telestream.net /screenflow).

New Level of Cognitive Complexity

This task or project would raise the assignment to the Create level on Bloom's revised taxonomy. Students would engage in the generating cognitive process as they brainstormed possible animals that would be able to survive. They would be carefully rejecting many ideas that wouldn't work. Students would be thinking using the planning and producing cognitive dimensions as they drew their animal and justified in their presentation how it would best survive in that environment.

Real-World Learning Framework for Elementary Schools © 2017 Solution Tree Press • SolutionTree.com
Visit **go.SolutionTree.com/instruction** to download this free reproducible.

Grades K–2 Critical-Thinking Rubric for Problem-Based Learning

I can explain why we are doing the project.

1. Still learning	2. Sometimes	3. Almost always

I can ask questions about the project.

1. Still learning	2. Sometimes	3. Almost always

I can use information I get from different places.

1. Still learning	2. Sometimes	3. Almost always

I can say why an idea is a good one.

1. Still learning	2. Sometimes	3. Almost always

I can use feedback from my friends and teacher to improve my work.

1. Still learning	2. Sometimes	3. Almost always

I can explain my idea using facts and details.

1. Still learning	2. Sometimes	3. Almost always

Sources: BIE, 2013a. Used with permission.

Grades 3–5 Critical-Thinking Rubric for Problem-Based Learning

CRITICAL-THINKING OPPORTUNITY AT PHASES OF A PROJECT	BELOW STANDARD	APPROACHING STANDARD	AT STANDARD	ABOVE STANDARD ✓
Launching the Project: Analyze Driving Question and Begin Inquiry	• I cannot explain what I would need to know to be able to answer the driving question. • I still need to learn how another person might think differently about the driving question. • I still need to learn how to ask questions about what our audience or product users might want or need.	• I can identify a few things I would need to know to be able to answer the driving question. • I can understand that another person might think differently about the driving question. • I can ask a few questions about what our audience or product users might want or need.	• I can explain what I would need to know to be able to answer the driving question. • I can explain how different people might think about the driving question. • I can ask lots of questions about what our audience or product users might want or need.	
Building Knowledge, Understanding, and Skills: Gather and Evaluate Information	• I still need to learn how to use information from different sources to help answer the driving question. • I still need to learn how to think about whether my information is relevant or if I have enough.	• I can use information from different sources to help answer the driving question, but I may have trouble putting it together. • I can think about whether my information is relevant and if I have enough, but I don't always decide carefully.	• I can use information from different sources to help answer the driving question. • I can decide if my information is relevant and if I have enough.	

CRITICAL-THINKING OPPORTUNITY AT PHASES OF A PROJECT	BELOW STANDARD	APPROACHING STANDARD	AT STANDARD	ABOVE STANDARD ✓
Developing and Revising Ideas and Products: Use Evidence and Criteria	• I still need to learn how to identify the reasons and evidence an author or speaker uses to support a point. • I still need to learn how to decide if an idea for a product or an answer to the driving question is a good one. • I still need to learn how to use feedback from other students and adults to improve my writing or my design for a product.	• I can identify some of the reasons and evidence an author or speaker uses to support a point. • I can tell when an idea for a product or an answer to the driving question is a good one but cannot always say why. • I can sometimes use feedback from other students and adults to improve my writing or my design for a product.	• I can explain how an author or speaker uses reasons and evidence to support a point that helps me answer the driving question. • I can explain how to decide if an idea for a product or an answer to the driving question is a good one. • I can use feedback from other students and adults to improve my writing or my design for a product.	
Presenting Products and Answers to Driving Question: Justify Choices	• I still need to learn how to explain my ideas in an order that makes sense. • I still need to learn how to use appropriate facts or relevant details to support my ideas.	• I can explain my ideas, but some might be in the wrong order. • I can use some facts and details to support my ideas, but they are not always appropriate and relevant.	• I can explain my ideas in an order that makes sense. • I can use appropriate facts and relevant details to support my ideas.	

Source: Adapted from BIE, 2013b. Used with permission.

CHAPTER 3

Student Engagement

In the spring, kindergarten students are studying the role of community helpers. One student asks why there wasn't a community helper to rescue cats from a tree. The students giggle, and another asks why there aren't community helpers to carry a large snake. One student asks why they cannot invent a community helper. So the students work in pairs to draw an original community helper on the app Explain Everything on their iPads and record an audio narration about their community helper.

Student engagement happens when students take responsibility for their own learning and partner or collaborate with the teacher, other students, or outside experts to guide their learning. The concept of engaged learning has a well-established history that has morphed since the 1990s into much more than simply attention to the learning task. Research demonstrates that engagement in learning involves student interest (Dewey, 1913), effort (Meece, Blumenfeld, & Hoyle, 1988), motivation (Skinner & Belmont, 1993), time on task (Berliner, 1990), and high levels of active learner participation (Bulger, Mayer, & Almeroth, 2006). Students in highly engaging classrooms perform an average of nearly 30 percentile points higher than other students on standardized tests (Marzano, 2007). This chapter explains the five levels of student engagement, the elements of engaged learning, and standards for student engagement.

Five Levels of Student Engagement

The Create Excellence Framework's student-engagement component indicates the degree to which students take responsibility for their own learning; partner or collaborate with the teacher, other students, or outside experts; and use resources such as teachers, experts in the discipline, and tools and technology. The five levels of engagement are described in the following sections.

Knowing

At level 1, students engage very little. The teacher may lecture or question while students take notes. Usually, this type of instruction or assessment expects one correct answer to questions.

Practicing

Students at the Practicing level are working on a task or project the teacher designs and directs. Unlike Knowing, where there is only one correct answer, multiple solutions are possible and accepted in the Practicing level. A task or project in which the teacher tells students to write a paragraph on their iPad about the early explorers in their state, using at least five of their ten vocabulary words, is an example of a Practicing-level activity.

Investigating

At level 3, Investigating, the teacher directs a task or project in which students have choice and that differentiates content, process, or product. An example of a level 3 task or project is a teacher directing students to select any famous African American scientist, author, or politician and create an Animoto video from the African American's point of view describing how he or she accomplished what made him or her famous, and what a day was like in his or her life at the time he or she became famous.

Integrating

At level 4, Integrating, students partner with the teacher to define the content, process, or product; students use an inquiry-based approach; and students collaborate with other students. An example of an Integrating activity is a class that has been studying various health habits. When a student comes into class one day with a foot injury after falling on a gravel road, the teacher capitalizes on the teachable moment. The class discusses the absence of safe walking trails, brainstorms options for solving the problem, studies zoning regulations, interviews community members, and writes letters to the mayor and council members. The students then work with professionals from the community to create a proposal to build safe walking and running trails and propose their ideas in a community forum.

Specializing

In the highest level, Specializing, students initiate their own inquiry-based learning projects. They are thoroughly immersed in the project, conduct full implementation from topic to solution, and initiate appropriate collaborations pertaining to their project. For example, students become upset after watching a documentary about students in a Kenyan school who do not have chairs for their classroom. The documentary deeply moves these fourth graders. The students want to raise funds for chairs for the African students. The teacher and students use Coggle (https://coggle.it), an online mind-mapping tool, to brainstorm ways to raise the funds. One student's idea is to sponsor a hat day at school where students pay one dollar for the privilege of wearing a hat at school. Another student contacts his uncle, a member of a civic club, to help them. The students also participate in an event at the county fair to raise funds. The teacher contacts an international humanitarian group for the students to work with to purchase and ship the chairs. The humanitarian group delivers the chairs (with desktops) and makes a video of the excited African students to share with the fourth graders.

Table 3.1 provides the student-engagement component at the five levels as well as an example at each level.

Table 3.1: The Student-Engagement Levels of the Create Excellence Framework

CREATE LEVEL	DESCRIPTION	SAMPLE TASK OR PROJECT
1: Knowing	Teacher lectures or questions while students take notes or expects only one correct answer from the students.	Students determine whether the following statement is true or false: The trumpet is an essential instrument to the 1940s and 1950s jazz movement.
2: Practicing	Students are engaged in a teacher-directed task or project, and multiple solutions for one task or project are accepted.	After reading the diary of a 1950s young girl, students summarize how music affected her life.
3: Investigating	There is student choice for a task or project, and content, process, product, or differentiation, such as addressing learning preferences, interests, or ability levels for the task or project.	After watching a performance of a jazz ensemble, students determine the conductor's most important movements that the jazz ensemble has to follow. Students answer the questions, What hand movements are irrelevant? and What hand movements help the ensemble stay together? Then, they present their findings in a Prezi presentation and distinguish why it is important to focus and listen when working in an ensemble.
4: Integrating	Students partner with the teacher to define the content, process, or product; students take an inquiry-based approach; and students collaborate with other students.	After viewing a video about contemporary jazz music in the 1950s, the fifth-grade students begin discussing how much their grandparents enjoyed this music. Some of the students who play musical instruments want to play some of the jazz music. Another student suggests that they play the music for the seniors at the nursing home down the street. Some students learn to play the music, and others learn the dances. So the students and teacher plan the concert and dance where they perform and get some of the seniors involved in the dances.
5: Specializing	Students initiate their own inquiry-based learning projects with thorough immersion and full implementation from topic to solution, and students initiate appropriate collaborations pertaining to their project.	After the concert and dance at the nursing home, students are so excited that they want to learn more about jazz music and how it evolved into today's music. The students discover and contact the Jazz Foundation of America. Through this organization, they discover a famous jazz musician who is now older and not performing anymore. The students contact him and offer to play jazz with him if he is willing. He visits the school and is excited to play jazz with the students. He and the students organize a benefit concert for their new jazz musician friend so that he can begin to travel and play jazz again.

Elements of Engaged Learning

Student engagement has become an important quality in creating effective schools and advancing student achievement. Educators know now that students simply staring at the teacher or completing worksheets does not equal engaged learning, and just because students are quiet and busy, that does *not* mean they are engaged in their learning. Activities that focus on procedures and rudimentary tasks as opposed to cognitively demanding learning opportunities have been found to actually impede student engagement (Blumenfeld & Meece, 1988). Engaged learning involves students solving problems or creating solutions to ill-structured, multidisciplinary, real-world problems. There are several facets of engaged learning, including the following.

- **Inquiry-based learning:** Students are engaged in solving problems or creating solutions to develop deep understandings.
- **Student-directed learning:** Students are active learners, take responsibility for their own learning, and have voice and choice.
- **Collaboration within and beyond the classroom:** Students collaborate or partner with other students, teachers, or outside experts.
- **Differentiated learning:** Students' interests, ability and readiness, and learning preferences are taken into consideration, and instruction is differentiated accordingly.

Inquiry-Based Learning

Student engagement is connected to a movement in education toward inquiry-based learning. With inquiry-based learning, students are engaging with real-world issues while solving problems or creating solutions to develop deep understandings. According to biology instructor Douglas Schamel and research associate Matthew P. Ayres (1992), students learn in a more effective manner when they generate their own questions based on their observations rather than developing a solution to a situation or problem with a predetermined answer. The National Science Education Standards state, "Inquiry is something that students do, not something that is done to them" (National Research Council, 1996, p. 21). Since inquiry-based learning is student directed, it would be placed at the Integrating level (4) of the Create Excellence Framework if students are collaborating with the teacher and other students. It would be considered level 5 (Specializing) if students are collaborating beyond the classroom.

The basis of inquiry-based learning is that students are key planners and designers in the learning process. Table 3.2 shows the comparisons between traditional and inquiry-based learning, with students directing the learning, the teacher facilitating the learning, and students having input in the assessment.

Table 3.2: Comparison of Traditional and Inquiry-Based Learning

TRADITIONAL	INQUIRY BASED
Teacher directed	Student directed
Teacher as giver of knowledge	Teacher as facilitator of learning
Content mastery	Content mastery and beyond
Vertical and linear learning path	Learning is more web-like; concept development ranges from linear to spiral
Teacher-created assessment	Assessment requires student input

Source: Adapted from Crie, 2005.

With inquiry-based learning, students first explore the topic and identify a question. In collaboration with the teacher, students establish the learning target for the project and the assessment. An atmosphere of intellectual and emotional safety is essential so that students have the freedom to take risks without fear of embarrassment, punishment, or implications that they are inadequate. Students need the freedom to take unpopular risks and explain why their answer is plausible (Antonetti & Garver, 2015).

Second, students investigate through designing the plan, selecting information, and formulating the focus. Third, students analyze, evaluate, and organize the information to process it. Finally, students create a product or presentation to demonstrate their learning, an authentic-performance task. While this model moves away from the rote memorization of concepts, there is supporting evidence that students learn as many basic facts through this model as in a teacher-directed lecture. The benefit with this model is that students tend to be able to recall their learning for a longer time (Gabel, 1994). *Inquiry-based learning* is the umbrella term that encompasses the ideas of design thinking, problem-based learning, and project-based instruction.

Design Thinking

Design thinking is a student-driven, problem-solving model that requires high levels of student engagement. In design thinking, students identify a school or community issue and gather information about the problem. Next, they brainstorm solutions to the problem and research the best ideas. They then create a prototype for a select solution, gathering feedback from experts who review their work. Finally, they implement the solution and present their findings. Design thinking is perfect for the STEAM (science, technology, engineering, art, and mathematics) disciplines. It provides ways for students to structure their thinking to develop solutions.

Problem-Based Learning

Closely connected to design thinking is problem-based learning (PBL). The PBL model clearly connects to high levels of student engagement as it emphasizes the learning process, student choice, student-directed learning, inquiry-based approaches, student collaboration, and multidisciplinary, authentic problems that are not always well defined or clearly structured. The following is a summary of the eight PBL steps (BIE, 2014).

1. Explore the problem.
2. Record what you know that can help you solve the problem.
3. Develop a problem statement.
4. Identify possible solutions.
5. List actions to complete to solve the problem.
6. Research information to help solve the problem.
7. Record a solution that includes the data gathered, data analysis, and support for the solution.
8. Present and defend your conclusion.

See figures 3.1, 3.2, 3.3, and 3.4 (pages 60–67) for tools to assess PBL projects.

Source: Adapted from BIE, 2013e. Used with permission.

Figure 3.1: Grades K–2 collaboration rubric for PBL.

CCSS ELA–Aligned Individual Performance for Grades 3–5			
	BELOW STANDARD	**APPROACHING STANDARD**	**AT STANDARD**	**ABOVE STANDARD** ✓
Takes Responsibility	• I need to prepare for and join team discussions. • I need reminders to do project work. • My project work is not done on time. • I need to learn how to use feedback from others.	• I am usually prepared for and join team discussions. • I do some project work but sometimes need to be reminded. • I complete most project work on time. • I sometimes use feedback from others.	• I am prepared for work with the team; I have studied required material and use it to explore ideas in discussions (3–5.SL.1a). • I do project work without having to be reminded. • I complete project work on time. • I use feedback from others to improve my work.	
Helps the Team	• I need to cooperate with my team and help the team solve problems. • I need to learn how to help make discussions effective. • I need to learn how to give useful feedback to others. • I need to learn to offer to help others if they need it.	• I cooperate with the team but do not help it solve problems. • I usually help make discussions effective but do not always follow the rules, ask enough questions, or express ideas clearly. • I give feedback to others, but it may not always be helpful. • I sometimes offer to help others if they need it.	• I help the team solve problems and manage conflicts. • I help make discussions effective by following agreed-upon rules, asking and answering questions, and clearly expressing ideas (3–5.SL.1b, c, d). • I give helpful feedback to others. • I offer to help others do their work if needed.	

Figure 3.2: Grades 3–5 collaboration rubric for PBL.

Continued →

	BELOW STANDARD	APPROACHING STANDARD	AT STANDARD	ABOVE STANDARD ✓
Respects Others	• I am sometimes impolite or unkind to teammates (may interrupt them, ignore others' ideas, or hurt their feelings). • I need to learn how to listen to other points of view and disagree kindly.	• I am usually polite and kind to teammates. • I usually listen to other points of view and disagree kindly.	• I am polite and kind to teammates. • I listen to other points of view and disagree kindly.	

CCSS ELA–Aligned Team Performance Rubric for Grades 3–5

	BELOW STANDARD	APPROACHING STANDARD	AT STANDARD	ABOVE STANDARD ✓
Makes and Follows Agreements	• We need to learn how to talk about how the team will work together. • We need to learn how to follow rules for collegial discussions, decision making, and conflict resolution. • We need to learn how to talk about how well agreements are being followed.	• We try to talk about how the team will work together but do not make agreements. • We usually follow rules for discussions, decision making, and conflict resolution but not always. • We sometimes talk about how well agreements are being followed but need help from the teacher to take appropriate steps when they are not.	• We make agreements about how the team will work together. • We follow rules for discussions (3–5.SL.1b), decision making, and conflict resolution. • We honestly talk about how well agreements are being followed and take appropriate steps if they are not.	

Organizes Work	• We get to work without creating a task list. • We need to learn how to set a schedule and track progress toward goals and deadlines. • We need to learn how to assign roles. • We need to learn how to use time and run meetings well and organize our materials, drafts, and notes.	• We create a task list that divides project work among the team, but it may not be in detail or followed closely. • We set a schedule for doing tasks but do not follow it closely. • We assign roles but do not follow them, or we pick only one "leader" who makes most decisions. • We usually use time and run meetings well but may occasionally waste time; we keep our materials, drafts, and notes but not always organized.	• We create a detailed task list that divides project work fairly among the team (3–5. SL.1b). • We set a schedule and track progress toward goals and deadlines. • We assign roles based on team members' strengths (3–5. SL.1b). • We use time and run meetings efficiently; we keep our materials, drafts, and notes organized.	
Works as a Whole Team	• We need to learn how to recognize or use special talents of team members. • We need to learn how to do the project as a team.	• We try to use special talents of team members. • We do most project tasks separately and put them together at the end.	• We recognize and use each team member's special talents. • We develop ideas and create products as a team; tasks done separately are brought to the team for feedback.	

Source: Adapted from BIE, 2013c. Used with permission.

Source: BIE, 2013d. Used with permission.

Figure 3.3: Grades K–2 creativity and innovation rubric for PBL.

Process				
CREATIVITY AND INNOVATION OPPORTUNITY AT PHASES OF A PROJECT	BELOW STANDARD	APPROACHING STANDARD	AT STANDARD	ABOVE STANDARD ✓
Launching the Project: Define the Creative Challenge	• I may just follow directions without understanding why something needs to be created. • I still need to learn how to think about what people might need or like when they use or see what is created.	• I know that something needs to be created but cannot give detailed reasons why. • I have a basic idea of what people might need or like when they use or see what is created.	• I understand the reasons why something needs to be created. • I understand the needs and interests of the people who will use or see what is created.	
Building Knowledge, Understanding, and Skills: Identify Sources of Information	• I use only the usual sources of information (website, book, or article).	• I find one or two sources of information that are unusual.	• I find unusual ways to get information.	
Developing and Revising Ideas and Products: Generate and Select Ideas	• I think of ideas for the product that are not new or original. • I pick an idea without deciding which one is best. • I still need to learn how to improve on the idea. • I still need to learn how to use feedback from others to improve written products.	• I think of some new ideas for the product. • I quickly decide which idea is best. • I might think about how to improve on the idea but might not. • I use some feedback to make small changes in written products.	• I think of many new ideas for the product. • I carefully decide which idea is best. • I ask new questions and think about how to improve on the idea. • I use feedback from others to improve written products (3–5.W.5).	

Figure 3.4: Grades 3–5 creativity and innovation rubric for PBL.

Continued →

CREATIVITY AND INNOVATION OPPORTUNITY AT PHASES OF A PROJECT	BELOW STANDARD	APPROACHING STANDARD	AT STANDARD	ABOVE STANDARD ✓
Presenting Products and Answers to Driving Question: Present Work to Users or Target Audience	• I present ideas and products in just the regular ways (show Power Point slides and read notes). • I have no audience involvement.	• I try to add some interesting touches to visual aids, but they may not add much, or they may be distracting. • I try to involve the audience actively in the presentation, but it is very quick or does not work well.	• I create visual aids that are interesting to see and hear. • I involve audience members actively in the presentation (ask them questions and have them do an activity).	

Product

CREATIVITY AND INNOVATION OPPORTUNITY AT PHASES OF A PROJECT	BELOW STANDARD	APPROACHING STANDARD	AT STANDARD	ABOVE STANDARD ✓
Originality	• My product looks like things that have been seen before; it is not new or unique.	• My product has some new ideas, but it still looks mostly like things that have been seen before.	• My product is new, unique, and surprising; it shows a personal touch.	
Value	• My product is not useful or valuable to the people who use or see it. • My product would not work in the real world.	• My product is somewhat useful, but it may not exactly meet the needs of people who use or see it. • My product might work in the real world, but it might have problems.	• My product is seen as useful and valuable by the people who use or see it. • My product would work in the real world (not too hard, expensive, or time-consuming to create).	

| Style | • My product looks like other things like this; it is made in a traditional style.
• My product has several pieces that do not fit together; it is a mishmash. | • My product has some interesting touches.
• My product has some pieces that may be too much or do not fit together well. | • My product is well made, impressive, and designed with style.
• My product's pieces all go well together. | |

Note: The term *product* is used in this rubric as an umbrella term for the result of the process of innovation during a project. A product may be a constructed object, a proposal, a presentation, a solution to a problem, a service, a system, a work of art or piece of writing, an invention, an event, an improvement to an existing product, and so on.

Source: Adapted from BIE, 2013d. Used with permission.

While many books, websites, and professional developers train teachers to completely design project-based learning units before rolling them out to students, the Create Excellence Framework encourages teachers to include their students in the planning. Students can help add novelty and variety to the project. Projects can have a myriad of content, processes, or products; they can address diverse perspectives; and they can include competitions to instill excitement (Antonetti & Garver, 2015). Beyond novelty and variety, students can share perspectives that teachers may have overlooked or disregarded, which may be keys to engaging students.

The teacher can do some preliminary planning but should be willing to change the course of the project after hearing student suggestions. Even in kindergarten or first grade, students may ask questions that inspire the teacher to integrate the students' ideas and interests into the project. Teachers who are not as comfortable with letting go of the reins may need to take smaller steps. Professor Gerald Grow (1991) outlines four stages of self-directed learning (table 3.3).

Table 3.3: Stages of Self-Directed Learning

STAGE	STUDENT	TEACHER	EXPLANATION	EXAMPLES
1	Dependent	Authority coach	Coaching with immediate feedback, drill, and informational lecture; focus on overcoming deficiencies and resistance	Worksheets, skill tests, and reading groups
2	Interested	Motivator, guide	Inspiring teacher-led presentation plus guided discussion, goal setting, and learning strategies	Student discussion and projects follow the teacher's presentation

Continued →

STAGE	STUDENT	TEACHER	EXPLANATION	EXAMPLES
3	Involved	Facilitator	Teacher partner who collaborates as an equal facilitates discussion; students engage in Socratic seminars and group projects	Literacy circles and Socratic questioning; hosting a mock Congress with students writing bills
4	Self-directed	Consultant, delegator	Student-directed study group, individual work, and projects	Student-directed projects; students identify an authentic problem in their school, community, or world and design a plan of action to address it

Source: Adapted from Grow, 1991.

The teacher's purpose is to match the learner's stage of self-direction and prepare the learner to advance to higher stages. The process of inquiry-based learning involves a learning curve for the teacher and the students, but with practice, both teachers and students can become proficient at partnering for learning.

Project-Based Instruction

Project-based instruction (PBI) involves students designing a project or presentation as a demonstration of their understanding. Students gain knowledge and skills by working for an extended period of time to investigate and respond to a complex question, problem, or challenge. They are given some voice and choice in how they can complete the assignment, and they plan a rigorous project through which the teacher assesses key academic content and an authentic product or presentation conveys the knowledge they have gained (BIE, 2014). BIE (n.d.) further explains that essential elements of PBI include the following:

Significant Content—At its core, the project is focused on teaching students important knowledge and skills, derived from standards and key concepts at the heart of academic subjects.

21st Century Competencies—Students build competencies valuable for today's world, such as problem solving, critical thinking, collaboration, communication, and creativity/innovation, which are explicitly taught and assessed.

In-Depth Inquiry—Students are engaged in an extended, rigorous process of asking questions, using resources, and developing answers.

Driving Question—Project work is focused by an open-ended question that students understand and find intriguing, which captures their task/project or frames their exploration.

Need to Know—Students see the need to gain knowledge, understand concepts, and apply skills in order to answer the Driving Question and create project products, beginning with an Entry Event that generates interest and curiosity.

Voice and Choice—Students are allowed to make some choices about the products to be created, how they work, and how they use their time, guided by the teacher and depending on age level and PBL experience.

Critique and Revision—The project includes processes for students to give and receive feedback on the quality of their work, leading them to make revisions or conduct further inquiry.

Public Audience—Students present their work to other people, beyond their classmates and teacher.

Student-Directed Learning

Student-directed learning is another key component of student engagement. Student-directed learning places the learning focus directly on the students and less heavily on the teacher's actions. As incorporated in all elements of inquiry-based learning, students are active learners, take responsibility for their own learning, and constantly formulate new ideas and refine them through their collaboration with others (Hung, Tan, & Koh, 2006). In project-based learning, students have voice and choice. Students help teachers set clear expectations so that they know what success looks like. Students articulate the targets or goals and examine targets in their own work (Antonetti & Garver, 2015).

Finding the spark—a real-world subject, idea, or project that makes a student light up—is the key to customizing learning experiences and engaging individual students. In order to tailor learning to meet students' educational needs and aspirations, teachers seek and develop knowledge of each student's unique tendencies, circumstances, and interests through both formal processes (such as surveys or advisories) and informal processes (casual conversations and insight from partner or cooperating organizations, community members, or other teachers; Martinez, 2014). For example, on a level 4 project, students might partner with the teacher to decide which tasks they need to complete or determine what type of products they might produce.

Student-directed learning in comparison to teacher-directed approaches increases students' depth of understanding, increases critical-thinking skills, improves long-term retention, and increases students' positive feelings toward the subject studied (Crie, 2005). At the highest levels of student-directed learning, students establish the learning goals based on their interests or questions they pose. At this level of self-directed learning, students may also co-construct knowledge, assume varied roles and tasks, and participate in self-monitoring and assessment.

The inquiry process identifies several levels based on the level of student input. In figure 3.5 (page 70), open inquiry involves the top level of student engagement in the learning process with *no predetermined questions since students propose and pursue their own questions*. This level could correlate with Create framework level 4 or 5 in the student-engagement component, depending on the amount of student initiation of inquiry and collaboration. In the second level, guided inquiry, the teacher decides on the topic, but the students can decide how they will approach the topic and investigate the problem. This level could connect with Create framework level 3 or 4, depending on the amount of teacher input or student collaboration. At the third level, structured inquiry, the teacher determines the topic and method for investigation, and students explore various solutions. This level could correlate with Create framework level 2 or 3, depending on task choices and differentiation. In the lowest level, limited inquiry, students follow the directions and make sure their results match those given in the text. This level would be Create framework level 2 since students are engaged in a teacher-directed task.

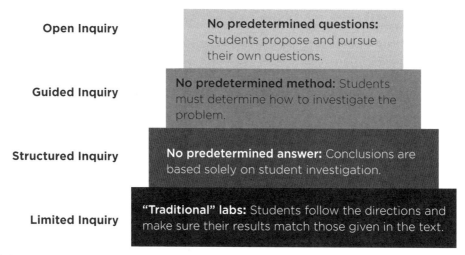

Open Inquiry — **No predetermined questions:** Students propose and pursue their own questions.

Guided Inquiry — **No predetermined method:** Students must determine how to investigate the problem.

Structured Inquiry — **No predetermined answer:** Conclusions are based solely on student investigation.

Limited Inquiry — **"Traditional" labs:** Students follow the directions and make sure their results match those given in the text.

Source: Stewart & Rivera, 2010.

Figure 3.5: Levels of student input in student-directed learning.

Collaboration Within and Beyond the Classroom

Collaboration is the third key component to student engagement. In engaging tasks, students should collaborate within the classroom with other students and teachers or beyond the classroom with outside experts. Teachers and experts provide real-world tools, techniques, and support that allow for open communicating and sharing (Hung et al., 2006).

Extending learning beyond the traditional classroom provides students with real-world learning experiences that allow them to communicate with experts, take ownership of their learning, and extend their support networks. Educators, including principals, act as consummate networkers throughout the process—searching for meaningful resources that meet the school's learning goals and student interests in places like museums, colleges, and community organizations. For many educators, tapping these resources has been done to arrange internships or mentorships, but the Create Excellence Framework encourages teachers and principals to use their networking skills for deeper learning (Martinez, 2014).

Student-Student Collaboration

Within the classroom, students can work in teams on problems through cooperative-learning tasks. When structured effectively, cooperative-learning tasks can teach students collaborative social interaction and team-building skills. Student collaboration works best when shared and flexible roles are defined, and accountability for the task or project is determined (Abrami, Lou, Chambers, Poulsen, & Spence, 2000). See figures 3.1 and 3.2 (pages 60–63) for rubrics to assess individual performance and collaboration with a team.

Student-Teacher Collaboration

Prensky (2010) promotes a partnering pedagogy where teachers and students collaborate on what to learn, how to learn, and how to assess. Each party in the collaboration draws on its own strengths to improve student learning. Student roles include researcher, technology user and expert, thinker, world changer, and self-teacher. The teacher roles include coach and guide, goal setter and questioner, learning designer, context provider, rigor and quality assurer, and assessor. There must be mutual trust and respect among students and teachers for true partnering to prosper. The teacher can guide students in locating resources to support their work.

Student-Expert Collaboration

Finally, collaboration can occur with outside experts, as is the case with projects at level 5 of the Create Excellence Framework. Communicating with experts through email, Skype, and other technologies can bridge the divide and provide up-to-date, real-world information to students. Education researchers Monica Bulger, Richard E. Mayer, and Kevin C. Almeroth (2006) assert that an engaged learning design should include a real-world task or project presented via directed interactive activities, collaborative group work, teacher facilitation, or role modeling and a requirement to reference and integrate resources from beyond the classroom's boundaries. This process allows students to benefit from the most up-to-date information as well as reconcile any misconceptions or inconsistent information from other sources as they collaborate with experts.

Students are more careful in their work if they know others are going to read it, especially if it is someone outside the school. An outside audience also instills a sense of responsibility to group work (Antonetti & Garver, 2015).

Differentiated Learning

Opportunities for choice combined with a broad variety of instructional strategies result in the highest levels of engagement (Raphael, Pressley, & Mohan, 2008). When students are given choices, they have a sense of ownership of their personal learning. A diverse collection of instructional strategies should be paired with students' prior knowledge and readiness to learn in order to promote student engagement. However, the level and complexity of the varied instructional strategies and activities must also be challenging (Gregory & Chapman, 2007). Table 3.4 presents three types of differentiation with examples of how they may be applied in a statistics project. Differentiation begins at level 3 with the teacher differentiating content, process, or product. At level 4, students partner with the teacher to define their own content, process, or product. At level 5, students design and implement their own inquiry-based projects from topic to full implementation to solution. Students initiate their own outside collaborations with field experts. With both of these top levels, instruction is differentiated as students choose what content to examine, what processes they will use to find the solution, and how they will demonstrate their learning (product).

Table 3.4: Three Types of Differentiation

TYPE OF DIFFERENTIATION	EXAMPLES OF A STATISTICS PROJECT
Differentiation of Content via Interests: Appealing to students' interests is one of the easiest and quickest ways to differentiate content. However, one must keep the content in mind to ensure that students' interests do not take them down rabbit holes too far away from learning the content. The teacher must make expectations and learning criteria clear to the students.	Most students are interested in pets and animal shelters. After studying the animal adoption process, a class visits the local animal shelter and selects an animal it likes. Using the animal's biographical description, some student teams decide to develop a persuasive video public service announcement (PSA) to persuade community members to adopt their animal. Other student teams decide to design an original enclosure or toy for their animal. (Level 4 on the Create Excellence Framework)

Continued →

TYPE OF DIFFERENTIATION	EXAMPLES OF A STATISTICS PROJECT
Differentiation of Process via Ability and Readiness: Another differentiation tactic is through addressing students' ability and readiness level. This method can provide focused instruction, and it aligns well with response to intervention. Students' educational needs differ in regard to pace and complexity; therefore, this method gives students an opportunity to achieve at their own cognitive level (Gavin, Casa, Adelson, Carroll, & Sheffield, 2009). All students can be studying the same content topic at the same time, yet some will experience and learn on different levels than others. Preassessment of the content is necessary to plan and focus on meeting students' needs.	Students are in different groups based on ability or readiness level. Continuing the example of the animal shelter, the teacher may give information to one group at a lower readiness level and assign it a project such as listing reasons that some animals end up in animal shelters and brainstorming ways to convince the students' parents to adopt from the animal shelter. (Level 2)\n\nThe second group of average ability or readiness may choose a dog or cat breed and research how often it ends up at animal shelters. Students could create a small multimedia presentation to persuade the class that rescuing animals from animal shelters is better than getting them by other means. (Level 3 or 4, depending on the amount of teacher direction versus student direction in project decision)\n\nThe third group with higher ability may design an online interactive questionnaire that would match potential adopters with the best dogs or cats up for adoption. (Level 4)
Differentiation of Product via Learning Preferences: Differentiation based on learning preferences can be realized through choice in product. Student products may be technological (blogs, webpages, and PowerPoints), visual (posters, pamphlets, and drawings), written (essays, vignettes, and articles), oral (speeches, interviews, and monologues), or kinesthetic (models, dioramas, and role play; Roberts & Inman, 2009).	Students have choice in their product for their project based on learning preferences; they will create an original product. Groups may be formed based on learning styles. Project choices can be based on learning styles (determined by a learning styles inventory). For example, a group of kinesthetic learners may bring in or print pictures of shelter animals and make a collage, matching animals to potential adopters. Students who prefer writing may select to write a newspaper editorial on the benefits of adopting pets from the animal shelter. Visual learners may create graphs or infographics depicting animals that need adopting and their characteristics. (Level depends on the amount of teacher direction and student voice in product selection and creation: if the teacher tells them what to create, it is level 3; if students are allowed to decide and create an original product, it could be level 4.)

Standards and Student Engagement

Content standards and teaching standards emphasize student engagement. In each content area, the standards indicate that students should be actively involved in learning. The content standards direct student engagement in having discussions, writing, solving problems, assessing options, and evaluating solutions. For example, the NGA and CCSSO (2010a) literacy standards state that students should "engage effectively in a range of collaborative discussions" (SL.8.1). In social studies, the C3 Framework states that students should "assess options for individual and collective action to address local, regional, and global problems by engaging in self-reflection, strategy identification, and complex causal reasoning" (D4.7.9–12; NCSS, 2013). These content standards are heavily focused on ways students can engage in and demonstrate their learning.

The emphasis on student engagement is also mirrored in the teaching standards. In the Danielson Framework for Teaching (Danielson, 2014), for a teacher to be scored exemplary for the indicator "Using Questioning and Discussion Techniques Within Domain 3: Instruction," students must initiate higher-order thinking questions, extend the discussion, and invite comments from their classmates. In this domain, an indicator is also dedicated to measure student engagement in the learning. To score exemplary on this indicator, students must be intellectually engaged in the lesson and take initiative to improve the lesson by modifying a learning task or project to make it more meaningful or relevant to their needs, suggesting modifications to the grouping patterns, or suggesting modifications or additions to the materials.

These indicators focus on student voice as a key component in leading the instruction, as opposed to in the past when the teacher planned the complete lesson without student input. See table 3.5 for examples of additional standards that focus on student engagement.

Table 3.5: Additional Standards That Focus on Student Engagement

SOURCE OF STANDARDS	STANDARD INDICATORS
STUDENT STANDARDS	
English language arts: Common Core English language arts standards	SL.4.3: "Identify the reasons and evidence a speaker provides to support particular points" (NGA & CCSSO, 2010a). W.5.10: "Write routinely over extended time frames (time for research, reflection, and revision) and shorter time frames (a single sitting or a day or two) for a range of tasks, purposes, and audiences" (NGA & CCSSO, 2010a).
Mathematics: Common Core mathematics standards	5.MD.C.5: "Relate volume to the operations of multiplication and addition and solve real world and mathematical problems involving volume" (NGA & CCSSO, 2010b). 4.OA.A.3: "Solve multistep word problems posed with whole numbers and having whole-number answers using the four operations, including problems in which remainders must be interpreted. Represent these problems using equations with a letter standing for the unknown quantity. Assess the reasonableness of answers using mental computation and estimation strategies including rounding" (NGA & CCSSO, 2010b). MP3: "Construct viable arguments and critique the reasoning of others" (NGA & CCSSO, 2010b).
Social studies: C3 Framework	D2.Eco.15.3–5: "Explain the effects of increasing economic interdependence on different groups within participating nations" (NCSS, 2013). D2.Geo.4.3–5: "Explain how culture influences the way people modify and adapt to their environments" (NCSS, 2013). D1.1.K–2: "Explain why the compelling question is important to the student" (NCSS, 2013). D1.4.3–5: "Explain how supporting questions help answer compelling questions in an inquiry" (NCSS, 2013).

Continued →

SOURCE OF STANDARDS	STANDARD INDICATORS
Science: Next Generation Science Standards	3–5-ETS1–2: "Generate and compare multiple possible solutions to a problem based on how well each is likely to meet the criteria and constraints of the problem" (Achieve, 2013).
	3–5-ETS1–1: "Define a simple design problem reflecting a need or a want that includes specified criteria for success and constraints on materials, time, or cost" (Achieve, 2013).
	K–2-ETS1–1: "Ask questions, make observations, and gather information about a situation people want to change to define a simple problem that can be solved through the development of a new or improved object or tool" (Achieve, 2013).
	K-ESS3–3: "Communicate solutions that will reduce the impact of humans on the land, water, air, and/or other living things in the local environment" (Achieve, 2013).
	K-ESS3–2: "Ask questions to obtain information about the purpose of weather forecasting to prepare for, and respond to, severe weather" (Achieve, 2013).
	MS-PS2–4: "Construct and present arguments using evidence to support the claim that gravitational interactions are attractive and depend on the masses of interacting objects" (Achieve, 2013).
TEACHER STANDARDS	
Danielson Framework for Teaching	Domain 3: Instruction—Using Questioning and Discussion Techniques (3b) Critical Attributes
	• "Students initiate higher-order questions. Students extend the discussion, enriching it. Students invite comments from their classmates during a discussion and challenge one another's thinking. All students are engaged in the discussion" (Danielson, 2014, p. 63).
	Domain 3: Instruction—Engaging Students in Learning (3c) Critical Attributes
	• "Virtually all students are intellectually engaged in the lesson. Students take initiative to adapt the lesson by (1) modifying a learning task to make it more meaningful or relevant to their needs, (2) suggesting modifications to the grouping patterns used, and/or (3) suggesting modifications or additions to the materials being used" (Danielson, 2014, p. 69).

Critical Questions for Student Engagement

It is ultimately the teacher's responsibility to select curriculum standards that will be incorporated into the unit. However, the goal is for teachers and students to partner together to select curriculum. Real-world learning projects provide numerous options for standards students can meet. For example, in this chapter's opening vignette, here are opportunities in the students' project to learn several social studies standards (community helpers and their tools, volunteer service, and collaboration), language arts standards (many writing, speaking and listening, and language standards), and technology, critical-thinking, and career-readiness standards.

When planning instruction to maximize student engagement, teachers should reflect on the following critical questions.

- Are students given choices in tasks? Does content, process, or product differentiate the task? (Level 3)
- Are students partnering with the teacher to define the content, process, and product? Are students using an inquiry-based approach to learning? Are students collaborating with each other? (Level 4)

- Are students initiating their own inquiry-based projects? Are they thoroughly immersed in the problem? Are students engaged in full implementation from topic development to solution? Do students initiate appropriate collaborations pertaining to their project? (Level 5)

Curriculum mapping is key to achieving the necessary curriculum standards within lessons and units throughout the year. If a teacher partners with and guides students on four to five authentic projects during a school year, interspersed among required topics and standards, students will reap amazing benefits of real engagement in their own learning on authentic projects that interest them.

Conclusion

Student engagement is probably the Create Excellence Framework's most misunderstood component. Teacher flexibility in controlling (or allowing students to responsibly take more control of) the learning environment is a key to successful student engagement. As with all the Create components, student engagement to achieve at the higher levels of the Create Excellence Framework takes planning and collaboration, resulting in student learning that is much deeper, richer, and longer lasting.

Discussion Questions

Answer the following six questions to summarize the chapter's concepts.

1. Why should we channel students toward more self-directed learning at the elementary level?
2. How does students' self-directed learning change the way we teach primary students? Intermediate students?
3. How might increasing student engagement to the upper levels of the Create Excellence Framework help students beyond the classroom?
4. Which student-engagement attributes do you think you are the strongest in implementing? Why? Give examples.
5. Which student-engagement attributes do you think you implement the least? What are some changes you could make to implement this attribute of engagement with your students?
6. In what ways do you need to plan for engagement differently depending on primary versus intermediate grade levels?

Take Action

Consider the following eight tasks and activities to help you toward implementing the Create Excellence Framework.

1. Develop an idea for a highly engaging task or project for your students. How will you incorporate the four characteristics of engaged learning?
2. Identify an assignment or project your class was involved in last year that you thought involved a high level of student engagement. What level would it be on the Create Excellence Framework's student-engagement component? Why do you think so? How could you modify your assignment to increase the level of engagement?

3.   Which instructional task or project idea in the student-engagement component of the Create Excellence Framework (table 3.1, page 57) could you adjust to use in your classroom? Describe how your students would react and what changes you would make.

4.   Review the reproducible "Analyzing a Task or Project for Student Engagement." Answer the questions to analyze the task. Then compare your analysis to the sample analysis at the end of the reproducible.

5.   Review the rubrics from this chapter (pages 60–67). What would you modify to apply one of these rubrics to your students' projects, to your subject area, or both? Is there anything in the rubrics that is in violation of your school's policies or ways of operating? Explain and tell how you could still use a similar rubric to encourage high levels of student engagement.

6.   Review three online web 2.0 collaborative tools such as PrimaryPad, Wiggio, Skype, Wallwisher, or Google Drive. Describe how you can use these tools to increase student engagement for your students.

7.   Select one of the Create Excellence Framework projects in part II. How could you modify the project to use in your classroom? How could you improve one project to increase engagement? Have a conversation with a colleague about implementing the project in either of your classrooms.

8.   Select another sample project in part II. Rate the level of each component on the Create Excellence Framework. Compare your ratings to the rating table following the sample student work. How do they compare?

Analyzing a Task or Project for Student Engagement

Examine the scenario in the following table, and answer the questions. Then, compare your answers to the authors' responses.

Scenario: After studying different cultures' food, teams of students select a different ethnic style of food. One team likes Chinese food, and it decides to research the healing properties of rice in Chinese culture. The team picks the best recipe for its healing properties and creates a multimedia presentation to justify its selection to the class. Students are so excited that they cook the recipe at home and bring it to the class for other students to sample.	
Level of Student Engagement	What is the level of engagement of this task? Why do you think so?
Ways to Raise the Level of Student Engagement	What are some ways to increase the student-engagement level for this task?
New Level of Student Engagement	What is the new level of engagement?

Authors' Responses

Compare your answers to the authors' responses to the scenario questions.

Level of Student Engagement

This task is at level 4. The students decide on their content, process, and product through collaboration with other students and the teacher. It is an inquiry-based approach since students decide on the question and direct the research toward the healing properties of rice on their own.

Ways to Raise the Level of Student Engagement

This activity could reach a higher level if the students initiate collaborations beyond the classroom, such as with a cook from a local Chinese restaurant, to learn more original and authentic cooking methods. Finally, the teacher and students could collaboratively create an assessment rubric for the student-designed projects.

New Level of Student Engagement

This level of engagement could be level 5, depending on activities the students choose to complete.

CHAPTER 4

Technology Integration

In Ms. Denning's second-grade mathematics class, the students examine examples of symmetry in nature and human creations. Students are instructed to use symmetry to design a beautiful picture that will inspire students in their class. Using Picreflect, students practice uploading pictures and create a reflection of various images. Groups discuss what makes the picture visually pleasing. Students use Picreflect or Doodle Buddy to design their images. Groups evaluate the various images and select one image to display in the classroom.

With advances in technology doubling every eighteen months (McGinnis, 2006), there is a plethora of technologies available to schools. Schools must have a planned approach in order to maximize the impact of these technologies to enhance student learning (Pence & McIntosh, 2010). Educators, however, struggle to integrate technology in meaningful ways that involve higher-order thinking, collaborative tasks, and authentic problem solving (the United Nations Educational, Scientific and Cultural Organization [UNESCO], 2004). Optimally, technology integration is a seamless component of instruction to engage students in authentic, creative-thinking tasks, as demonstrated in this chapter's opening scenario.

Our research shows a high correlation of technology integration with the other three components of the framework (Maxwell, Stobaugh, & Tassell, 2011). Technology should be used not simply as an add-on but to meaningfully support the work to more efficiently and effectively accomplish the task, just as it is in the professional world. In the sections that follow, we explore traditional technology use and research-based technology integration and demonstrate the supportive relationship between technology integration and real-world learning, cognitive complexity, and student engagement. In addition, we discuss the alignment of technology integration in the Create Excellence Framework to national and provincial technology standards and provide examples of instructional tasks.

Because we look at how students interact with the content using higher-level thinking before we look at technology use, we also examine how technology integration relates to the levels of Bloom's taxonomy. Authors Ian Jukes, Ted McCain, and Lee Crockett (2010) state that the revised Bloom's taxonomy reflects the "new era of creativity that has been facilitated by the emergence of the online digital world" (p. 69). Technology paired with critical thinking, student engagement, and real-world learning provides opportunities for students to produce novel products to address authentic problems.

Five Levels of Technology Integration

When classifying a task or project on the technology-integration dimension, an assignment could be anywhere from level 0 to level 5. If a lesson or instructional plan does not use technology, it would be considered a level 0 for technology integration. Following are descriptions of levels 1–5. The hope is that teachers are teaching a majority of the lessons at the Investigating and Integrating levels of the Create Excellence Framework with a few lessons each year at the Specializing level (level 5).

Knowing

At the Knowing level, a teacher may use technology for demonstration or lecture. This could include showing a video, presenting a PowerPoint presentation, or using web technology to demonstrate how to dissect an animal. Students may use technology for low-level thinking tasks at the Remember level such as taking an online quiz of vocabulary terms. At the Knowing level, using technology may be merely optional for students. Technology use may be limited to simple keyboarding tasks. In these examples, technology is not meaningfully contributing to real-world learning.

Practicing

At the Practicing level, students use technology for Understand- or Apply-level thinking tasks or for gathering information. The instruction is still teacher directed but at a higher level of cognitive complexity than level 1. Examples of Practicing-level tasks are students searching the Internet for information on a topic, using technologies to summarize information, or using websites to practice mathematics skills.

Investigating

At level 3, students are using technology for higher-level thinking assignments at the Analyze, Evaluate, and Create levels. However, the technology appears to be an add-on and not essential for completing the task. For example, students may make an audio recording explaining a mathematical mistake in a complex mathematics problem. While adding the technology may pique students' interest in completing the assignment, students could have written their explanation on paper. The technology might be an afterthought, added after planning the lesson, to meet state teaching standards that require technology's inclusion in the lesson.

Integrating

At the Integrating level, teachers are adept at infusing technology into their classroom, and student technology use includes content standards essential to project completion, promotes collaboration among students and partnership with the teacher, and helps them solve authentic problems at Bloom's Analyze, Evaluate, or Create levels. This level engages all four Create Excellence Framework components with (1) real-world applications of knowledge, (2) critical thinking at the highest cognitively complex levels, (3) student engagement through collaboration and partnerships, and (4) technology infused in a meaningful way. Technology at this level is not an add-on but is infused while designing the assignment. Students partner with the teacher to design the assignment and rubric, and the teacher is more of a coach than a leader of direct instruction. For example, students in a mathematics class can discuss a recent futuristic movie and how mathematics was used to create the movie. Students might then ask the teacher if their project could be to create a video showing how multiplication and division could help solve a real-world problem twenty years in the future. For example, today you play electronic games twice as many minutes a day as you did five years ago. Using this function, how many minutes a day would you play electronic games twenty years from now?

Specializing

At the highest level on the Create Excellence Framework, students continue to direct their technology use. The Specializing level involves students designing projects that are integrated seamlessly in content at the Create level, include several technologies, and incorporate collaboration with field experts or global organizations to find solutions to real, complex problems. As with level 4, all four of the Create Excellence Framework components are engaged in this level. Students complete projects at the highest level on Bloom's taxonomy: Create. Students must consider the constraints of the problem, situation, or task and use their knowledge to produce a high-quality solution or product, employing several appropriate technologies to accomplish the task. In addition, students collaborate with experts to develop solutions to authentic problems. This level requires classrooms to be structured as collaborative-learning environments in which students' interests and passions are nurtured to engage in rich, deep thinking tasks. For example, students in one class decide to help hurricane victims in Bangladesh. They use their smartphones and tablets to look up organizations providing relief. One team of students Skypes with international hurricane relief organization Direct Relief and discovers the organization's needs, which include a flashy announcement for its website. That team creates a public service announcement in Adobe Flash for the website. Direct Relief's webmaster works with this group in training, consultation, and evaluation of its work. After researching needs in the country, another team creates a survey on Google Forms to determine student interest in helping the hurricane victims and the best type of fundraiser to hold. Members ultimately hold a running event and raise money to send to Direct Relief. A third team uses Prezi to design a snazzy presentation to show to three local civic groups that donate to the cause. A fourth team designs a spreadsheet and charts to keep up with the funds the other teams raised.

Table 4.1 showcases each of the technology-integration levels within the Create Excellence Framework along with task and project examples aligned to each level.

Table 4.1: Technology-Integration Levels of the Create Excellence Framework

CREATE LEVEL	DESCRIPTION	SAMPLE TASK OR PROJECT
1: Knowing	Teacher uses technology for demonstration or lecture, student technology use is at the Remember level, or technology is a student option but not required or used for keyboarding.	• Students complete a teacher quiz on Google Forms, a polling technology, on vocabulary terms for the unit. • The teacher plays a Hello Slide presentation to summarize the author's background prior to studying a book.
2: Practicing	Students use technology for Understand or Apply thinking tasks, or students use technology for gathering information.	• Students play Sushi Monster to practice their multiplication skills. • Students search the web for information on E. B. White, author of *Charlotte's Web*, or for primary students, Don Freeman, author of *Corduroy*. • Students take digital pictures of architectural features in their community that show ancient Greece's influence on current architecture. • Using an interactive web-diagram graphic organizer, students identify five ways their day would be different if U.S. colonists lost the war to Britain. • Students solve real-world mathematics problems using the Classkick app, allowing the teacher to see everyone's work and provide immediate feedback.

Continued →

CREATE LEVEL	DESCRIPTION	SAMPLE TASK OR PROJECT
3: Investigating	Technology use appears to be an add-on or alternative—not essential for task or project completion—and students use technology for Analyze, Evaluate, or Create thinking tasks.	• After reading Shel Silverstein's *The Giving Tree*, students use an online newspaper generator to write an article taking a stance on whether the tree gave too much. • Students describe three changes they would make and the positive long-term effects they would have if they could go back in time and positively change the world by affecting Martin Luther King Jr.'s actions. They create a Prezi account and use Screencast-O-Matic to record their presentation. • Students create a music video about their favorite teacher, expertly integrating two poetic devices (for example, rhyme and onomatopoeia). • Students find two online historical sources and determine each source's reliability. • Students conduct a web search for five images related to westward expansion and in groups create a graphic organizer showing how these images help them better understand the time period.
4: Integrating	Student-directed technology use is embedded in content and essential to project completion, student-directed technology use promotes collaboration among students and partnerships with the teacher, and student-directed technology use helps students solve authentic problems using Analyze, Evaluate, or Create thinking tasks.	• To encourage students to read a variety of books from diverse perspectives, students use WeVideo to create a persuasive video convincing their friends to read a book few have read. Students post videos on the school's website for students to review when they don't know what book to check out. • When studying other countries, students decide to plan a holiday celebration from another country, such as Chinese New Year, for the school. They create a collaborative document on Google Docs to prepare and inform school officials and students of the activities. • In English class, students and the teacher hatch the idea of writing a poem and creating a video using Animoto profiling their poem, which celebrates either a family member or someone important to them, to be shown at the school's heroes celebration.
5: Specializing	Student-directed technology use is seamlessly integrated in content at the Create level; student-directed technology use incorporates several technologies; and student-directed technology use includes collaboration with field experts or global organizations to find solutions to an in-depth, real problem.	• After a Skype session with their pen-pal class in England, students realize that they have a common challenge in their countries—childhood obesity. The students inquire how they can make a positive impact on this issue. The two classes identify an organization in their country that addresses this issue. Their research reveals Healthy Kids, Healthy Communities and the British Obesity Society. The classes skype the organizations to determine ways their classes can support the organizations' mission. Both organizations mention that they need materials that would appeal to kids and be informative. The classes form groups to brainstorm ideas. Some groups plan to write and film a commercial, while others want to develop a child-friendly website to accompany the organization's site. Groups present their proposals and evaluate plans from both classes. Groups review the feedback from their own class and their pen-pal class and edit their project idea. Students then develop their project and present it to the organizations.

Meaningful Application of Technology

Most students are well versed in technology. Prensky (2001) coins the term *digital natives* to describe those students who, throughout their lives, have always had exposure to using digital technology, Internet connectivity, and social networking. These students favor technology-based learning tasks that provide for collaboration on real-life application of concepts (Oblinger, 2003).

While students live in a media-based environment, many of the instructional tasks in classrooms do not include opportunities for students to use technology. In fact, a 2007 joint report from ISTE, the Partnership for 21st Century Skills, and the State Educational Technology Directors Association (2007) indicates that of all industries in the United States, the education sector is the least infused with technology. Additionally, the National Center for Education Statistics reports that 97 percent of teachers had access to a computer in 2009, but only 72 percent of all teachers used the computers for instruction (Gray, Thomas, & Lewis, 2010).

Internationally, there is quite a variance of integration of technology based on factors including access to technology, government prioritizing and investing in technologies, and varying comfort levels and beliefs in the importance of utilizing digital tools for K–12 learning. According to a report by the European Commission (2013), in the European Union, 63 percent of nine-year-olds do not study at a "highly digitally equipped school." Among the European countries, there is a large variation in the average ratio of computers available for educational purposes. For example, the average for the European Union is 5:1, but in Greece, it's 21:1.

Traditional Technology Integration

Traditionally, technology in classrooms has been a gadget to obtain students' attention or an add-on to instruction to meet curriculum or teaching standards, but it fails to meaningfully impact instruction when teachers use it in that capacity. Technology used to deliver teacher-directed content (as a glorified blackboard) and digital worksheets has not delivered the rate of return expected for the millions of dollars spent on technology (Schwartzbeck & Wolf, 2012). Without sound application of technology integration, money spent on technology is wasted. Authors Thomas W. Greaves, Jeanne Hayes, Leslie Wilson, Michael Gielniak, and Eric L. Peterson (2010) state, "Although educational technology best practices have a significant positive impact, they are not widely and consistently practiced" (p. 12). Technology is a *tool* to reach an educational goal; technology is not the goal itself. Author, educator, and technology administrator Will Richardson (2013) comments, "It's not about the tools. It's not about layering expensive technology on top of the traditional curriculum. Instead, it's about addressing the new needs of modern learners in entirely new ways" (p. 12).

Effective Technology Integration

Effective technology integration involves using technology tools in a new way. It involves transforming the classroom into an environment where students engage in real-world, critical-thinking tasks that involve students and teachers collaborating together. Through these tasks, students are inspired to innovate. Technology provides tools that enable users to process their thinking and be effective and efficient. The Create Excellence Framework's technology-integration component advocates for this new approach, incorporating real-world tasks that are naturally infused with critical thinking and student engagement. Effective technology integration seamlessly embeds technology tools as part of the instructional design in order to engage students with significant content at high levels of thinking, whereby students use varied technologies to collaborate with others, explore solutions to real-life problems, and share their results in an authentic manner. Pentucket Regional School District, which was noted in the 2016 National Education Technology Plan from the U.S. Department of Education, is a good example. All elementary schools in the district provide multiple opportunities for student choice and learning opportunities beyond the school walls. By reconfiguring their school day and year, elementary students experience online and blended coursework, off-campus academic opportunities, internships and apprenticeships, and hands-on experiential learning (Office of Educational Technology, 2016).

The web provides an unlimited source of information and opportunities to connect with others that is changing the way we view what is important in education. Knowledge and remembering were critical when there were limited sources of information. Now, with more readily accessible information, education can focus on new areas: real-world interactions, cognitive complexity, student engagement, and technology integration. Unfortunately, many of these foci are not present in classrooms. Psychology professor Daniel T. Willingham (2009) finds a lack of student engagement in many schools due to teacher-directed instruction, often at lower thinking levels, without authentic applications. However, when critical thinking, real-world applications, and student engagement are combined with technology integration, powerful learning can occur. While some may view technology as helpful in building basic foundations of knowledge through online games that reinforce basic applications of content, students more effectively use technology to design solutions and create new products, which are high-level thinking activities. Technology tools have the potential to enhance student learning, but they must be implemented in a research-based framework to ensure sound implementation. See table 4.2 for a comparison of traditional ways of using technology to supplement curriculum and research-based ways to infuse technology as a part of high-level learning.

Table 4.2: Traditional Technology Versus Research-Based Technology Approaches

TRADITIONAL TECHNOLOGY APPROACH	RESEARCH-BASED TECHNOLOGY APPROACH
Technology is used to search for information or practice skills.	Technology is used to expand students' learning as it is embedded with high-quality instruction requiring students to critically think, solve complex real-world problems, and create products. Students engage in deep project-based learning tasks.
Teacher plans instruction that meets the needs of students with average ability.	Technology is used to customize and individualize instruction, making learning personalized or learner centered.
Teacher uses textbook to guide instruction.	Students use technology to address relevant and authentic tasks aligned to content standards.
Teacher leads instruction.	Teachers are coaches or facilitators of the learning process.
Teacher uses technology to plan lessons or present information.	Students use multiple technology tools to address real-world problems.

Source: Adapted from Wolf, 2012.

The Create Excellence Framework embraces the view that technology integration can bolster real-world learning through the areas of cognitive complexity and student engagement. Technology is not merely an add-on but is the vehicle through which teachers can accomplish the other Create Excellence components. Effective digital learning engages students in high-level thinking tasks with real-world applications to improve student achievement.

Standards and Technology Integration

A knowledge-based society depended on people memorizing information before the abundance of technology, but we can now quickly search for facts on the Internet. Digital learning resources challenge students to engage in deeper learning as they analyze and evaluate information to employ complex, authentic problem solving that promotes the transfer of learning to other contexts. As students engage in digitally rich environments, they can become self-driven, independent thinkers prepared for the real world. Technology affords students opportunities to collaborate beyond the classroom with peers or experts in a digital environment to develop original products. Students can share their work with a wider global audience to impact change (Richardson, 2013).

Groups such as ISTE and the Partnership for 21st Century Learning have identified best practices to establish a framework for effective technology integration. The ISTE (2016) standards embrace a holistic view of technology integration, focusing on the empowered learner, digital citizen, knowledge constructor, innovative designer, computational thinker, creative communicator, and global collaborator. P21 (2011) identifies information, media, and technology skills as supporting arches for 21st century learning in the core subjects. The Create Excellence Framework similarly asserts that technology resources can support critical thinking, communication, collaboration, and creativity as students master the core subjects.

Further, key points for the Common Core standards for English language arts state, "Just as media and technology are integrated in school and life in the twenty-first century, skills related to media use (both critical analysis and production of media) are integrated throughout the standards" (NGA & CCSSO, 2010a). Technology is also included in the revised science standards. The Next Generation Science Standards conceptual framework states, "New insights from science often catalyze the emergence of new technologies and their applications, which are developed using engineering design. In turn, new technologies open opportunities for new scientific investigations" (NGSS Lead States, 2013). In science, teachers are naturally expected to use the technologies that support the learning, whether they be probes, microscopes, or other technologies. Of course, technology use varies greatly in each discipline, as we will see in the following text and supporting examples.

Real-World Learning

When students engage in real-world problems focused on research and inquiry, teachers can guide them to select and utilize appropriate technologies to address the problem (Jones, Valdez, Nowakowski, & Rasmussen, 1995). Project-based learning experiences can combine multimedia projects with authentic audiences and purposes.

There are several indicators within the ISTE standards that link technology and authentic learning. The critical-thinking, problem-solving, and decision-making standard states that "students use critical-thinking skills to plan and conduct research, manage projects, solve problems, and make informed decisions using appropriate digital tools and resources" (ISTE, 2007). It also specifies that students should be able to "identify and define authentic problems and significant questions for investigation" (ISTE, 2007). Technology standards like this clearly reflect that technology must be appropriately integrated with real-world issues.

Students can use technology to solve problem-based learning challenges surrounding real community or world issues. They can use technology to research, collaborate, and present their group's findings. Following are examples of technology integration paired with real-world learning.

- Working in groups, students brainstorm potential businesses for their school entrepreneur fair. After solidifying their idea, groups collect materials and sell their items at the fair. Throughout the project, groups track their expenses and profits using Excel worksheets and develop commercials about their products to show on the school news channel. In this student-directed task at level 4 on the Create Excellence Framework, the technology is appropriately supporting the project. Students are designing their own business, thus working at the Create level while collaborating with others.

- Students select a school policy or social cause that they want to positively impact. After consulting with experts knowledgeable about their selected topic, they research the best way to communicate with the public about their cause. Students create presentations, websites, and blogs. This project is level 5 in the Create Excellence Framework, as students are impacting a real community problem and utilizing several technologies to accomplish the purpose. Students are collaborating with experts to gain valuable information.

- Students utilize the online tools iBrainstorm and MindMeister to brainstorm ideas for redesigning a playground, utilize Excel to develop a budget and raise funds, and sketch a layout using SketchUp. Students can then present a proposal using Animoto for the school council to consider. This project is level 4 in the Create Excellence Framework. Students in the project are developing their own ideas; hence, it is a student-directed task. Students are collaborating with technologies for brainstorming and budgeting, which appropriately supports the purpose of the task.

- Students use technology to improve a current product and prepare a sales presentation using Haiku Deck to pitch their ideas. This project would be on the fourth level of the Create Excellence Framework, as students are designing a solution to a current problem and then utilizing technologies to present their ideas.

- Students identify a problem in their school and, in groups, discuss ways of using their writing skills and digital abilities to solve the problem. This project is at the fourth level of the Create Excellence Framework, as students are defining the problem and identifying appropriate technologies to support their work. As they solve an authentic school problem, they utilize technologies like bubbl.us to brainstorm solutions or create digital presentations and use SlideShare to showcase their solution.

Critical Thinking

Critical thinking and technology are emphasized in ISTE's 2016 technology student standards. The ISTE (2016) standards include students using technology to create and innovate, solve problems, and make decisions. The ISTE technology standards for students were revised in 2016 to portray expectations of 21st century learning, which include principles of effective technology integration embedded with critical thinking. The ISTE standards reinforce the effective integration of technology with high-level thinking that the Create Excellence Framework and the revised Bloom's taxonomy embrace. While cognitive complexity is evident throughout the 2016 ISTE student standards, the following highlights one ISTE standard that promotes technology use along with cognitive complexity:

Standard 3 Knowledge Constructor—

Students critically curate a variety of resources using digital tools to construct knowledge, produce creative artifacts and make meaningful learning experiences for themselves and others.

3a: Students plan and employ effective research strategies to locate information and other resources for their intellectual or creative pursuits.

3b: Students evaluate the accuracy, perspective, credibility and relevance of information, media, data or other resources.

3c: Students curate information from digital resources using a variety of tools and methods to create collections of artifacts that demonstrate meaningful connections or conclusions.

3d: Students build knowledge by actively exploring real-world issues and problems, developing ideas and theories and pursuing answers and solutions. (ISTE, 2016)

Ian Jukes et al. (2010) developed a list of 21st century competencies that include students thinking creatively to address real-world issues, critically assessing the quality of digital content, and creating their own digital projects.

Many other organizations beyond those focused solely on education support this need to integrate cognitive complexity and technology. The U.S. 21st Century Workforce Commission's (2000) National Alliance of Business maintains that "the current and future health of America's 21st century economy depends directly on how broadly and deeply Americans reach a new level of literacy—21st century literacy" (p. 5). Their alliance identifies 21st century literacy as including digital literacy, inventive thinking, and results-based thinking. As routine jobs transition to high-skill positions, students must possess 21st century skills to meet workforce demands (Chao, 2001). Employers comment that, despite young employees' knowledge of technology, they are unable to use their thinking skills and technology on the job. Dan Gordon (2011) notes:

Work readiness is no longer just about the three Rs; now it's also about turning information into knowledge through web searching and vetting . . . developing effective multimedia presentations . . . [and] . . . seamlessly using digital tools to collaborate and problem-solve. (p. 32)

Teachers can partner with students to design open-ended assignments that have no single right answer, require students to design solutions to problems that require higher-level thinking, and naturally embed technology. Students can provide feedback on other students' work through peer editing as they add comments to a digital document on Google Docs or using Microsoft Word. Students can also engage in inquiry learning focused on answering a question. Following are some examples that exemplify the natural connection between cognitive complexity and technology integration.

- Students design a proposal for a school club. They collect and analyze survey data and then prepare a persuasive presentation using basic calculations to show why the club will be successful. (Level 4)
- Students propose a new way to do scheduling at their school. They use their writing skills to construct logical arguments to support their ideas. Students use Wix (www.wix.com), a website builder, to create a persuasive presentation to show their principal. (Level 4)
- Students are frustrated with a poorly designed school garden and decide to design a more functional garden for students and staff using their mathematics skills. Students use SketchUp to create a diagram depicting their proposed plan. (Level 4)

Student Engagement

When there are real-world classroom tasks and projects, there are often high levels of technology integration and student engagement. Digital tasks can invite students to emotionally invest in learning as they learn in their "native" (digital) language. Teachers can ignite students' passion and purpose as students define their own problems and create content with technology. It involves shifting the ownership of the learning to make instruction self-directed and self-paced. The teacher's role then becomes a partner and co-learner with students as they are immersed in the content together. Students are able to approach learning in a differentiated way by investigating their interests and passions. This individualized approach to learning enhances students' intrinsic motivation as they select and examine areas of concentration instead of the teacher directing the learning. At the elementary level, students have formative opportunities for student engagement and self-directed learning. This formative preparation can further support self-directed learning often expected in secondary school, university, and the workplace.

ISTE standards endorse the view that technology should be connected to student engagement in learning. The communication and collaboration standard states that students will "contribute constructively to project teams, assuming various roles and responsibilities to work effectively toward a common goal" (ISTE, 2016). Also related to engagement, the digital citizenship standard asserts that students should "engage in positive, safe, legal, and ethical behavior when using technology, including social interactions online or when using networked devices" (ISTE, 2016). The following list features a sampling of additional ISTE standards of technology and student engagement:

> Standard 7 Global Collaborator—
>
> Students use digital tools to broaden their perspectives and enrich their learning by collaborating with others and working effectively in teams locally and globally.
>
> 7a: Students use digital tools to connect with learners from a variety of backgrounds and cultures, engaging with them in ways that broaden mutual understanding and learning.
>
> 7b: Students use collaborative technologies to work with others, including peers, experts or community members, to examine issues and problems from multiple viewpoints.
>
> 7c: Students contribute constructively to project teams, assuming various roles and responsibilities to work effectively toward a common goal.
>
> 7d: Students explore local and global issues and use collaborative technologies to work with others to investigate solutions. (ISTE, 2016)

Beyond ISTE's recommendations, other researchers and authors support using technology to increase student engagement. Research shows that when teachers integrate technology into classrooms, such as with interactive whiteboards, students remain passive learners unless teachers purposefully plan higher-level thinking and student-directed instructional tasks (Lemke, Coughlin, & Reifsneider, 2009). Thus, simply integrating technology without purposely planning for rich student engagement can produce little impact on student achievement. Online partnerships are one method teachers can use in planning student engagement through technology. There are many successful online partnerships, including classrooms from different parts of the world skyping or having pen pals who digitally communicate. In these experiences, students can discover different perspectives as they pose questions and seek understanding. Students' curiosity is piqued as they have a real-world audience engage in higher-level thinking as they formulate questions and consider different viewpoints. The partnership is student centered as students' interests and questions drive the conversation and communication. Research shows that schools using online collaboration find reduced disciplinary actions and dropout rates (Greaves, Hayes, Wilson, Gielniak, & Peterson, 2012). Therefore, technology enhances student collaboration in a meaningful way while positively impacting student achievement and other measures of school success.

As teachers infuse technology into their daily teaching, researchers find that the teacher and student have become adaptable and enhanced, with both parties introducing additional content. Technology use minimizes traditional issues of space and time, thus increasing student engagement (Forkosh-Baruch, Mioduser,

Nachmias, & Tubin, 2005). In short, the focus on student engagement reflects contemporary learners' need to use digital tools to locate information, assimilate meaning, create products, and collaborate during the learning process (Maxwell, Constant et al., 2011). Technology-infused classrooms can transform students' role from passive consumers to active producers of products as they engage in hands-on, collaborative work that replicates the workplace. This student-centered learning meets students' individual learning needs. Following are a few examples of technology integration fused with high levels of student engagement.

- Fifth-grade students plan a webinar to discuss ways to improve habitats for threatened species in their community. Students research the issue and invite community members to attend. Students present their findings and plan questions for the participants. Students use Piktochart (https://piktochart.com) to prepare an informational graphic to depict the challenges of the species. (Level 4)
- The school has a flooding issue near the school's entrance. Via Skype, fourth- and fifth-grade students interview several city-planning officials and school-district leaders. Students use the interview information and research to design an effective way to address the problem. In groups, students use a web presentation tool, Projeqt (https://projeqt.com), to design their presentation. (Level 5)

See table 4.3 for examples of additional teaching and content standards that align to technology.

Table 4.3: Alignment of Standards to Technology Integration

SOURCE OF STANDARDS	STANDARD INDICATORS
STUDENT STANDARDS	
Social studies: C3 Framework	D4.3.3–5: "Present a summary of arguments and explanations to others outside the classroom using print and oral technologies (e.g., posters, essays, letters, debates, speeches, and reports) and digital technologies (e.g., Internet, social media, and digital documentary)" (NCSS, 2013).
Science: Next Generation Science Standards	Science Practice 3: Planning and Carrying Out Investigations • "Make observations (firsthand or from media) to collect data that can be used to make comparisons" (Achieve, 2013). Science Practice 4: Obtaining, Evaluating, and Communicating Information • "Read grade-appropriate texts and/or use media to obtain scientific information to describe patterns in the natural world" (Achieve, 2013).
Mathematics: Common Core mathematics standards	Mathematical Practice 5 • "Use *appropriate tools* strategically" (NGA & CCSSO, 2010b). • "When making mathematical models, they know that *technology* can enable them to visualize the results of varying assumptions, explore consequences, and compare predictions with data. Mathematically proficient students at various grade levels are able to identify relevant external mathematical resources, such as *digital content located on a website*, and use them to pose or solve problems" (NGA & CCSSO, 2010b). • "Mathematically proficient students at various grade levels are able to identify relevant external mathematical resources, such as *digital content located on a website*, and use them to pose or solve problems. They are able to use *technological tools* to explore and deepen their understanding of concepts" (NGA & CCSSO, 2010b).

Continued →

SOURCE OF STANDARDS	STANDARD INDICATORS
English language arts: Common Core English language arts standards	SL.4.5: "Add audio recordings and visual displays to presentations when appropriate to enhance the development of main ideas or themes" (NGA & CCSSO, 2010a). SL.5.5: "Include multimedia components (e.g., graphics, sound) and visual displays in presentations when appropriate to enhance the development of main ideas or themes" (NGA & CCSSO, 2010a). W.5.6: "With some guidance and support from adults, use technology, including the Internet, to produce and publish writing as well as to interact and collaborate with others; demonstrate sufficient command of keyboarding skills to type a minimum of two pages in a single sitting" (NGA & CCSSO, 2010a).
TEACHER STANDARDS	
Danielson Framework for Teaching	Domain 2: Classroom Environment—2E Organizing Physical Space "The classroom environment is safe, and learning is accessible to all students, including those with special needs. The teacher makes effective use of physical resources, including computer technology. The teacher ensures that the physical arrangement is appropriate to the learning activities. Students contribute to the use or adaptation of the physical environment to advance learning. (Distinguished rating description)" (Danielson, 2014, p. 51).

Critical Questions for Technology Integration

When planning instruction for technology integration, teachers should reflect on the following critical questions.

- Have I planned for students' use of technology?
- If the technology is an add-on (level 3), what can I do to make it more integrated (levels 4–5)?
- Does technology promote collaboration among students and the teacher (level 4)?
- Do students use several technology tools (level 5)?

Conclusion

While students increasingly desire to learn with technology, some classrooms still resist integrating student use of technology to increase student achievement. Others see technology integration as superficial as teachers check off that they have integrated it into instruction. It is critical that educators integrate technology in a purposeful, research-based way to avoid wasting instructional time. The ISTE standards and other documents support the use of technology seamlessly integrated in content to challenge students to think at high levels while collaborating with others to solve authentic tasks. The Create Excellence Framework also embraces the holistic view of technology integration. The technology-integration component focuses on students using technology to cooperatively solve real-world problems while challenging students to think critically. This view of technology integration can truly make strides toward advancing student learning. The Create Excellence Framework is different from the ISTE standards in that it provides a system for educators to analyze lesson plans and instructional tasks and projects to determine the levels of cognitive complexity, student engagement, and technology integration into real-world learning.

Discussion Questions

Answer the following five questions to summarize the chapter's concepts.

1. How do you define technology integration? How might this chapter's definition of technology cause schools to change how they allocate money for technology?

2. How would teaching critical thinking be different in a primary versus intermediate elementary classroom?

3. What instructional projects or tasks in this chapter could you adapt for your classroom?

4. Are you better at integrating technology with cognitive complexity, real-world learning, or student engagement? How so?

5. Review one of your lessons, and identify the level of technology integration in the Create Excellence Framework. How could you move it to a higher level?

Take Action

Consider the following five tasks and activities to help you toward implementing the Create Excellence Framework.

1. Visit the Create Excellence Framework's resources webpage (http://create-excellence.com/resources), and examine the technology links to projects. What idea can you adapt to improve student learning in your classroom?

2. Examine the reproducible "Analyzing a Task or Project for Technology Integration" (page 92), and answer the questions in the blank form. Then, examine the sample classroom scenario in the reproducible, and compare your responses to the authors' responses.

3. Explore the technology tools in the reproducible "Websites With Lessons Embedding Technologies" (page 94) and on the Create website (http://create-excellence.com/resources). Which tool or tools could help you better meet your students' learning needs as well as more effectively address your learning targets?

4. Select one of the Create Excellence Framework projects in part II. How could you modify the project to use in your classroom? How could you improve the technology integration in one project? Have a conversation with a colleague about implementing the project in your or the colleague's classroom.

5. Select one Create Excellence Framework project for technology integration in part II. Rate the level of each component on the Create Excellence Framework. Compare your ratings to the rating table following the project's sample student work. How could you increase the ratings for each framework component?

Analyzing a Task or Project for Technology Integration

Examine the scenario in the following table, and answer the questions. Then, compare your answers to the authors' responses.

Scenario: After studying causes of bullying, students create a digital book using Storybird (https://storybird.com) about a time when they observed bullying.	
Level of Technology Integration	What is the level of technology integration on the Create Excellence Framework?
Ways to Raise the Technology Integration	What are some ways to raise the level of technology integration?
New Level of Technology Integration	What is the new level of technology integration on the Create Excellence Framework?

Authors' Responses

Compare your answers to the authors' responses to the scenario questions.

Level of Technology Integration

This assignment is on level 2 (Practicing) of the Create Excellence Framework. Students are using technology for a reflection activity. There is no collaboration required for this task or attempt to solve a real-world problem.

Ways to Raise the Technology Integration

After studying causes of bullying, collaborative teams of students propose a plan (cognitive complexity) to address bullying in their school or community (real-world learning). Students must collaborate with community resources (student engagement) and use two or more appropriate technologies (technology integration).

New Level of Technology Integration

This assignment is on level 4 (Integrating) of the Create Excellence Framework.

- **Cognitive complexity:** Students use complex thinking in analyzing the type and frequency of bullying that affects students and decision-making skills regarding what to include in the character education skit (the team creates multiple versions of a skit appropriate for each grade level and acts out the skits for classes).
- **Student engagement:** Students design their message and presentation format, and seek out counselors for advice and assistance in mentoring the elementary students on the *Safe Zone* blog.
- **Real-world learning:** Bullying is a real issue; students present to a group outside their own school, creating an impact beyond their own school through interactions with the students.
- **Technology integration:** The electronic blog format is chosen as a more inviting anonymous method for posting bullying concerns; the team also creates a screencast for training purposes for students, demonstrating how to use the blog.

Websites With Lessons Embedding Technologies

LearnZillion is a free learning site that provides Common Core–aligned lessons with video explanations, assessments, and progress reporting. The site offers more than two thousand teacher-created lessons.   Visit http://learnzillion.com to access the site.
Open Tapestry is a website that helps teachers select, organize, and share resources. Users can alter the content to meet their students' needs and add information to the site.   Visit www.opentapestry.com to access the site.
PowerMyLearning is a web platform with more than one thousand digital learning activities. This free teacher resource provides an opportunity for educators to design their own playlist of activities and contribute information to the site.   Visit http://powermylearning.org to access the site.
Share My Lesson is an online portal of more than 250,000 digital learning resources reviewed and created by two hundred teachers.   Visit www.sharemylesson.com to access the site.
EdTechTeacher offers a variety of assignments under their "Tools for Teachers" tab that include digital projects.   Visit www.edtechteacher.org/index.php/teaching-technology/presentation-multimedia/lesson-plans to access the site.
University of South Florida shows examples of digital projects with varying levels of technology integration.   Visit http://fcit.usf.edu/matrix/gradelevel.php to access the site.
appoLearning is a website that ranks education apps by experts.   Visit www.appolearning.com/?cg=4 to access the site.

CHAPTER 5

Implementation of the Create Excellence Framework

*At a second-grade team meeting, teachers are discussing their difficulties with plan-
ning meaningful projects, especially in an elementary school where the teachers are
responsible for instruction of multiple content areas. Sara shares a recent epiphany.
She had always thought that if students were doing a project, then at least they were
involved in work that enhanced their curriculum at that time. However, she confides
that she often felt that something was missing—some projects seemed shallow or
felt like an add-on to the curriculum, without any meaningful connection to the real
world. Her team agrees. Nita shares that she always strives to engage students during
a project, but sometimes the project does not connect seamlessly to the curriculum.
Lee shares how he is frustrated with how to incorporate student use of technology.
He knows that he, himself, is excellent at teaching and modeling with technology, but
he cannot figure out how to take the time out of the instruction and curriculum to
give the students the opportunity to stretch and grow personally with the content.
The teachers agree that they want to find an instructional-planning tool for real-world
projects that could help them move forward together.*

Planning is paramount when implementing the Create Excellence Framework in a classroom, school, or
district. Once educators understand the rationale behind the framework, they need tools to implement the
instructional changes successfully. Through this chapter, you will learn about instructional design and logistics
and gain tips and critical questions to consider for designing Create Excellence Framework projects. You will
also learn how professional development could look at a school or district level, and interact with the sample
meeting agendas, tables, and helpful implementation instruments throughout this chapter and in the Take
Action section. Here you will find many discussion tools and templates to help with this journey.

Instructional Design and Logistics

The Create Excellence Framework can help teachers adjust or even overhaul instructional planning.
Although Create Excellence Framework projects do and will take more time than a typical lesson or task,
we recommend that you still use them because they facilitate meaningful and deep learning. When you ask
students to tell you what the most memorable learning experience they have had as a student is, or even if

you consider this question in regard to your own learning, most often, the answer will involve the Create Excellence Framework elements. Simulations are a good starting point. Nature and training give K–5 teachers an expertise in integration, which can help in planning projects. In other words, the foundation is ripe and ready for elementary teachers to capitalize on this framework.

Frequency

When trying to determine how often to interweave a high-level Create Excellence Framework project into your instruction, we recommend once per grading period or every six to nine weeks at the beginning of implementation, and then adding more each year. This is manageable and works well to maintain your students' excitement throughout the year rather than giving them the feeling that you will never do this again. You will also find that as students have more experience with Create Excellence Framework projects, they will not take as much time. As students learn and practice these skills, they can apply them to other projects, as well.

Introductions

It is important to consider the classroom's climate. How are you going to get your students on board and involved in the task planning? How are you going to gather ideas that meet their interests? How are you going to communicate to parents about this way of connecting with your students? Remember to involve the students—they are your target audience! Refer to the reproducible personal learning surveys in the introduction (pages 13 and 14).

When introducing the Create Excellence Framework to students, teachers have shared the components with the students by having a discussion about an actual task or project itself. This is the key behind a successful implementation of a Create Excellence Framework design. Begin by generating ideas from the class for the activity. You may decide to begin with the content standards in mind, or you may choose to begin with a classroom, school, or community idea or issue. Then continue the conversation by discussing the targeted level of framework components. Focus the conversation with the students on developing an understanding of the rubric for assessing the task or project, as this will address the four components of the Create Excellence Framework. The discussion should involve how the task or project always focuses on the entire Create Excellence Framework comprehensively—involving all the components. Emphasize to students any opportunities for the project to be student driven.

Collaboration With Colleagues

A great way to thoroughly think through the task or project planning is to work together with colleagues. Begin with the list of critical questions in the Create Task or Project Planning Chart (see table 5.1). Teachers can use this tool as a checklist as they develop their instruction or after the development. This is helpful to use in a peer-discussion format as well.

While real-world learning is the goal, sometimes it is challenging to make the real-world connection to the required curriculum and standards. In that case, consider beginning with cognitive complexity or student engagement in planning tasks or projects. Notice that technology integration is not the initial focus in planning a Create Excellence Framework project but should be considered as flowing from the natural development of the instruction. For example, if you know that you would like your task or project to focus on a particular content standard and be at a certain level of Bloom's revised taxonomy, this may be a case where you would like to design your task or project with cognitive complexity. If you are interested in a particular topic at your school or in your community that you believe your students would want to study, you may want to plan

Table 5.1: Create Task or Project Planning Chart

DESIGN ANGLE	CRITICAL QUESTIONS
INITIAL TASK OR PROJECT PLANNING	
• Identify the standard, or determine the real-world problem that connects to students' lives. • Develop the objectives. • Determine the task or project.	• Is the task or project teacher or student directed? (Note that, to make a stronger impact, student-directed instruction is the goal.) • Does the task or project involve all four components at level 3 or higher?
PROJECT PLANNING FOR STUDENT LEARNING	
Real-World Learning • Examine the level of authentic learning required in the standard. Remember that standards are a minimum expectation; learning can go beyond the standard.	• Did you begin with ideas from your students or from something you know they are concerned or passionate about? • What is the authentic-learning connection? • Does the learning provide a solution to an open-ended problem? • Does the content connect to the students' lives? • How can the students have an emotional connection to the project? • Does learning investigate and simulate the real world (level 3), or does learning really affect the real world? • Are students really having an influence on the classroom, school, or community (level 4)? • Are students really having an impact on a national or global issue or problem (level 5)? • Are students really collaborating (not just cooperating) with field experts (level 5)?
Cognitive Complexity • Examine the level of thinking the standard requires. What verb is in the standard? If students are supposed to infer, then develop a task or project that aligns to this cognitive skill. • Identify which cognitive-complexity level on the Create Excellence Framework you will be working on. ⌃ The revised Bloom's thinking skills build on each other. If the standard calls for a student to infer (a cognitive process within the Understand level), the teacher can design an assignment at a higher thinking level than the standard. The student will learn the inferring standard and go beyond that level to learn at the Analyze level. • Determine if the project aligns to curriculum or standards.	• What is the Bloom's level of student thinking in the task? • Will the student work produce this level of thinking? • Is the project standards based and part of the curriculum? • Is the project teacher directed (level 3) or student directed (level 4)? • Do students have opportunities to generate open-ended, high-level thinking questions (level 5)?

Continued →

DESIGN ANGLE	CRITICAL QUESTIONS
Student Engagement • Focus on significant content. ⌃ Define the problem with the students. ⌃ Determine what they need to know about the problem. Use digital tools to research the problem. • Examine the level of student engagement required in the problem and in the standards. Remember that standards are a minimum expectation—learning and student engagement can go beyond the standard.	• Are students given choices in tasks or projects? • Does content, process, or product differentiate these tasks or projects (level 3)? • Are students using an inquiry-based approach to learning? Are students collaborating with each other (level 4)? • Are students initiating their own inquiry-based projects? Are they thoroughly immersed in the problem? Are students engaged in full implementation from topic development to solution? Do students initiate appropriate collaborations pertaining to their project (level 5)?
Technology Integration • It is best to consider the other components first and then select technology to support the task or project. ⌃ Focus on student use of technology, rather than teacher use, when solving the problem. ⌃ Students should have a choice as to what technology to use, but the use of technology should be seamless in solving the problem. • The technology needs to be a necessary and integral method of accomplishing the task or project. • Objectives need to support the task or project requirements.	• Is student use of technology planned? • If the technology is an add-on (level 3), what could be done to make it more integrated (levels 4–5)? • Does technology promote collaboration among students and teacher (level 4)? • Are several technology tools used (level 5)?
ASSESSMENT DEVELOPMENT	
• Develop the appropriate type of assessment to match student learning in the task or project. Incorporate the key components of the framework for the level targeted for the task or project. • Develop assessment criteria. Rubrics are needed to help in assessing open-ended portions of the project, such as the solution to an open-ended mathematics problem, a presentation, or a written project. • Utilize the Student Work Management Chart (table 5.2, page 100) that outlines steps to complete the project and the time line for the project, and identifies students' responsibilities.	• What is the student product, and how is it going to be assessed? • Does the assessment of the project align to the objectives and the intended Create Excellence Framework levels? • Were students involved in developing the assessment criteria?

*Visit **go.SolutionTree.com/instruction** for a free reproducible version of this table.*

from the real-world learning focus. If you are focusing on differentiations for content, process, or product, and collaboration techniques, you would probably want to begin by thinking about the student-engagement angle. Regardless, it is best to avoid starting your plan by considering which technology you want students to use. Because technology is the vehicle through which the other elements can be delivered, starting with technology inherently and unnecessarily limits the level of student learning, student engagement, and student decision making.

Communication With Parents or Guardians

Parents will be both excited and possibly nervous about this opportunity for their child. It is important to remember to emphasize that you are trying to offer a student-driven task or project versus a teacher-driven task or project. Consider communicating with parents via a letter to explain the Create Excellence Framework and how you will use it to improve learning and help students develop skills so they can become prepared for middle and secondary school, and then become college and career ready. (See a sample parent letter in figure 5.1; a reproducible version of the letter is also available on page 114.) It is also important to be sure that you monitor the work that the student does as an individual versus in a group. Oftentimes, parents perceive group projects negatively due to certain students always ending up doing all the work. It is important to ensure individual accountability and learning for all.

Dear Parent or Guardian,

During this school year, your child will experience a new way of learning. We will be having lots of conversations and taking many ideas from the students' interests to drive the learning when possible.

The Create Excellence Framework lesson-planning tool for real-world learning will guide how we strive to complete the projects and tasks and push our learning.

- Your child will be striving to learn at levels beyond rote memorization and instead will be creating new connections and evaluating his or her learning.

- Your child will be experiencing meaning from his or her own life and world and incorporating it into the tasks and projects.

- Your child will be working with the teacher as a partner in learning, consulting with experts (which may include many of you!), interacting with students in teams, and having choice in products, process, and content.

- Your child will be using technology to complete tasks and projects in a seamless fashion while enhancing learning.

The goal is that throughout the course of the year your child will be able to experience student-directed tasks and projects in addition to the typical teacher-directed tasks and projects.

The exciting part of using a lesson-planning tool of this kind for this class is that I can make sure all the vital learning components are included and that your child is experiencing challenging and well-rounded tasks and projects.

I appreciate your support in this endeavor of my instruction and of your child's inevitable growth! Please contact me if you would like to volunteer to help with this learning adventure. I welcome your help! Also, feel free to contact me about any questions that you may have.

Sincerely,

Teacher

Figure 5.1: Sample parent or guardian letter.

Teacher's Role in Facilitating Tasks and Projects

When you implement the task or project, the students will need facilitation and partnering from you. What this role looks like varies depending on the type of class and students' age, independence, and capability level. One example is a teacher meeting with the students to brainstorm ideas for how to narrow their interests for their topic of study. Another partnering example is a teacher meeting with a pair or group of students to help the students organize how they are going to design their study. This help may be in different forms, such as helping students consider ways to engage with peers and topic experts or providing students with genuine yet reasonable product options. Another way to partner with students is to work with them to develop a rubric that outlines criteria for success. Groups should outline the tasks that need to be completed with due dates and determine the person responsible. As groups check off items completed, teachers can formatively identify if the groups are on target.

To help students manage the magnitude of tasks, projects, and scenarios, you can use tools to organize their group work. See *Students Taking Charge* (Sulla, 2011) for great organizational tools. We suggest utilizing a student work management chart (table 5.2) adapted from that resource. Students can use the chart to define their tasks and organize the work to be done in the responsibilities and design time lines for the completion of the learning. With primary-age students, we suggest teachers support students with defining their role assignment so as not to get bogged down with this process. Not all tasks and projects will necessarily be around one-week in length as on this chart, but some will. The example provides an idea of how a small group notes members' jobs and how the work is completed.

Table 5.2: Student Work Management Chart

	NOTE CARDS	GRAPHIC ORGANIZER	DESIGN PROTOTYPE	SKYPE WITH OUTSIDE EXPERT	PEER EDITING WITH TWO STUDENTS	FINAL COPY
Ainsley	X—Oct. 1			X—Oct. 4		X—Oct. 8
Noel		X—Oct. 3		X—Oct. 4		X—Oct. 8
Parker			X—Oct. 4-7		X—Oct. 6	X—Oct. 8
Darby			X—Oct. 4-7		X—Oct. 6	X—Oct. 8

Source: Adapted from Sulla, 2011.

Professional Development Support

As seen in this chapter's opening scenario, teachers are seeking opportunities for collaboration and professional growth. If you are a principal or teacher who wants to have your school or professional learning community implement the Create Excellence Framework at the grade level, program level, or school level, some considerations need to be incorporated in the planning. The following three steps outline a professional development plan that leaders could use to train teachers on the Create Excellence Framework and for implementation.

1. Train all the targeted teachers on the Create Excellence Framework—ensure all those using the Create Excellence Framework in the classroom understand the different components in the same way.

    Day 1 learning targets:

- ◆ Identify the Create Excellence Framework components.
- ◆ Describe the revised Bloom's taxonomy skills.
- ◆ Classify assignments at various Bloom's levels.
- ◆ Create assignments and assessments at the highest three levels of Bloom's revised taxonomy.
- ◆ Describe the levels of real-world applications.
- ◆ Analyze the level of real-world applications in sample assignments.
- ◆ Design assignments and assessments at the highest three levels of the Create Excellence Framework's real-world learning component.

Day 2 learning targets:

- ◆ Identify the different student-engagement levels.
- ◆ Classify assignments based on their student-engagement level.
- ◆ Create assignments and assessments at the highest three levels of the Create Excellence Framework's student-engagement component.
- ◆ Describe the technology-integration levels.
- ◆ Determine the technology-integration level in featured sample projects.
- ◆ Describe assignments and assessments at the highest three levels of the Create Excellence Framework's technology-integration component.

Follow-up sessions:

- ◆ Share assignments implemented in classes.
- ◆ Identify ways to address implementation challenges.
- ◆ Leave with ideas of additional Create Excellence Framework projects.

2. Provide sample lessons for the teachers to score together and discuss. Emphasize the difference between the teacher-driven task or project levels and the student-driven task or project levels.

3. Incorporate study-group discussions throughout the school year about:

- ◆ Tasks and projects that the teachers have designed (see table 5.1, page 97).
- ◆ Student work after completion of the framework tasks and projects (see figure 5.2).

Figure 5.2 is a tool for teachers to use in study groups to discuss whether their task or project was designed in such a way that it produced the desired and targeted student outcomes. This essential tool is critical to review student work because although teachers can do all kinds of planning, until they look critically at a student's level of work on the assessment, they do not truly know the student's level of achievement. Visit **go.SolutionTree.com/instruction** for a free reproducible version of the discussion tool. Also, see the "Create Excellence Framework Task or Project Template" reproducible on page 112 for an additional tool to plan a lesson or project using the Create Excellence Framework.

Student Product	• Did the students in the class work through the task or project as teacher or student directed? • Was the task or project low- or high-level learning? • Did the product designed to assess student learning align with the task or project? • Did your scoring instruments align with the learning targets of the task or project? • What needs to be revised? • Does the student product align with each planned level of each component in the Create Excellence Framework?

Figure 5.2: Discussion tool for student work.   Continued →

Real-World Learning	• Did students connect to the task or project? • In what ways did students make the task or project more authentic as they worked through the solution? • Did you find them adding in their own ideas? • What would you strengthen or do differently?
Cognitive Complexity	• Did the students perform at the level designed for the task or project? • What revisions are needed? • What revised Bloom's taxonomy level do you believe the task or project ended up being at? Do you believe the student work met the thinking level intended? • Did students have opportunities to raise questions?
Student Engagement	• What choices did students have? • How did partnering with the teacher work out? • In what ways did students work with others in and out of the classroom?
Technology Integration	• What variety of technology was used? • Did students use multiple technologies within a single task or project? • Did the technology feel seamless, or was it an add-on? • If the technology was an add-on, what could be done to make it more integrated?

Visit **go.SolutionTree.com/instruction** *for a free reproducible version of this figure.*

District-Level Implementation

For a district to implement the Create Excellence Framework in schools, it is first and foremost important to have buy-in from all administrators and building leaders. Then, we also recommend having a districtwide philosophy-building session about why you would choose this initiative. Suggested inspiration for this would be to show a presentation that explains the rationale and inspiration behind choosing the Create Excellence Framework as a district initiative. See http://create-excellence.com/resources for additional resources.

A couple of districts that have implemented the framework host competitions for using this framework with their teachers. They ask all their K–12 teachers to participate in designing and implementing a lesson. (See the reproducible "Create a Lesson-Plan Template" on page 110 and at **go.SolutionTree.com/instruction** for an example of one district's lesson-plan template.) After designing and submitting a lesson plan, teachers participate in rating the lessons with the framework and give suggestions for improvement. The objective is to increase real-world learning in the classroom, while enhancing the other components of cognitive complexity, student engagement, and technology integration.

Tools for Designing and Managing Create Excellence Framework Tasks and Projects

It will probably take more time to develop a Create Excellence Framework task or project than a typical assignment. However, when implementing the task or project, students will take charge of learning, and the classroom will be more student led. Elizabeth A. City, Richard F. Elmore, Sarah E. Fiarman, and Lee Teitel (2009), authors of *Instructional Rounds in Education*, state that the "task predicts performance" (p. 30). Thus, if assignments are of low quality and not aligned to standards, then learning also will be negatively impacted.

However, if teachers take the time to design high-quality tasks and projects, there can potentially be better learning results.

When students are working in groups, it can be challenging for the teacher to determine a grade or score for the work and hold each student accountable. First and foremost, it is important to remember that the learning is the most critical part of the task or project—more so than the grading of it! Do not let the scoring get in the way of the learning! The Group Collaboration Feedback Instrument (figures 5.3 and 5.4, page 104) is a tool that students can use to help give informal feedback on how the group performed and on how members contributed (see pages 116–117 for free reproducible versions of these figures). However, this is something that needs to be considered with the classroom environment and within a positive culture. Students need to understand that this is a way to provide feedback to classmates to help them improve and to point out their strengths. The teacher needs to consider this as part of how the overall task or project is assessed and should emphasize that the students need to work together and support each other's growth.

Primary

Directions: Each group member should rate the following statements independently. Read each statement and place a check mark under your rating. Be honest in your ratings!

	No	**Maybe or I Am Not Sure**	**Yes**
The group began working right away. The teacher did not have to remind the group to get started.			
The group made a plan and brainstormed ideas before members began working.			
Each group member worked on the project the entire time.			
Each member had a chance to explain his or her thoughts and ideas for each part of the project.			
Group members worked together and got along.			
The group researched to find a solution to this project.			

Figure 5.3: Group collaboration feedback instrument for primary grades.

Intermediate

Directions: Each group member should rate the following statements on a scale of 1 to 4, with 1 being the lowest score and 4 being the highest. Read each statement and place a check mark under your rating. Rate independently. Be honest in your ratings!

	1 BEGINNING	2 DEVELOPING	3 ACCOMPLISHED	4 EXEMPLARY
The group actively began working on the task or project without prompting from the teacher.				
The group interacted to organize, plan, and generate ideas and plans for the task or project solution.				
The group used the Student Work Management Chart (table 5.2, page 100) to plan its work and divide responsibilities and keep track of its time line.				

Figure 5.4: Group collaboration feedback instrument for intermediate grades.

Teachers may also need a tool to help them determine if their task or project is a well-rounded, project-based scenario that will lend itself well to the underlying base of the Create Excellence Framework components. Figure 5.5 provides a tool to preassess a project for these features. A free reproducible version of this tool is available on page 118.

THE TASK OR PROJECT IS . . .	YES	NO
1. Stemming from an idea important to the students		
2. Designed within the student's level of success		
3. Content related and relevant to the learner's needs		
4. Designed to stretch the student's achievement level		
5. Devised to engage the student in researching and processing information		
6. Designed to fit the time frame		
7. Providing the student experience with new learning		
8. Filled with opportunities to self-guide students' learning		
9. Including accessible resources and materials		
10. Designed with a framework for students to add progress checkpoints		
11. Designed with an assessment tool that is included		

Figure 5.5: Checklist for preassessing a task or project.

The teacher may find it helpful for the students to use a clarification questionnaire to help them determine what roles they want to assume during the project and to help the teacher meet students' individual learning needs (see figure 5.6). A free reproducible version of this questionnaire is available on page 119.

For help with project planning, have students complete this questionnaire, and review the responses to determine your students' interests.

Questions to get ideas for a project from students:

- What are the most interesting topics of this study for me?
- Consider the content being studied in class currently. Which part would make a good project?
- If I could design any project, what would I want to do? What do I want to learn? What would be the time line?
- How do I typically like to work on a project—alone, in partners, or in groups?
- Do I like to collaborate or work with people beyond the classroom?

Questions to refine the project designed by the teacher:

- Which part of the project am I most excited about?
- What do I want to learn most from this project?
- What will be my time line?
- How will I meet the requirements of the progress checkpoints?
- Where can I find the material and resources?
- What are my greatest concerns or needs related to the assignment?
- What do I need to do before I begin the project?
- How will I collaborate with my peers? Will I want to work alone, with a partner, or in a group?
- How will I partner with my teacher? Others?
- How will the project look when it is finished?
- How will technology be involved in my project?
- How will I present the project?
- How will my work be assessed?

Figure 5.6: Sample student clarification questionnaire for an engaging, real-world project.

Visit **go.SolutionTree.com/instruction** *for a free reproducible version of this figure.*

Case Study of a Project in Action

In this section, we present a case study to show how the ideas originated from the teacher and students in the classroom, blossomed into a project, and played out into the instruction. We encourage you to take time to interact with the case study and consider the Take Action activities (page 108).

A fourth-grade classroom of students becomes very upset once it learns that a classmate, Michael, has been diagnosed with leukemia. When the students find out he is going to receive homebound instruction while going through cancer treatment, they ask the teacher what they can do to help Michael still be able to come to school on occasion and feel like a part of the class. As students brainstorm ideas and information they need, each student adds ideas to Etherpad (http://etherpad.org) so the ideas will be visible to all students on the projector from the teacher's computer. Ideas from the class include the following: learn about leukemia, study how to cope with serious illness, look for ways to arrange the classroom to fit the reclining chair, consider the cleanliness of the room and school, understand the health of the classmates, make a schedule of the days when visiting, draft rules for caring for and visiting with Michael, and consider arrangements regarding food menus, recesses, lessons, and exercise.

As the students continue their brainstorming, they realize many areas of concern. They need to know more about leukemia and how serious this disease is so they can remain aware of the gravity of the situation. They are concerned about making sure that Michael's parents can transport him and his wheelchair in and out of his home and school. They realize they need a special form of transportation. As they plan, concerns arise about financial expenses for the transportation. The students want to talk with local businesses to see if they can convince any to donate funds for the cause. The classmates are also concerned about Michael's feelings. Will he want to come to school? He always did before, but now he is sick. The class realizes it will need to research how to help children going through cancer and chemotherapy and see if it can form a support group. The class also understands the importance of reaching out to Michael and his parents to get their opinion on the class's plan.

It is quickly evident that students have interests in different aspects of the problem. The students split themselves into teams according to task. The emotional support team works on the emotional aspect, forming the support group and researching how to help form a mentally healthy environment for Michael and for each other. A funding and logistical support team works on the transportation aspect, organizing the vehicle, parking, special recliner chair, and fundraising or sponsors. A third team, the healthy-school team, organizes the health aspect. This angle includes setting up a plan and checking on the room's cleanliness, planning the meals and snacks for the day, and figuring out how to incorporate exercise and activities. The environment team works on the environment aspect of the room for welcoming Michael, both at the school and in the classroom especially. It makes sure to attend to the floor plan and decorations to be inclusive and mindful of where his recliner will be located.

The whole class discusses tasks, projects, and assessments. Everyone has input into the self-monitoring (each student will keep a personal blog that only the teacher has access to) and assessment rubrics for the project as a whole. The teacher coaches each team and facilitates the creation of a list of tasks and responsibilities that the recorder enters into List After List (http://listafterlist.com) during the discussion, and all members design and sign a team contract. The teams use either Tracky (http://tracky.com) or Timetonote (http://timetonote .com) to manage their project. Most teams use Creately (http://creately.com) or Mind42 (http://mind42.com) to map out their network of ideas and Google Docs to write up their documents so different team members can contribute to the writing. The funding and logistical support team decides to use Google Forms for its survey, and members obtain email addresses of organizations and businesses that can aid in this project.

The teacher consults with the teams on designing appropriate interview or survey questions. The environment team talks with an interior designer and a health supply store manager, who provides a special recliner chair. These two aspects are most helpful in pointing out which design aspects to look for, what types of barriers to overcome, the importance of electricity, and maintenance tips. When the team finishes, the two experts remotely review and critique the team's design.

Once collecting, compiling, and analyzing the survey and interview data in an Excel worksheet, the teacher takes the opportunity for a whole-class mathematics lesson on graphing with this authentic student-collected data. The funding and logistical support team then uses Google Drive to compose a letter of proposal to community businesses and civic organizations. Some students visit businesses and civic groups in person to promote their cause.

They then begin working on ReviewStudio (www.reviewstudio.com), a collaborative video site, and scouring the Internet for royalty-free photos to use for the campaign.

The funding and logistical support team meets with a mentor from a local university to learn how to raise funds for a not-for-profit project. The team then designs its campaign plan for how to raise funds from local donors and businesses. Team members research and develop a multifaceted plan for gathering donations. They meet with businesses, conduct a phone campaign, and write emails and letters.

Since the funding and logistical support team has secured financial commitment for half the cost of the special recliner chair, the town council approves its plan. The environment team organizes a workday for many of the students to volunteer on Saturdays to help rearrange and decorate the classroom with the new chair and floor plan. The healthy-school team inspects the room upon completion of the redesign. The team also promotes and shares the menu for meals and snacks and the recess plans with the class so the students have an understanding of the rationale for the design. The emotional support team holds a Monday morning meeting before Michael comes to school to brief fellow classmates on how to support him and each other in dealing with illness and overcoming the feeling of isolation and depression.

Conclusion

Thoughtful planning of the Create Excellence Framework implementation is critical because it is important to engage students and ensure they are learning. We provide the steps and tools suggested in this book for implementing the framework at the classroom, school, or district level to help facilitate a smoother path to your instructional success.

Discussion Questions

Answer the following six questions to summarize the chapter's concepts.

1. What are some ways students can generate ideas for a Create Excellence Framework project based on a topic they are studying?
2. What is your style as a teacher? Would you tend to begin with the standards or the real-world topic to generate your task or project?
3. How comfortable are you in involving your students with developing a rubric and targets for a task or project?
4. What concerns might you have about communicating with parents about the Create Excellence Framework?
5. What is a simulation you are already doing that you could improve with the Create Excellence Framework?
6. How would implementation be different in the primary classroom versus the intermediate classroom?

Take Action

Consider the following seven tasks and activities to help you toward implementing the Create Excellence Framework.

1. Consider an idea for a Create task or project. Use table 5.1 (page 97) for brainstorming. Use the "Create a Lesson-Plan Template" reproducible (page 110) to jot down your idea. Share your idea with a colleague.

2. Use figure 5.2 (page 101) or the reproducible on page 115 to discuss completed student work from a Create Excellence Framework project to see if the work correlates to the project's targets.

3. Choose a group of students to use the Group Collaboration Feedback Instrument (see figure 5.3, page 103, or figure 5.4, page 104, and the reproducibles on pages 116 and 117). How does the group perform with this format? Does it like working in a group? After you see how it works with the one group, now consider what you will need to do for implementing the instrument with your whole class.

4. Another angle that can help you discern whether your task or project is ready for use with your class is the "Checklist for Preassessing a Task or Project" reproducible (page 118). Pair with a colleague, and apply this checklist to your tasks or projects. Discuss the checklists, and note the framework elements. In what areas are you strong, and in what areas are you lacking?

5. Using the "Sample Student Clarification Questionnaire for an Engaging, Real-World Project" reproducible (page 119), have students give you feedback in general about what kind of project they would like to do. Then have students give specific ideas for a preliminary project idea. How can you incorporate their ideas?

6. Using the Create Excellence Framework, rate the level of the case study in this chapter for each framework component, and justify its rating. What suggestions would you give to bump it even higher?

7. Analyze the case study, and answer the following questions.
   - How would you describe the real-world learning scenario and connection to the students?
   - What standards are addressed?
   - How is each Create Excellence Framework component addressed?
   - How could you convert this scenario to a lesson plan?
   - What assessment would you design for this scenario?
   - What formative assessments would you use with this scenario?

Final Thoughts

So why change instructional practices? *Real-World Learning Framework for Elementary Schools* was designed out of passion and a need to share great changes that are happening in education. With the Create Excellence Framework, teachers are transforming their ways of thinking—focusing on how to connect with students through real-world learning. Even though this kind of real-world instruction does not necessarily happen every day in each classroom, educators have an appreciation for each component and how the pieces combine to form a comprehensive lesson. Amid a world of constant change, the Create Excellence Framework can provide a foundation to manage this change and ensure high-level, real-world, standards-based instruction that remains at the forefront for our students.

The Create Excellence Framework is a lesson-planning framework that guides students, teachers, and parents in thinking about learning in a different yet comprehensive way. Teachers can aspire to the upper levels of the framework, levels 4 and 5, which are student directed. Teachers can use the framework to plan lessons that will deeply engage students in self-directed learning experiences, resulting in students being eager to come to school, intrinsically motivated to learn more, and prepared for the rigor of higher education or high-skill workplaces.

When knowledge and skills are embedded in real-world learning, students will see the connections in content knowledge and skills in the standards. While many teachers and principals are highly concerned with the acquisition of this knowledge and these skills, we believe that intentionally designing learning experiences to be unified around real-world concepts and ideas is the key. By using real-world themes and essential questions to integrate their learning objectives and align content standards, students have an authentic context for the projects and tasks they undertake. Also, integration of the standards in real-world themes and experiences helps students achieve a deeper level of learning. Students will begin to see that subjects are related and life is full of interconnected relationships to content (Martinez, 2014).

National and provincial content standards and teacher standards emphasize students leading their own learning while engaging in critical-thinking tasks and projects and applying their knowledge in real-world contexts using 21st century tools. Therefore, educators must plan instructional experiences that involve real-world learning, high levels of cognitive complexity, student engagement, and technology integration. Students and teachers can be confident that learning targets will be met if teachers embed these components into their teaching.

If teachers are going to demonstrate being highly effective and students are going to take responsibility for their own learning, then teachers need a planning framework to help organize instruction for student learning of these new standards. We suggest addressing these challenges with quality instructional planning through the Create Excellence Framework. To design a comprehensive project that truly encompasses real-world learning and all components for student learning and growth in the 21st century classroom, we assert that the Create Excellence Framework is an integral design framework that complements any set of curriculum standards. Our research, framework, and sample projects demonstrate a design for student learning with more depth and breadth than simply teaching the standards in isolation. With the real-world learning component tying it all together, we believe that comprehensive student learning will have far-reaching results such as higher test scores, increased student excitement about learning, and improved student responsibility for their own learning.

Change needs to happen. Many leading educators have been admired for innovation and educational initiatives for change. Now is the time to press onward with highly effective instructional experiences that incorporate authentic-learning opportunities connected to the real world. This is an exciting time in education. We have the opportunity to partner with students to encourage them to take responsibility for their own learning, generate their own questions, design projects, facilitate discussions, assess peers, and meet with outside experts. Embrace the challenge. Let the Create Excellence Framework transform your classroom!

Create a Lesson-Plan Template

Teacher: _____ Grade Level: _____ Create Level: _____

School: _____ Course or Class: _____ Date of Lesson: _____

Content Connection (Standards section):
Overall Unit Goal:
Learning Targets/Objectives:
Lesson Description (Brief overview of this specific lesson as it relates to the overall unit and a general description of how the lesson is to be implemented):

Create Excellence Framework Rating

CREATE ANALYSIS		
CREATE COMPONENT	**LEVEL**	**JUSTIFICATION**
Real-World Learning		
Cognitive Complexity		
Student Engagement		
Technology Integration		

Sequence of Strategies and Activities

STRATEGY OR ACTIVITY	TIME REQUIRED	SPECIFIC SKILL OR CONTENT CONNECTION	STUDENT ASSESSMENT (DESCRIBE AND SPECIFY FORMATIVE OR SUMMATIVE)	PLANNED DIFFERENTIATION

Source: Adapted from Hart County School District, 2011.

Attachments

- Please attach three student work samples associated with this lesson (required).
- Please attach any supporting files or resources (PowerPoint files, graphic organizers, and so on; encouraged but not required).

Questions for Reflection

1. What went especially well with this lesson, and why?

2. What lesson components would you refine when or if you deliver the lesson again?

3. How did (or could) the use of technology impact student engagement, delivery of content, or student performance associated with this lesson?

Real-World Learning Framework for Elementary Schools © 2017 Solution Tree Press • SolutionTree.com
Visit **go.SolutionTree.com/instruction** to download this free reproducible.

Create an Excellence Framework Task or Project Template

On the first page of the lesson plan, include the following information.

Project title: Create a fun and interesting, catchy title.

Grade level or course: List the grade level for K–8 assignments, but list the course for high school.

Learning objectives: Start each objective with "Students will . . ." followed by a verb and the learning goal. You can have more than one objective.

Standards: List the standards being addressed, such as the Common Core State Standards, Next Generation Science Standards, and so on.

Project options: Give students multiple choices for completing the assignment. Consider offering several technology options.

Resources needed: List items, including software and web tools, needed for the assignment.

On the second page of the template, include the project title again and the following.

Scenario: Create a real-world learning scenario that establishes the context of the project. This could be where students simulate real-world roles or actually do something like writing a public service announcement that will be shared with the school.

Project tasks: Insert student directions for the assignment. This is what will be copied and given to students. Add extensions to the project (not required).

Scoring rubric: For younger students, you may want to use a checklist; for older students, a four-point rubric. On the four-point rubric, put the objective in the first column, and then identify rubric headings.

Scoring Rubric

	1 SIGNIFICANT REVISION NEEDED	2 SOME REVISION NEEDED	3 PROFICIENT	4 EXCEEDS EXPECTATIONS
Write the first learning objective in this space.				
If applicable, write the second learning objective in this space.				
If applicable, write the third learning objective in this space.				

Sample student work: Include a sample project with the lesson plan illustrating what the finished product should look like.

Create Excellence Framework rating: Use the following table to evaluate the project for each component of the framework. At what level does each component rate: 1 (Knowing), 2 (Practicing), 3 (Investigating), 4 (Integrating), or 5 (Specializing)?

Create Excellence Framework Rating

CREATE ANALYSIS		
CREATE COMPONENT	LEVEL	JUSTIFICATION
Real-World Learning		
Cognitive Complexity		
Student Engagement		
Technology Integration		

Sample Parent or Guardian Letter

Dear Parent or Guardian,

During this school year, your child will experience a new way of learning. We will be having lots of conversations and taking many ideas from the students' interests to drive the learning when possible.

The Create Excellence Framework lesson-planning tool for real-world learning will guide how we strive to complete the projects and tasks and push our learning.

- Your child will be striving to learn at levels beyond rote memorization and instead will be creating new connections and evaluating his or her learning.
- Your child will be experiencing meaning from his or her own life and world and incorporating it into the tasks and projects.
- Your child will be working with the teacher as a partner in learning, consulting with experts (which may include many of you!), interacting with students in teams, and having choice in products, process, and content.
- Your child will be using technology to complete tasks and projects in a seamless fashion while enhancing learning.

The goal is that throughout the course of the year your child will be able to experience student-directed tasks and projects in addition to the typical teacher-directed tasks and projects.

The exciting part of using a lesson-planning tool of this kind for this class is that I can make sure all the vital learning components are included and that your child is experiencing challenging and well-rounded tasks and projects.

I appreciate your support in this endeavor of my instruction and of your child's inevitable growth! Please contact me if you would like to volunteer to help with this learning adventure. I welcome your help! Also, feel free to contact me about any questions that you may have.

Sincerely,

Teacher

Discussion Tool for Student Work

Student Product	• Did the students in the class work through the task or project as teacher or student directed? • Was the task or project low- or high-level learning? • Did the product designed to assess student learning align with the task or project? • Did your scoring instruments align with the learning targets of the task or project? • What needs to be revised? • Does the student product align with each planned level of each component in the Create Excellence Framework?
Real-World Learning	• Did students connect to the task or project? • In what ways did students make the task or project more authentic as they worked through the solution? • Did you find them adding in their own ideas? • What would you strengthen or do differently?
Cognitive Complexity	• Did the students perform at the level designed for the task or project? • What revisions are needed? • What revised Bloom's taxonomy level do you believe the task or project ended up being at? Do you believe the student work met the thinking level intended? • Did students have opportunities to raise questions?
Student Engagement	• What choices did students have? • How did partnering with the teacher work out? • In what ways did students work with others in and out of the classroom?
Technology Integration	• What variety of technology was used? • Did students use multiple technologies within a single task or project? • Did the technology feel seamless, or was it an add-on? • If the technology was an add-on, what could be done to make it more integrated?

Group Collaboration Feedback Instrument for Primary Grades

Each group member should rate the following statements independently. Read each statement and place a check mark under your rating. Be honest in your ratings!

	No	Maybe or I Am Not Sure	Yes
The group began working right away. The teacher did not have to remind the group to get started.			
The group made a plan and brainstormed ideas before members began working.			
Each group member worked on the project the entire time.			
Each member had a chance to explain his or her thoughts and ideas for each part of the project.			
Group members worked together and got along.			
The group researched to find a solution to this project.			

Group Collaboration Feedback Instrument for Intermediate Grades

Each group member should rate the following statements on a scale of 1 to 4, with 1 being the lowest score and 4 being the highest. Read each statement and place a check mark under your rating. Rate independently. Be honest in your ratings!

	1 BEGINNING	2 DEVELOPING	3 ACCOMPLISHED	4 EXEMPLARY
The group actively began working on the task or project without prompting from the teacher.				
The group interacted to organize, plan, and generate ideas and plans for the task or project solution.				
The group used the Student Work Management Chart (table 5.2, page 100) to plan its work and divide responsibilities and keep track of its time line.				
Each group member contributed and participated for the duration of the task or project planning and work.				
Each member was encouraged to voice his or her opinions for how to achieve each component of the task or project.				
The group discussed options to reach a consensus in order to work through conflicts.				
Group members used their time efficiently.				
Each group member collaborated well with the others.				
The group learned, initiated, and used the inquiry-based approach for finding its solution.				

Checklist for Preassessing a Task or Project

THE TASK OR PROJECT IS . . .	YES	NO
1. Stemming from an idea important to the students		
2. Designed within the student's level of success		
3. Content related and relevant to the learner's needs		
4. Designed to stretch the student's achievement level		
5. Devised to engage the student in researching and processing information		
6. Designed to fit the time frame		
7. Providing the student experience with new learning		
8. Filled with opportunities to self-guide students' learning		
9. Including accessible resources and materials		
10. Designed with a framework for students to add progress checkpoints		
11. Designed with an assessment tool that is included		

Sample Student Clarification Questionnaire for an Engaging, Real-World Project

For help with project planning, have students complete this questionnaire, and review the responses to determine your students' interests.

Questions to get ideas for a project from students:

- What are the most interesting topics of this study for me?
- Consider the content being studied in class currently. Which part would make a good project?
- If I could design any project, what would I want to do? What do I want to learn? What would be the time line?
- How do I typically like to work on a project—alone, in partners, or in groups?
- Do I like to collaborate or work with people beyond the classroom?

Questions to refine the project designed by the teacher:

- Which part of the project am I most excited about?
- What do I want to learn most from this project?
- What will be my time line?
- How will I meet the requirements of the progress checkpoints?
- Where can I find the material and resources?
- What are my greatest concerns or needs related to the assignment?
- What do I need to do before I begin the project?
- How will I collaborate with my peers? Will I want to work alone, with a partner, or in a group?
- How will I partner with my teacher? Others?
- How will the project look when it is finished?
- How will technology be involved in my project?
- How will I present the project?
- How will my work be assessed?

PART II

While the following projects are divided into the subject areas of English language arts (pages 123–180), mathematics (pages 181–225), social studies (pages 227–266), and science (pages 267–317), all projects are interdisciplinary, and readers should consider perusing projects from other subject areas for ideas. The projects include specific grade-level standards, but we encourage you to scaffold or modify the projects for use in a lower or higher grade level. Each project's grade level is noted in the standard alignment. Many of the mathematics projects are adapted from Garlic Press (www.garlicpress.com) with permission.

The structure for projects is as follows.

- The first segment of each project lists content standards, learning objectives, project options, and resources needed. This segment explains the background of the lesson for the teacher. Some include vocabulary or technology-integration tools students need to complete the lesson.
- The second segment of each project contains a short introduction, project tasks, and a scoring rubric. This segment is reproducible for students because it provides project directions and a rubric. Projects for grades K–2 provide a checklist rather than a rubric for ease of use with younger children. (Visit **go.SolutionTree.com/instruction** to access free reproducible versions of each.)
- The third segment contains sample student work to show a final product. To help readers critically examine each project, an analysis table explains how the project aligns to each of the four framework components.

DISCOVER THE AUTHOR IN YOU!

Source: Adapted from Sheriden Edwards. Used with permission.

Content: English language arts

Learning Objectives:

1. Students will create a sequel to a well-known children's classic or historical story.
2. Students will become authors through writing, editing, and publishing a book.

Standards:

Common Core English language arts—

- RL.5.5 Explain how a series of chapters, scenes, or stanzas fits together to provide the overall structure of a particular story, drama, or poem (NGA & CCSSO, 2010a).
- W.5.3 Write narratives to develop real or imagined experiences or events using effective technique, descriptive details, and clear event sequences (NGA & CCSSO, 2010a).
- W.5.6 With some guidance and support from adults, use technology, including the Internet, to produce and publish writing as well as to interact and collaborate with others; demonstrate sufficient command of keyboarding skills to type a minimum of two pages in a single sitting (NGA & CCSSO, 2010a).

Project Options: Students will use word processing software such as Microsoft Word. Online publishing tools may need some adult intervention to set up accounts on book-creation sites such as CreateSpace or Lulu.

- Primary options include Lulu Jr. for intermediate grades, and Storybird is great for online publishing.
- As an optional extension to the project, students can draw and scan in their own illustrations. These can be done in a particular historical or artistic style to add authenticity to the masterpiece!
- This project has worked well as a Victorian project, reading *The Railway Children* by E. Nesbit, or an ancient Greek project, using a range of ancient Greek myths.

Resources Needed: Computer with Internet access; word processing software; access to online publishers; sample Author Night schedule; writing utensils

Discover the Author in You!

Everyone can write, and everyone can publish. Yes, *you* can publish your own writing! Great readers often make great writers. You have been reading books for years, and you have been writing for yourself, your family, and your teachers. Here is your chance to study a classic children's story or a historical story. You will then write a different version or continuation of the story and publish this for your parents and other students. Remember your audience; you will be publishing your writing like a real author!

Project Tasks

1. We have been reading books over the last few weeks. Some have been linked to a historical period, and some were classic books. Let's discuss the language use or styles that connect these books to particular genres. Complete part one on your "Writing Worksheet."

2. Choose a classic novel or book about a historical event. The book should be one you are familiar with, so choose a book you have read in previous weeks. You will write a continuation of the story or create a different version. Complete part two on your "Writing Worksheet," the Planning Chart (page 126).

3. Create your first draft, using a similar style and language. As authors, you must write with the audience in mind and with a consistent and authentic style to match the original novel or time period. Use of setting, characterization, and plot should be considered. You will work with a partner to help each other with the creating and editing process. You will use word processing software for all drafts of your book.

4. After you have created a draft, we will work as a class to develop a set of criteria that you will use to edit your own and each other's work. For example, you may decide to review each other's writing for development of ideas; organization; use of language similar to that in the original story; use of correct grammar, punctuation, and spelling; how you stick to your plan; and so on.

5. Critique each other's and your own work against the set of criteria, and remember to make sure the story is sympathetic to the style and genre of the original book. You should include features that you have learned from your study of historical events at the time in which the story is set.

6. Once your story is free of errors, it is time to publish it! This can be done in a variety of ways. Options include Lulu (www.lulu.com), Storybird (https://storybird.com), Scribble Press (https://app.scribblepress.com), Nanowrimo (http://nanowrimo.org), Launch Pad (www.launchpadmag.com), Amazon (www.amazon.com), 48 Hour Books (http://48hrbooks.com), Studentreasures Publishing (http://studentreasures.com), and Mixbook (www.mixbook.com).

Publishing on the Internet

Plan for an Author Night, during which the class will present its books to parents and the community. You may even be asked to sign your book copies! You'll need to consider the following.

- Decide on a date, time, and location for the event.
- Decide whether each student will take a turn on stage to tell about his or her book or if each student will set up at a different table (and guests will go around the room to visit the authors).
- Decide whether you will serve food and drinks. If so, where will you get the funding?
- Plan a schedule for the evening.
- Create a program to give to all guests with each student's name and book title.
- Create a plan to advertise Author Night.
- Discuss the students' dress code for the event.

Writing Worksheet

Name: _____

Part 1: Define the following terms.

- **Genre:**

- **Audience:**

- **Purpose:**

- **Style:**

- **Sequel:**

- **Plot:**

- **Characters:**

Part 2: Complete the following planning chart to plan your story.

Writing Worksheet Planning Chart

	BOOK YOU ARE WRITING A SEQUEL TO: _____	PLAN YOUR SEQUEL OR DIFFERENT VERSION OF THE SAME STORY
Genre		
Characters		
Setting		
Plot		
Conflict		
Resolution		
Conclusion or Ending		

Scoring Rubric

	1 SIGNIFICANT REVISION NEEDED	2 SOME REVISION NEEDED	3 PROFICIENT	4 EXCEEDS EXPECTATIONS
Objective 1: Students will create a sequel to a well-known children's classic or historical story.	Story does not use language features consistent with the original author or historical period.	Story uses language features consistent with the historical period, but the style lacks consistency.	Story uses language features consistent with the original author and historical period.	Story uses language features and style of writing mirroring the original author and historical period.
	Story has disorganized sentence constructions. There is a lack of any literary techniques.	Story uses mostly simple sentences. Literary techniques are predictable or are sometimes not consistent with the genre.	Story uses varied sentence patterns and complex sentences. The author has attempted to use literary techniques such as imagery and dialogue.	Story uses a wide range of sentence structures including complex sentences and a good range of figurative language.

Real-World Learning Framework for Elementary Schools © 2017 Solution Tree Press • SolutionTree.com
Visit **go.SolutionTree.com/instruction** to download this free reproducible.

	1 SIGNIFICANT REVISION NEEDED	2 SOME REVISION NEEDED	3 PROFICIENT	4 EXCEEDS EXPECTATIONS
Objective 2: Students will become authors through writing, editing, and publishing a book.	Story is not well edited; there are errors in spelling, grammar, and punctuation.	Story is edited but lacks flow; there are few errors in spelling, grammar, and punctuation.	Story is well edited; spelling, grammar, and punctuation are correct.	Story is well edited, and spelling, grammar, and punctuation are correct. Punctuation and syntax are at a highly mature level of sophistication.
	Student's work is not well organized for publication. Significant revision is needed.	Student's work is complete for publication, although some intervention for organization is required.	Student's work is well organized for publication.	Student's work is well organized for publication and includes features such as appropriate illustrations, which add authenticity.
	Student's work is unable to establish a sense of style and has no sense of audience.	Student's work has difficulty establishing a style appropriate to the purpose with little sense of audience.	Student's work can establish and maintain a style mostly appropriate to the purpose with a sense of audience.	Student's work can establish and maintain a style appropriate to the purpose with a strong sense of audience.

Sample Student Work

Writing Worksheet

Look inside students' published books.

Harlaxton CE School Year 6's (2014) *The Further Adventures of the Railway Children*: http://tinyurl.com/railwayH A book written by a student at Harlaxton Church of England Primary School School website: www.harlaxton-lincs.co.uk	Denton CE School Class 3's (2013) *The Further Adventures of the Railway Children*: http://tinyurl.com/railwayD A book written by a student at Denton Church of England Primary School School website: www.dentonceschool.co.uk

---

Name: **Jenny Smith**

Part 1: Define the following terms.

- **Genre:** This is the category of book—in this case, historical children's fiction.
- **Audience:** This is who the writing is aimed at; this book is for children aged ten and up.
- **Purpose:** This is what the book is for; the purpose of the book is to give pleasure.
- **Style:** Style is the type of writing; this book is written in a narrative style.
- **Sequel:** This is where there may be several stages or episodes to a story.
- **Plot:** This is the main occurrence in the story.
- **Characters:** These are the main people or beings in a story.

Part 2: Complete the following planning chart to plan your story.

Writing Worksheet Planning Chart

	BOOK YOU ARE WRITING A SEQUEL TO: _____	PLAN YOUR SEQUEL OR DIFFERENT VERSION OF THE SAME STORY
Genre	Historical fiction	Historical fiction
Characters	Bobby, Phyllis, and Peter (children and brothers and sisters); Mother; Mr. Perks, the station master	Bobby, Phyllis, and Peter (children and brothers and sisters); Mother; Mr. Perks, the station master; and Father
Setting	Yorkshire, England	Yorkshire, England
Plot	The children and Mother leave London for Yorkshire because Father has been imprisoned for a crime he did not commit. The children adjust to country life with very little money and learn about the workings of a rural railway station.	This is their first Christmas with their father, and the children plan how to make it special. A visit from Queen Victoria interrupts their plan.
Conflict	One day, they find a bridge has collapsed. The next train is likely to crash into it.	The queen enters the house and slips by the fire; she is unconscious.
Resolution	The children set up some signals along the track to alert the driver, and all is saved.	The children find her and fetch the doctor, who revives her.
Conclusion or Ending	The children become local heroes, and their father is cleared and comes to live with them in Yorkshire.	The children are awarded with a special medal, and their mother and father are very proud of them. The children and their mother do get to spend Christmas with Father.

Create Excellence Framework Rating

CREATE ANALYSIS		
CREATE COMPONENT	**LEVEL**	**JUSTIFICATION**
Real-World Learning	4: Integrating	Students are authors who publish their writing either online or in print for a real audience. They present their work during Author Night at the school.
Cognitive Complexity	4: Integrating	Students are analyzing a children's classic story or historical story for characters, plot, and writing style. Students critique each other's story using a set of criteria the class developed.
Student Engagement	4: Integrating	Students collaborate and critique their own and each other's work. Students create the rubric or checklist to guide the peer critique. Students also get to select the book that will be the basis for their sequel.
Technology Integration	4: Integrating	Technology is an essential tool to help the students organize and edit their work effectively. The online publishing tool allows students to understand how the physical structure of electronic texts can be manipulated to suit a variety of outcomes.

MAKE OUR SCHOOL PLAYGROUND BETTER!

Source: Adapted from Katelyn Heupel and Sam Northern. Used with permission.

Content: English language arts

Learning Objectives:

1. Students will design a new playground incorporating reasons that support the proposed solutions.
2. Students will create a multimedia project (using Prezi, Animoto, or another tool) to present to their principal showing the problems they found with their school playground and possible solutions.

Standards:

Common Core English language arts—

- W.3.1 Write opinion pieces on topics or texts, supporting a point of view with reasons (NGA & CCSSO, 2010a).
- W.3.6 With guidance and support from adults, use technology to produce and publish writing (using keyboarding skills) as well as to interact and collaborate with others (NGA & CCSSO, 2010a).
- W.3.8 Recall information from experiences or gather information from print and digital sources; take brief notes on sources and sort evidence into provided categories (NGA & CCSSO, 2010a).

Project Options: Students will choose a problem that they believe exists in their school. Each group will create a multimedia project to present to the principal showing the problems they found and possible solutions to those problems. Students will choose their multimedia presentation's format, including the possibilities of an Animoto video, Prezi, PBS Storyboard, or another presentation tool. Animoto allows students to turn photos and video clips into a professional-quality video. Students can use Prezi to design a visually compelling presentation that integrates multimedia content. With PBS Storyboard, students can create a dynamic presentation by incorporating videos, graphics, and text. These project options are web-based presentation tools that can be accessed from any Internet-ready device.

Resources Needed: Resources depend on the research the students conduct as well as the presentation format each group chooses. A computer with Internet access and a digital camera are necessary.

Make Our School Playground Better!

Successful businessman Lindsay Fox once said, "If you believe you can make a difference, then you will make a difference. Believe in yourself, your family, and your community, and you will win." You and your classmates are a school family that is setting out to make a difference. Together, we will win by making our school a better place for everyone. In class, we have been learning about writing to persuade an audience. You have been asked to think about problems with your school and ways your school could be improved. The class has decided to help the school playground solve its problems with litter, graffiti, and overall appearance. So, let's get to work!

Project Tasks

1. First, in groups of four, investigate the playground for the problem you would like to target. Recording your observations of the problems in the playground using the "Observation Guide" will achieve this goal.

2. Next, your group needs to agree on the one problem you believe you could fix. Obtain the digital camera from the teacher to take pictures of the problem you have decided to focus on.

3. You will brainstorm with your group possible solutions to that problem. Your group will then research the solutions listed. Interview teachers and students in your school to get their points of view on the problem you are addressing. Record your questions and answers on the "Interviewing Guide" (page 134).

4. Design a new playground, which implements your solution. The design should include four elements of a new playground (for example, gardens, equipment, play areas, and trash receptacles). Include the design in your presentation. Create your design using digital photography, a model, or a sketch.

5. You will know you are finished with your research when you are able to put the following things into the presentation.

   * Problems with the school playground, including evidence
   * Your solution to the problems
   * A point of view from a teacher at the school
   * Points of view from students at the school
   * A plan to implement the solution
   * The cost for implementing the solution
   * A design of a new playground incorporating your solution to the problems

   Keep record of these questions and prompts throughout the project using the "Task Sheet" (page 135).

6. You can choose what program to use to create your presentation. I would suggest two programs you have practiced with in the library and the computer lab: Animoto (https://animoto.com) and Prezi (https://prezi.com). However, your group can use another electronic format for your multimedia presentation that I (the teacher) approve.

page 1 of 6

7. Once you have completed your presentation, save and email the link to me. I will then embed the videos or presentations in the classroom blog. I will arrange for the principal to come to the classroom so each group can present its project. It is your job to convince the principal that your solution needs to be implemented.

Use this form to investigate the playground for the problems that you observe. Record observations for four different problems of our school playground.

Observation Guide

Problem 1: _____

Describe the problem. List three or more details about the problem.

_____

_____

_____

Problem 2: _____

Describe the problem. List three or more details about the problem.

_____

_____

_____

Problem 3: _____

Describe the problem. List three or more details about the problem.

_____

_____

_____

Problem 4: _____

Describe the problem. List three or more details about the problem.

_____

_____

_____

What are the challenges of these problems?

Real-World Learning Framework for Elementary Schools © 2017 Solution Tree Press • SolutionTree.com
Visit **go.SolutionTree.com/instruction** to download this free reproducible.

Use this form to plan and conduct your interview.

Interviewing Guide

Before the Interview

Person's name: _____

Date: _____

Purpose of interview: _____

_____

_____

Questions I Want to Ask

Question: _____

Answer: _____

_____

_____

Question: _____

Answer: _____

_____

_____

Question: _____

Answer: _____

_____

_____

After the Interview

What did you learn? (Draw conclusions.)

_____

_____

_____

Complete this form with your group throughout the project to help you create a strong solution and presentation.

Task Sheet

The problem with the school playground, including evidence:
Your solution to the problem:
A point of view from a teacher at the school:
Points of view from students at the school:
A plan to implement the solution:
The cost of implementing the solution:
A design of a new playground incorporating your solution to the problem:

Scoring Rubric

Acceptable student performance is level 3 or higher.

Objective 1: Students will design a new playground incorporating reasons that support the proposed solutions.				
	1 **SIGNIFICANT REVISION NEEDED**	**2** **SOME REVISION NEEDED**	**3** **PROFICIENT**	**4** **EXCEEDS EXPECTATIONS**
Evidence	Evidence of the problem is minimal with only one picture. No details are provided with the evidence.	Product contains some evidence of the problem with few details and contains only two pictures.	Product contains evidence and some details of the problem and contains three pictures.	Product contains evidence and details of the problem and contains four or more pictures.
Research and Solution	Product contains little research on a solution to the problem. No teacher or other students' points of view are included. There is no information on how the solution could be implemented.	Product contains some research on a solution to the problem. No teacher or other students' points of view are included. Product contains little information on how the solution could be implemented.	Product contains research on a solution to implement to solve the problem. Teacher and other students' points of view are included. Product contains some information on how the solution could be implemented.	Product contains thorough research on a solution to implement to solve the problem. Points of view from a teacher and other students in the school are included. Product contains information on how the solution could be implemented.
Playground Design	Product does not contain a playground design for the presentation.	Product contains a design with little detail but leaves a solution out of the design.	Product contains a somewhat detailed design of a new playground with a solution included.	Product contains a detailed design of a new playground with a solution included.

Objective 2: Students will create a multimedia project (using Prezi, Animoto, or another tool) to present to their principal showing the problems they found with their school playground and possible solutions.

	1 **SIGNIFICANT REVISION NEEDED**	**2** **SOME REVISION NEEDED**	**3** **PROFICIENT**	**4** **EXCEEDS EXPECTATIONS**
Originality	Presentation is a rehash of other people's ideas or graphics. It shows very little attempt at original thought.	Presentation shows an attempt at originality and inventiveness in one or two areas.	Presentation shows some originality and inventiveness. The content and ideas are presented in an interesting way.	Presentation shows considerable originality and inventiveness. The content and ideas are presented in a unique and interesting way.
Effectiveness	Presentation is lacking several key details and has inaccuracies that make it poor at persuading the audience.	Presentation is missing at least two key details. It is incomplete in persuading the audience.	Presentation includes most material needed to gain a comfortable understanding of the problem and chosen solutions but is lacking one or two key details. It is adequate at persuading the audience.	Presentation includes all material needed to gain a comfortable understanding of the problem and chosen solutions. It is highly effective at persuading the audience.
Presentation	Delivery is not smooth, and the audience's attention is often lost.	Delivery is not smooth but able to maintain the audience's interest most of the time.	Presentation was rehearsed and has a fairly smooth delivery that holds the audience's attention most of the time.	Presentation was well rehearsed and has a smooth delivery that holds the audience's attention.
Technology Use	Product makes use of font, color, graphics, effects, and such, but these distract from the presentation's content. There is no audio use. Transitions are a distraction to the content.	Product makes use of font, color, graphics, effects, and such, but occasionally these distract from the presentation. There is no audio use. Transitions distract from the presentation.	Product makes good use of font, color, graphics, effects, and such to enhance the presentation. There is good use of audio. There is good use of transitions.	Product makes excellent use of font, color, graphics, effects, and such to enhance the presentation. There is excellent use of audio. There is excellent use of transitions.

Sample Student Work

In this sample, a group of students investigated the school playground for a problem to target. Students recorded their observations of the problems in the playground using the "Observation Guide."

Observation Guide

Use this form to investigate the playground for the problems that you observe. Record observations for four different problems of our school playground.

Problem 1: Plants

Describe the problem. List three or more details about the problem.

1. There are large trees in the garden area.

2. The leaves from the trees give students shade when it is really hot outside.

3. The grass stays mowed.

4. There are no colorful flowers around the playground.

5. Weeds and grass are growing in the mulched areas.

Problem 2: Equipment

Describe the problem. List three or more details about the problem.

1. The playground has a lot of equipment for playing.

2. There are three jungle gyms and two swing sets.

3. Students also have a large grass area to play games like kickball and football.

4. The swing set looks old. There is rust on some of the chains.

5. The grassy area for games is one big area, so only one game can be played at a time.

6. People have drawn inside the towers and on the slide.

Problem 3: Play areas

Describe the problem. List three or more details about the problem.

1. There is a lot of room between playground equipment.

2. There is not a lot of grass growing in each play area.

3. The grassy area for games is close to the swing sets.

4. Sometimes students catch balls near where people are swinging.

5. When it rains, the ground under the swings gets really muddy.

Problem 4: Safety

Describe the problem. List three or more details about the problem.

1. There is a sign in the parking lot that says, "Slow, Children at Play."

2. Teachers sit on benches and watch students play.

3. If students fall off the jungle gym or swing, they land on hard ground.

4. Some students run back and forth through the areas where others are playing.

5. Trash flies out of the dumpster close by, which could spread germs and make kids trip.

What are the challenges of these problems?

The challenge with planting flowers in the playground is that they will need to be watered and cared for by someone. Staff or a team of students could help water the new plants and pull unwanted weeds. Replacing the rusty swing set may be challenging because of its cost. It is hard to keep students from drawing inside the slide's towers because you can't see people when they are in there. A challenge for improving the play areas is that they will likely be worn down again because of students playing in them.

Interviewing Guide

Use this form to plan and conduct your interview.

Before the Interview

Person's name: John Maxwell

Date: August 20

Purpose of interview: To get a student's point of view on our problem (playground litter, graffiti, and overall appearance).

Questions I Want to Ask

Question: What do you think is the biggest problem with our school playground?

Answer: Trash on the ground. There are no garbage cans near the playground to throw trash away either.

Question: What area of the playground needs the most improvement?

Answer: The swing set. The spot for your feet is always muddy, and it ruins your shoes.

Question: What would you like to see changed about our school playground?

Answer: There needs to be more places to play games like catch and football.

After the Interview

What did you learn? (Draw conclusions.)

Students want a clean playground and are willing to help keep it looking nice.

Something needs to be done about the areas that sometimes get muddy.

Areas of the playground need be separated better so that other games can be going on.

Task Sheet

Complete this form with your group throughout the project to help you create a strong solution and presentation.

The problem with the school playground, including evidence:

Litter, graffiti, and overall appearance

Your solution to the problem:

Student cleanup crew

Mulch for swings and playground equipment area

Continued →

A point of view from a teacher at the school:

Mulch will prevent injuries if falls occur.

A cleanup crew will give students the opportunity to exhibit school leadership.

Points of view from students at the school:

Picking up trash will make the playground look nicer.

Writing on the equipment makes things look dirty and old.

A clean playground will increase school pride and impress visitors.

A plan to implement the solution:

Students will complete an application for being part of the playground cleanup crew.

The cleanup crew will collect trash twice a week and clean graffiti.

Trash bags and gloves will be provided by the school.

The cleanup crew and volunteers will help the school custodians spread mulch.

The cost of implementing the solution:

64' playground border costs $599

1,000 pounds of redwood playground mulch costs $499

A design of a new playground incorporating your solution to the problem:

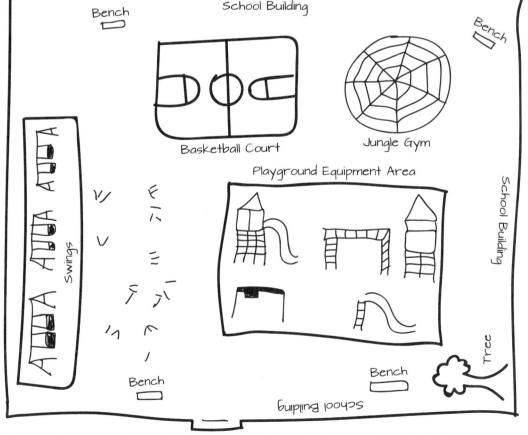

Visit "Playground Safety and Appearance" at https://youtu.be/MzO5T2UcKYQ (Northern, 2016) to access the Animoto video.

Create Excellence Framework Rating

CREATE ANALYSIS		
CREATE COMPONENT	**LEVEL**	**JUSTIFICATION**
Real-World Learning	4: Integrating	Learning emphasizes and impacts the classroom, school, or community. Learning is integrated across subject areas. The design and solutions to the problems the students find could affect their school in a positive way. The groups present to their principal in hopes that a solution could actually be implemented at their school.
Cognitive Complexity	3: Investigating	Students are planning a playground, which is at the Create level of the revised Bloom's taxonomy. The teacher directs the topic of school playground problems, and students create with that topic. Students use their research, observations, and interviews to design a new school playground.
Student Engagement	4: Integrating	Students partner with the teacher to come up with the content of problems with the school playground. Interviews reveal issues students and teachers face with the current playground. Students choose specific problems with the playground and decide what their solutions will be. Students take an inquiry-based approach to finding solutions to the problems. Students collaborate with their peers in a group setting.
Technology Integration	3: Investigating	Students' technology use is creating a multimedia presentation at the end of the project; therefore, it is an add-on. Technology is also an option in the design of a new playground.

BE THE CHANGE YOU WANT TO SEE IN YOUR SCHOOL!

Source: Adapted from Ashley Burnette and Shannon East. Used with permission.

Content: English language arts

Learning Objectives:

1. After researching, students will gather information to create a plan to solve a problem at their school through a shared research project.
2. Students will implement their plan in the school.

Standards:

Common Core English language arts—

- W.2.8 Recall information from experiences or gather information from provided sources to answer a question (NGA & CCSSO, 2010a).
- W.2.7 Participate in shared research and writing projects (e.g., read a number of books on a single topic to produce a report; record science observations; NGA & CCSSO, 2010a).
- W.2.6 With guidance and support from adults, use a variety of digital tools to produce and publish writing, including in collaboration with peers (NGA & CCSSO, 2010a).

Project Options: Students have the freedom to choose any issue for their project as long as it is something that can be improved and be implemented in their school. Students can choose to make a poster on Glogster or Canva or a video on Animoto to showcase the steps for implementing their plan. To extend the bounds for student choice, students could also develop and assign roles as well as a time line for the project tasks as they are designing their improvement plan.

Resources Needed: Computer with Internet access

Teacher Notes: In steps two and three of the project, you will need to help the students brainstorm ideas to get the students started on thinking about their school. Once two to three ideas have been shared, have students brainstorm with their group. (Preplanned groups are suggested.)

Be the Change You Want to See in Your School!

Every day, engineers create new inventions and products that improve our world. Hybrid cars (cars that use a combination of electricity and gas) were just a daydream before engineers Victor Wouk and Charlie Rosen made them a reality.

Imagine you are an engineer who wants to improve our school. What areas of the school need to be improved? Is our school environmentally friendly? Does our classroom need more organization? Does our lunch line flow smoothly? Does our school's landscaping need attention? Think about your daily activities and what changes could improve them.

Project Tasks

1. As a class, we will discuss the following questions.

   - What do engineers do?
   - What is an invention that makes your day flow smoothly?
   - What about it improves your day?

2. Watch the Disney Channel (2014) video "Friends for Change" (www.youtube.com/watch ?v=NyeGqAxEMHE), and answer the following questions with your group.

   - How did the community work with the volunteers to build the new classroom?
   - When planning your project with your group, how can you simulate their teamwork?
   - How important was planning and organization in building the classroom?
   - What are the first steps you and your group should take when planning your project?

3. Walk around your school to identify possible problems.

4. Begin planning using the "Project Planning Sheet."

   - Once you have identified a school problem that you would like to solve, create a plan for how to solve the problem.
   - After the plan has been created, make a list of steps to implement the plan.
   - Once the steps have been listed, create a poster on Glogster (www.glogster.com) or Canva (www.canva.com) or a video on Animoto (https://animoto.com) that showcases the steps of your plan.

5. After the teacher has reviewed all the groups' plans, the plans will be brought to the attention of the principal for implementation. If approved, the posters or videos will be hung around the school for other students to view or broadcasted on the school's closed-circuit TV or digital scrolling screens to play continuously for passersby to view.

Real-World Learning Framework for Elementary Schools © 2017 Solution Tree Press • SolutionTree.com
Visit **go.SolutionTree.com/instruction** to download this free reproducible.

Project Planning Sheet

Name: _____

Imagine you are an engineer who wants to improve your school. What areas need to be improved? Is your school environmentally friendly? Does your classroom need more organization? Does your lunch line flow smoothly? Does your school's landscaping need attention? Think about your daily activities and what changes could improve them. Write down your ideas.

1. _____

2. _____

3. _____

4. _____

Select one idea from the list that you think would make the best project. Circle the number. As a group, record why this idea is the best option for this project.

_____

_____

_____

_____

_____

It's time to put your idea into action! What steps are needed to implement your plan? Your plan needs to have at least four steps.

1. _____

2. _____

3. _____

4. _____

5. _____

6. _____

Now that you and your group have a plan, trade your steps with another group for peer review. Edit each other's plans until you believe that they are ready to be put into action.

You are now ready to put your plan to the test! Design and create a poster using Glogster or Canva, or create a video on Animoto to showcase the steps to implement your plan. Don't forget to add a catchy title and attention-grabbing poster or video by adding pictures and other visual aids. After you have created your poster or video, list the sources that you used to create your plan in a Word document.

After each group has hung up its poster in the classroom or broadcasted its video, walk around and vote for the project that you think is the best. You may not vote for your own project.

Scoring Rubric

Group Cohesiveness (ten points)

☐ Students work together and contribute to the group.

☐ Students discuss their ideas in a polite manner and do not argue.

☐ Students equally carry the project's workload.

☐ Students provide useful feedback for other groups.

Project Details (ten points)

☐ Students include at least four steps for their plan.

☐ The plan is practical and can be implemented in the school.

☐ Steps for the plan are in the correct order.

☐ Steps include enough detail for the reader to understand.

☐ Students provide a Word document with a list of their sources.

Poster (ten points)

☐ The poster includes all the steps needed to implement the group's plan.

☐ The steps displayed on the poster are easy to read.

☐ The poster is attention grabbing and visually pleasing.

Sample Student Work

Project Planning Sheet

Name: _Abby_

Imagine you are an engineer who wants to improve your school. What areas need to be improved? Is your school environmentally friendly? Does your classroom need more organization? Does your lunch line flow smoothly? Does your school's landscaping need attention? Think about your daily activities and what changes could improve them. Write down your ideas.

1. Recycling program for the lunchroom

2. Plant a garden in the front of the school

3. Compost program for the school

4. Establish new naming system for cubby holes

Select one idea from the list that you think would make the best project. Circle the number. As a group, record why this idea is the best option for this project.

This idea is best for this project because it helps the most people. It will also keep working for the longest period of time and will help the school for a long time. The compost will help the landscape and keep landfills from getting too big.

It's time to put your idea into action! What steps are needed to implement your plan? Your plan needs to have at least four steps.

1. Add a trash can for compost to the lunch line.

2. Post signs around the compost bin to tell students what to compost.

3. Have students show each lunch shift how to compost.

4. Add a compost bin outside our school.

5. Use the compost to improve the outside of our school.

6. _____

We used the following sources.

- Morrisey, B. (2016, May 19). A kids' guide to composting. Accessed at www.ecofriendlykids.co.uk/composting.html on June 29, 2016.

- Richter, R. (n.d.). Composting for kids! Accessed at http://aggie-horticulture.tamu .edu/kindergarden/kidscompost/CompostingForKids.pdf on June 29, 2016.

STEPS FOR COMPOSTING

WE CAN HELP!

1. Add a trash can for compost to the lunch line.

2. Post signs around the compost bin to tell students what to compost.

3. Have students show each lunch shift how to compost.

4. Add a compost bin outside our school.

5. Use the compost to improve the outside of our school.

Create Excellence Framework Rating

CREATE ANALYSIS		
CREATE COMPONENT	**LEVEL**	**JUSTIFICATION**
Real-World Learning	3: Investigating	The project impacts the classroom and school environment through having the students create an improvement plan and implement it within the school. Students have the freedom to incorporate any subject area into their improvement plan.
Cognitive Complexity	4: Integrating	The assignment includes student-generated projects that impact their school environment. As part of the project process, students are editing and evaluating their peers' work.
Student Engagement	3: Investigating	The students are engaged in a teacher-directed task. There are multiple solutions for the task since students are allowed to create an improvement plan for an area of their choice.
Technology Integration	3: Investigating	Student use of technology is embedded within the project and is essential to project completion. The project promotes collaboration among students and partnership with the teacher, and the students are working to solve authentic problems that exist in their school environment.

ART GALLERY

Source: Adapted from Randa Gary and Rhea Isenberg. Used with permission.

Content: English language arts

Learning Objectives:

1. Students will create artwork using three or more colors to distinguish different colors.
2. Students will answer questions from a peer to explain their painting.

Standards:

Common Core English language arts—

-   SL.K.2 Confirm understanding of a text read aloud or information presented orally or through other media by asking and answering questions about key details and requesting clarification if something is not understood (NGA & CCSSO, 2010a).

National Core Arts—

-   MA:Cr1.1.1.K Discover and share ideas for media artworks using play and experimentation (National Coalition for Core Arts Standards [NCCAS], n.d.).

Project Options: This lesson can be easily adapted to other grade levels. At intermediate grades, students can learn to complete their Aurasma project independently. At primary grades, teacher assistance is needed throughout the lesson.

Resources Needed: The book *Mix It Up!* by Hervé Tullet; donated paint samples or cards from a paint store; famous paintings online; paint, brushes, and paper; an iPad or Android video camera; the Aurasma app; materials to display artwork; gallery invitations; hors d'oeuvres (optional)

Art Gallery

Teacher Directions

1. Read aloud the book *Mix It Up!* by Hervé Tullet. (This book presents an invitation to mix up colors in an interactive and hands-on experience. Follow the artist's simple instructions, and suddenly colors appear, mix, splatter, and vanish as the reader interacts with the text.)

2. Display paintings about "play" from the Internet on the interactive whiteboard. Discuss with students how the paintings remind them of play, and have the students look for colors, such as red, blue, green, orange, and so on. Discuss with the class what type of questions you might like to ask the artist. Emphasize that students should ask questions that require an explanation, instead of simple yes or no answers. Questions help us learn more about something. Note: Remind students that questions help us learn more about something.

3. Students choose three or more colors for their painting. Students create a painting about "play" using their selected colors. Be sure each student puts his or her name at the bottom of the painting.

4. Students look at each other's paintings and select a peer's painting. Each student should choose a different painting so that all paintings will be reviewed. All students will write at least two questions to ask their peer artist about his or her painting.

5. The teacher and students use the iPad or other device's video camera and the Aurasma app from an iPad or other device to record the interview between the student and peer artist.

6. The teacher and students use the Aurasma app to attach the video interview to the student's image of his or her painting.

7. Students set up an art show in their classroom, the hallway, the library, or the school lobby. They present their paintings at the art gallery for other students, their parents, and community members. Parents and community members use the Aurasma app to scan the paintings, enabling them to see and hear the interview attached to each painting.

Aurasma App Directions

Aurasma is an augmented-reality application that provides digitally enhanced views of objects. It collects video, graphics, animation, audio, and 3-D content with the scanned object. You use it much like a QR code; you aim the iPad or device at a student's painting, and it automatically displays the video attached to the image of the painting.

Visit Aurasma (www.aurasma.com) to learn how to set up an Aurasma account and use the app.

The following section is for the K–1 student. The teacher may need to read or explain the scenario and directions to the students.

Project Tasks

Do you want to be a *real* artist and have people come to see your great work? I believe that you can do it! Let's have an art gallery show for other classes, parents, and the community. What ideas do you have for the art gallery show?

1. Paint your own piece of art using three or more colors. You are painting about what comes to your mind when you talk about play. When you are finished, be sure to either paint or write your name with a pencil at the bottom.

2. Set up your painting to dry around the room.

3. Walk around and look at all the paintings.

4. Pick one other student's painting and think about it. What is it? What was he or she thinking when painting it? Why did the artist use those colors? You can ask the artist any questions about it, but at least one should be about the colors he or she chose.

5. Now you are going to interview the student artist of the painting you selected with your written questions.

6. Use the iPad or other device to record the interview with your artist about his or her painting.

7. With your teacher's help, place the art and interview into the Aurasma app.

8. You and your teacher will plan the big art gallery for teachers, students in other classes, parents, and community members. When will you have the art show? Where? Will you have refreshments? Will visitors be able to view your Aurasma events? Will each student artist stand beside his or her painting to help visitors, or will you all roam the room to help? Can you explain how you made your aura and how to use the app? Can you explain your use of color and how the colors contributed to your painting?

9. Hold your big art gallery show. Afterward, answer the following questions as a class.

   * How did the event go?
   * How many people came? Did they enjoy it?
   * What did you learn from this experience?

Scoring Rubric

	1 SIGNIFICANT REVISION NEEDED	2 SOME REVISION NEEDED	3 PROFICIENT	4 EXCEEDS EXPECTATIONS
Objective 1: Students will create artwork using three or more colors to distinguish different colors.	Painting has fewer than three colors.	Painting has fewer than three colors.	Painting has three colors.	Painting has more than three colors.
Objective 2: Students will answer questions from a peer to explain their painting.	Student does not plan logical questions for a peer. Student does the interview but is difficult to understand, or it was not logical.	Student plans only one question for a peer. Student does the interview but is difficult to understand.	Student plans two questions for a peer. Student speaks mostly clearly and answers questions in order to have good interviews.	Student plans two or more thoughtful questions to ask the artist. Student speaks clearly and answers questions confidently in order to have good interviews.

Sample Student Work

Sample Student Paintings for the Art Gallery.

Alex's Painting

Alex's aura: https://youtu.be/ERON _2dcpUQ (Maxwell, 2016a)

Sofia's Painting

Sofia's aura: https://youtu.be /8incmYBBo9E (Maxwell, 2016b)

An example of an art gallery

Parents and students using Aurasma

Create Excellence Framework Rating

CREATE ANALYSIS		
CREATE COMPONENT	LEVEL	JUSTIFICATION
Real-World Learning	3: Investigating	With teacher direction, students are creating and asking the interview questions. Students are participating in a real art gallery show for the school, parents, and the community.
Cognitive Complexity	3: Investigating	Students design their own art piece for the art gallery. Students are posing interpretive questions about a peer's painting and doing the interview with teacher direction.
Student Engagement	3: Investigating	Students can choose the colors they use, and they choose what their painting looks like. The students pose questions to their peers about their artwork with teacher assistance.
Technology Integration	3: Investigating	Students collaborate with the teacher to use the iPad and Aurasma app. The app is a major part of the art gallery experience.

BECOME AN INTERNATIONAL AMBASSADOR

Source: Adapted from Ameliah Leonhardt. Used with permission.

Content: English language arts

Learning Objectives:

1. Students will persuade other students about the positive aspects of a country.
2. Students will propose an effective solution to a social issue of the chosen country and present their findings.

Standards:

Common Core English language arts—

- W.4.7 Conduct short research projects that use several sources to build knowledge through investigation of different aspects of a topic (NGA & CCSSO, 2010a).
- SL.4.4 Report on a topic or text or present an opinion, sequencing ideas logically and using appropriate facts and relevant, descriptive details to support main ideas or themes; speak clearly at an understandable pace (NGA & CCSSO, 2010a).
- SL.4.5 Add audio recordings and visual displays to presentations when appropriate to enhance the development of main ideas or themes (NGA & CCSSO, 2010a).

Project Options: Students will work with each other in groups for the preliminary research of the project. Then, they may choose to work individually or in groups on the single country they research further. Students may use teacher-suggested technology (for example, PhotoPeach or Animoto), or they may suggest another teacher-approved technology to use for their presentation.

Resources Needed: Students need computers with Internet access in order to research their countries and to access websites that will be used as the medium for their presentations (such as Animoto or PhotoPeach). For the international festival, students need access to several computers (for example, in a lab or library) to present their countries simultaneously.

Become an International Ambassador

The world is getting smaller every day! Because there are so many opportunities for international jobs and travel, we should know many things about the world we live in. For this project, you will choose another country you are very interested in; you will become an ambassador to represent that country. Then, you will research your country and create a persuasive presentation highlighting the country's amazing qualities.

Project Tasks

1. In groups of three to four students, determine what important things you should consider about other countries, such as the culture that makes each country unique and ways to promote tourism in that country. Complete step one on the "Student Task Sheet" for this project.

2. Decide which country you would like to choose for this project, and complete step two on the "Student Task Sheet." Begin your research on your country by completing step three on the task sheet.

3. You will be an ambassador for this country at our festival, and you will give a presentation. The goal is to convince your peers to visit that country. Complete step four on the "Student Task Sheet."

4. All countries have problems that keep people from wanting to visit or move there. If your peers don't want to go to your country because of those problems, you've got to be prepared with ideas to address the problems so they will still be interested in your country. Identify a problem with the country. Offer a solution to the problem you have chosen. Complete step five on the "Student Task Sheet."

5. Use presentation technologies such as Animoto (https://animoto.com) or PhotoPeach (http://photopeach.com) to showcase your research, problem, and solution. Be sure to include other interesting things about your country that will convince your peers to go. Complete step six on the "Student Task Sheet."

6. Present your information to your peers and parents at the international festival the class will host at your school. Your group will need to effectively represent your country as ambassadors, using your best speaking skills and relevant research to convince your peers to visit!

Real-World Learning Framework for Elementary Schools © 2017 Solution Tree Press • SolutionTree.com
Visit **go.SolutionTree.com/instruction** to download this free reproducible.

Student Task Sheet

1. With your group, brainstorm five aspects that would be important to you that must be represented in the country you choose (for example, the weather, type of government, or economy). Describe why each is important to you.

IMPORTANT ASPECT	WHY IS IT IMPORTANT TO YOU?

2. Using your list as things to consider, choose a country that you would be interested in representing as an ambassador with an explanation of why that country might include the aspects that are important to you.

Country:	Why does this country seem like a good place to represent?

3. As a group, choose and then research four aspects of your country. Review step one, where you brainstormed aspects that are important.

ASPECT	RESEARCH ON ASPECT
1.	 Source:
2.	 Source:
3.	 Source:
4.	 Source:

4. Brainstorm some ways that you could persuade your peers to visit.

Write down your brainstormed ideas here.

5. All countries have problems that keep them from being the perfect place to live. Some of your peers will probably not want to visit the country you are presenting because of that country's problems. Now that you know quite a bit about your country, you will research barriers that discourage visitors from coming.

BARRIER	SOURCE	NOTES
1.		
2.		

6. Now, you will need to find some solutions. Select one issue, and brainstorm at least one solution that uses at least five realistic steps to resolve it.

Barriers:	
Brainstorm ways to solve the barriers.	
List your steps of your solution. 1. 2. 3. 4. 5.	Explain why the steps would solve the problems.

7. Now that you have become an expert on your country, you will create a persuasive presentation to convince your peers to visit your country. You may use Prezi (https://prezi .com), PhotoPeach (http://photopeach.com), Animoto (https://animoto.com), or another presentation technology. Use the following checklist to make sure you include everything you need, but feel free to add extra information to your presentation.

8. Use the presentation checklist to assess your work.

☐ Technology is used to present information (Prezi, Animoto, PhotoPeach, or another presentation technology).

☐ Presentation includes relevant details about the country.

☐ Presentation includes country's social problem.

☐ Presentation includes a solution to the country's social problem.

☐ Presentation lasts at least three minutes.

☐ Student demonstrates presentation skills to effectively discuss the country.

☐ Student speaks at an appropriate volume and pace (not too fast or slow).

☐ Student speaks clearly; it is easy to hear the presentation.

☐ Student maintains eye contact with the audience for the majority of the presentation.

Scoring Rubric

	1 SIGNIFICANT REVISION NEEDED	2 SOME REVISION NEEDED	3 PROFICIENT	4 EXCEEDS EXPECTATIONS
Objective 1: Students will persuade other students about the positive aspects of a country.	Student does not complete the research covering student-generated questions; there are several incomplete areas. Technology presentation is incomplete.	Student uses at least one credible source to complete the research covering student-generated questions; some information is incomplete. Technology somewhat supports the presentation.	Student uses at least one credible source to complete the research covering student-generated questions; all aspects have been researched for the country. Technology is used to present information.	Student uses multiple credible sources to complete the research covering student-generated questions; all aspects have been researched for the country. Technology is effectively used to present information.
Objective 2: Students will propose an effective solution to a social issue of the chosen country and present their findings.	Student does not utilize research to find a solution; or the student-generated solution is highly unrealistic or ineffective.	Student utilizes questionable sources to find a solution, or the solution is not realistic; or the student-generated solution's relevancy or effectiveness is questionable.	Student demonstrates effective skills using at least one credible source to find a solution; or the student-generated solution is relevant and effective.	Student demonstrates highly effective research skills using credible sources to find a solution; or the student-generated solution is highly relevant and effective.

Sample Student Work

Visit https://prezi.com/_xe0bfjvdbgu/south-korea (Flores, 2016) for an example.

Create Excellence Framework Rating

CREATE ANALYSIS		
CREATE COMPONENT	**LEVEL**	**JUSTIFICATION**
Real-World Learning	4: Integrating	This project not only allows students to critically evaluate the world, but it also allows the students to share their findings with the school. Thus, students will be leading their nonclassmate peers into more understanding and knowledge about other cultures and countries. Students act as ambassadors.
Cognitive Complexity	3: Investigating	Students gather relevant research materials. In addition, students have to identify the problem a country faces and suggest ways to address the problem. Students develop a persuasive presentation to convince their peers that their selected country is an amazing nation.
Student Engagement	4: Integrating	This is inquiry based because the students have to seek out an issue and then a solution to the issue. Furthermore, students are able to complete work with peers or work on their own after looking at all the options.
Technology Integration	4: Integrating	Students must use effective research through the use of technology in order to determine various aspects of their country. Furthermore, students use technology to present their countries in a way that is persuasively appealing.

COMFORT BOOKS: SMILING KIDS

Source: Adapted from Morgan Tierney and Kelli Ralston. Used with permission.

Content: English language arts

Learning Objectives:

1. After visiting critically ill children, intermediate students will create a narrative using their narrative writing skills by scoring proficient or higher on the narrative writing rubric.

2. Using their written narratives, intermediate students will create a comfort book using StoryJumper by scoring a three or higher on the rubric.

Standards:

Common Core English language arts—

- W.4.3 Write narratives to develop real or imagined experiences or events using effective technique, descriptive details, and clear event sequences (NGA & CCSSO, 2010a).

- W.4.4 Produce clear and coherent writing in which the development and organization are appropriate to task, purpose, and audience (NGA & CCSSO, 2010a).

- W.4.5 With guidance and support from peers and adults, develop and strengthen writing as needed by planning, revising, and editing (NGA & CCSSO, 2010a).

- W.4.6 With some guidance and support from adults, use technology, including the Internet, to produce or publish writing as well as to interact and collaborate with others; demonstrate sufficient command of keyboarding skills to type a minimum of one page in a single setting (NGA & CCSSO, 2010a).

- RI.4.1 Refer to details and examples in a text when explaining what the text says explicitly and when drawing inferences from the text (NGA & CCSSO, 2010a).

- RI.4.2 Determine the main idea of a text and explain how it is supported by key details; summarize the text (NGA & CCSSO, 2010a).

- RI.4.5 Describe the overall structure (e.g., chronology, comparison, cause/effect, problem/solution) of events, ideas, concepts, or information in a text or part of a text (NGA & CCSSO, 2010a).

Project Options:

- Students may complete the project individually, in pairs, or in groups.

- Note that this project takes the course of a few weeks to be completed. This is a flexible project that can be shaped to fit your students' and school's needs. As a project option, after both visits to the hospital have been completed, students can create and present a final presentation on their own experiences and what they learned. Students can complete this project using PhotoPeach (http://photopeach.com), Prezi (https://prezi.com), Slideroll (www.slideroll.com), or Glogster (www.glogster.com). See the technology presentation rubric included in this project. Visit http://create-excellence.com/resources for even more presentation technology resources.

Resources Needed: Computer with Internet access and web tools: Google Forms, StoryJumper, Tween Tribune, and Padlet. You'll also need the StoryJumper tutorial (www.youtube.com/watch?v=1kWazFUFgP4).

Teacher Notes: Do the following while planning the activity.

- Communicate with a local hospital, and tell the staff about the service-learning project. Make sure to acquire all school and hospital approval before starting the project with students. You must also acquire parent and guardian permission from both the elementary school students and the patients.

If a student's parent or guardian does not approve participation in the hospital visit, make sure to have an alternative option available. One option could be for that student to write interview questions and send them with a fellow classmate. That student could also spend time researching online information related to writing children's comfort stories in lieu of visiting the hospital.

- Set up two dates and times for your students to visit children who are in the hospital. First, students will interact with critically ill children and discover their interests. Your students will write a storybook just for them. Second, students will return to read their storybook to the children they met before.

- Research and plan fundraising and financial options for the project. It may be more financially feasible for students to complete the projects in groups. Use StoryJumper (www.storyjumper.com) for publishing the storybooks. Hardcover books for up to twenty pages are $24.95 each. Paperback books for up to sixteen pages are $12.95 each. Delivery times are two weeks for the United States; three weeks for Canada, Australia, New Zealand, and Europe; and four weeks for Asia.

Project Hook Ideas:

- Have students read the following grade-level news articles in cooperative-learning groups. Both articles deal with the subject of students giving or doing something for other people.
  - "Students Gather Blankets for Syrians" (Associated Press, 2016; http://goo.gl/LBkMVi)
  - "Teen Honored by CNN for Launching Literacy Program" (Associated Press, 2015; http://goo.gl/BLi6Tb)

- While reading, have students generate questions within their groups on what they are reading. It may be best to give them question stems to help them formulate their questions.

- On a classroom Padlet wall, have students post their thoughts on the article, giving them the following guiding questions.
  - What is the main idea in the two articles? Give examples from the text using exact words and phrases to support your answer. (RI.4.1; RI.4.2)
  - Describe what problem the students saw and what solution they came up with in the article. (RI.4.5)
  - How can we do something similar for critically ill children in the local hospital? (RI.4.5)

Comfort Books: Smiling Kids

Have you ever been able to put a smile on someone's face? Do you remember how great it made you feel? In this project, you will be doing that exact thing! There are many kids in our community who need someone to comfort them and make them feel like someone truly cares for their well-being. You will be playing a large role in doing that!

Project Tasks

1. To prepare for our visit to a local hospital, your group of three to five students will create an interest survey using Google Forms (www.google.com/forms) to learn about the interests of the child you meet at the hospital. This is to help you write a book for that child. Please see the "Google Forms Survey Task Sheet" (page 165).

2. In class, we will work together to come up with a list of local organizations and businesses that we can ask to help support us with donations.

   - Do an online search for one of the businesses or organizations online. Find an email address for that business or organization, and write it down. Check with the teacher to make sure you have the correct contact information.
   - Write a rough draft on paper of an email to that business or organization asking it for support for our project. Please see the "Email Format Sheet" (page 167) for how to write your email.
   - Turn in your rough draft to the teacher to check it. Be sure to make any changes the teacher asks you to make.
   - Log on to your student email, and type out your message. Raise your hand before you are ready to send it to have the teacher read over your email one last time before clicking Send.

3. As a class, we will take our first visit to the hospital. You must be prepared to take your survey on an iPad. We will discuss proper manners and behavior before leaving, as well as some talking points to discuss with the patient you meet in the hospital.

4. Throughout this whole project, you will be keeping a journal to reflect on your experience. Please see the "Journal Reflection Task Sheet" (page 168) for directions on your journal entries. You will write a journal entry after our first hospital visit.

5. When we return from our first visit to the hospital, we will discuss in class some of the common interests of the patients we met. We will share our ideas for possible narratives. When your group has an idea ready to go, share it with the teacher before you begin writing your narrative.

6. As a class, we will discuss narrative writing and the narrative writing rubric to make sure you know what a strong narrative looks like. (See page 169 for the rubric.)

Real-World Learning Framework for Elementary Schools © 2017 Solution Tree Press • SolutionTree.com
Visit **go.SolutionTree.com/instruction** to download this free reproducible.

- With your group, begin writing your narrative on paper. Keep referring to the narrative writing rubric. The teacher will continue to check on your group to make sure you are on the right track with your story. Make sure you keep your story related to your focus student's interests.
- When all groups have a rough draft of their narratives, we will continue to use peer revision to strengthen the stories.
- Hang up your group's rough draft somewhere on the classroom wall.
- Go find another group's narrative to read and revise. The teacher will give you a copy of the rubric and a few sticky notes.
- Read through the narrative at least three times. Look at the narrative writing rubric while reading through the narrative, and check off parts of the rubric that the narrative includes. On a sticky note, write some ideas or suggestions for improvement, and place it on the narrative so the writer can see the feedback.
- Write at least three suggestions for improvement on the sticky note, based on the rubric.
- Mention at least two sections of the narrative that you enjoyed reading on the sticky note.
- We will continue through this process to strengthen our narratives.
- Turn in your group's narrative to the teacher. When the teacher returns your narrative with feedback for improvement, change any parts needed in order to make it a stronger story. Check your rubric and that your narrative matches at least the Proficient column.

7. In class, we will discuss how to log in to and use StoryJumper (www.storyjumper.com). You will also watch a how-to video at www.youtube.com/watch?v=1kWazFUFgP4. Refer back to the video if you need to throughout the project.

   - We will discuss the StoryJumper rubric in class. Keep checking this rubric to make sure your storybook matches at least the Proficient column.
   - Begin representing your narrative on StoryJumper. Make sure you save your work every time you exit the website.

8. When you are done representing your narrative on StoryJumper, raise your hand, and have the teacher read your story. Change any parts of your story that the teacher recommends you improve.

   - When all groups in class are finished with their story, your group will go sit at a different computer to read and suggest improvements for another group's story. The teacher will give you a copy of the StoryJumper rubric to evaluate that story.
   - Read through the story at least three times. Look at the StoryJumper rubric while reading through the story, and check off parts of the rubric that the narrative includes. On a sticky note, write some ideas or suggestions for improvement.
   - Write at least three suggestions for improvement on the sticky note, based on the rubric.
   - Mention at least two sections of the narrative that you enjoyed reading on the sticky note.
   - We will continue this process until our stories are ready to be ordered, published, and returned to us as actual books!

9. When we receive our books back from StoryJumper, we will be ready for our second trip to the hospital. Again, as a class, we will discuss proper manners and behavior, as well as some talking points to bring up during the visit with your focus child.

   - At the hospital, you will talk with a patient. You will also show him or her the book and read it to him or her. You will be giving your book to that child to keep. Lastly, thank the child for allowing you to be there, and tell him or her how you hope this experience has cheered him or her up.
   - When we return from the hospital, we will discuss our experiences as a class. Make sure to write a final journal entry that sums up your entire journey through this project and what you are taking away from the full experience.

Google Forms Survey Task Sheet

1. Think of some ideas on what you might need to know about the child you will meet in the hospital. You will write your book based on what that child's interests are.

   ▴ Favorite sports:

   ▴ Favorite hobbies:

   ▴ Favorite toys:

   ▴ Favorite colors:

   ▴ Favorite interests:

   ▴ Favorite animals:

   ▴ Favorite books:

2. Create at least six questions to ask the child you meet.
3. Go to Google Forms (www.google.com/forms), and click on the plus (+) button to create a new survey.
4. Give your survey a name, such as *interest survey*, and type it in the Title box.
5. In the Question Title box, type your question that you want to ask.
6. Click the drop-down box next to Question Title, and click Short Answer. This way, the patient can type in his or her answer to the question.

7. Click the plus (+) button to the right of the question to add the question.

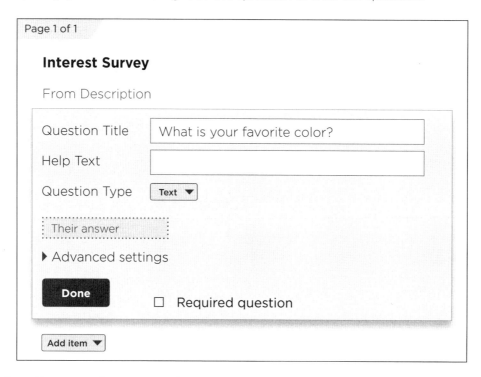

8. To add another question, repeat the same process.

9. When you're finished entering questions, click Send Form.

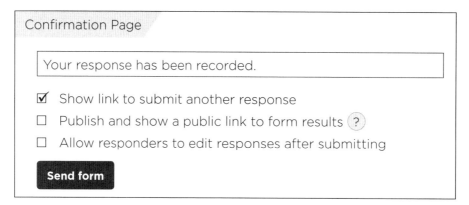

10. Click Send Via Link, and click Short URL. Copy the link on a piece of paper. You will type in this link on your iPad at the hospital to give the survey to the patient.

Send form

Link to share

| https://docs.google.com/forms/d/1l-6TsEB3J0ww | | Embed |

☐ Short Url

☒ Send form via email:

+ Enter names, email addresses, or groups...

Looking to invite other editors to this form? Add collaborators.

Done

Email Format Sheet

Directions: You are writing an email to a local business or organization asking it for support for our project. Please follow the following format when writing your email, and fill in the rest of the missing parts.

Dear _____ (Name of organization or business)

My name is _____, and I am a fourth grader at _____.

I'm writing to you to ask for help in a service project that we are doing at school . . . (explain what our class is doing in this service project, and tell the business how this will help other people).

We are looking for ways to raise money to publish our books for the children we meet in the hospital. We were hoping that you could support our classroom in this project . . . (explain how much you would appreciate any support the business could give us).

Thank you for taking the time to read this email. I hope that you will support our project in any way you can. Please contact the school at _____ (School's email address or phone number) to learn how you can give to this project.

Thank you,

_____ (Your full name)

Journal Reflection Task Sheet

You will be keeping a journal of your experience throughout this entire project. This is to help you reflect on your thoughts and feelings and what you are learning. Review the following reflection questions to help you write your journal entries and the checklist to make sure you have everything you need in your journal.

- What was it like to meet a critically ill child in the hospital?
- What did you learn about the child you are writing a book for?
- What kind of reaction did the child have when you told him or her what you were doing?
- How did it make you feel to be visiting this child in the hospital and getting to know him or her?
- What kind of impact do you think your storybook will have on this child?
- What has been your favorite part of this project so far? Why?
- What kind of story did you write about, and how did that story connect to the interests of your focus child?
- How did it make you feel to read your story to the child in the hospital?
- What has been the most challenging part of this project?
- What other projects could you do outside of class that have a similar purpose to this project's purpose?
- How has this experience changed you?
- What have you learned from this project?
- How could we expand this project to make it have a bigger impact?

Make sure that each journal entry includes the following information.

- ☐ Date of entry
- ☐ Creative title
- ☐ Update on what you have done recently in the project
- ☐ Reflection entry that shows that you have thought about your experience (see reflection questions to help you with this)
- ☐ At least three paragraphs
- ☐ Proper grammar and spelling
- ☐ At least five journal entries
    1. One before the project
    2. One after the first visit to the hospital
    3. One during the process of writing your narrative
    4. One after the second visit to the hospital
    5. One concluding entry summing up your entire experience

Narrative Writing Rubric

Objective 1: After visiting critically ill children, intermediate students will create a narrative using their narrative writing skills by scoring proficient or higher on the narrative writing rubric.				
	1 SIGNIFICANT REVISION NEEDED	**2 SOME REVISION NEEDED**	**3 PROFICIENT**	**4 EXCEEDS EXPECTATIONS**
Content	Topic is unfocused. Details do not develop setting, characters, or plot. Ideas do not meet the needs of the reader.	Topic is somewhat focused. Details somewhat develop setting, characters, and plot. Ideas sometimes meet the reader's needs.	Topic is mostly focused. Details develop setting, characters, and plot. Ideas frequently meet the reader's needs.	Topic is focused. Descriptive details develop setting, characters, and plot. Carefully selected ideas completely satisfy the reader's needs.
Organization	The writing is disorganized and hard to follow. Transition words and phrases are not used. There is no beginning or conclusion.	Events are out of order. Transition words are confusing or missing. The beginning or the conclusion is weak.	Some parts seem misplaced. Transition words and phrases somewhat help the organization. The beginning and conclusion work but may not be strong.	There is a logical order. Transition words and phrases help the organization. A strong beginning leads to a satisfying conclusion.
Voice	There is no voice. Mood and tone are absent. Dialogue, if used, does not sound right for some reason.	The voice sounds flat. Mood and tone are weak. Dialogue, if used, does not uniquely distinguish each character's voice clearly.	The voice, mood, and tone are right in places but inconsistent. Dialogue, if used, somewhat reveals each character's voice.	The voice, mood, and tone are just right for the purpose. Dialogue, if used, reveals each character's voice clearly.
Word Choice	Many words are used incorrectly, and readers cannot visualize characters and events. Word choice is distracting to readers.	Word choice is weak, which keeps readers from visualizing characters and events. Nouns and verbs are weak, and descriptive words are used too much or too little.	Most word choice helps readers visualize characters and events. Most nouns and verbs are used correctly and are supported by descriptive words.	Word choice helps readers visualize characters and events. Nouns and verbs are used correctly and are supported by descriptive words.
Fluency	Sentences lack structure and appear incomplete or rambling.	Most sentences are well constructed but have similar lengths and structures.	Most sentences are well constructed with different lengths and structures.	All sentences are well constructed with different lengths and structures.
Conventions	Writer makes more than four errors in grammar or spelling that distract the reader from the content.	Writer makes three or four errors in grammar or spelling that distract the reader from the content.	Writer makes one or two errors in grammar or spelling that distract the reader from the content.	Writer makes no errors in grammar or spelling that distract the reader from the content.

page 7 of 9

StoryJumper Rubric

Objective 2: Using their written narratives, intermediate students will create a comfort book using StoryJumper by scoring a three or higher on the rubric.

	1 SIGNIFICANT REVISION NEEDED	2 SOME REVISION NEEDED	3 PROFICIENT	4 EXCEEDS EXPECTATIONS
Creativity and Design	• Not an original or creative product • Lacks use of color and space • Theme is inconsistent • Not neat and unprofessional looking • No visual appeal to the audience • Information or content being presented does not support research or pictures	• Somewhat original and creative product • Lacks use of color and space • Theme is inconsistent • Somewhat neat and professional looking • Lacks visual appeal to the audience • Information or content being presented somewhat supports research and pictures	• Original and creative product • Good use of color and space • Same theme carried throughout product • Neat and professional looking • Mostly visually appealing to the audience • Information or content being presented mostly supports research and pictures	• Original and creative product • Excellent use of color and space • Same theme carried throughout product • Neat and professional looking • Visually appealing to the audience • Information or content being presented supports research and pictures
Organization and Grammar	• Not accurate • Missing parts, not neat, or unorganized • Six-plus grammatical errors	• Not accurate • Detailed, neat, or organized • Three to five grammatical errors	• Has accurate information • Detailed, neat, and organized • One or two grammatical errors	• Has accurate information • Detailed, neat, and organized • No grammatical errors
Use of Technology Features	• Many technical problems • Very inconsistent navigation • Two or fewer graphics and pictures	• Some technical problems • Inconsistent navigation • Three or four graphics and pictures	• Few technical problems • Consistent navigation • Five to six graphics and pictures	• No technical problems • Easily navigated • Seven or more graphics and pictures
Content	• Includes little valuable information and only one or two facts	• Includes some important information with three to five facts	• Includes important information that is mostly clear, correct, and relevant to the audience • Grabs the audience's attention	• Covers content in great detail, leaving out no important information • Has information that is clear, correct, and relevant to the purpose and audience; grabs the audience's attention

Technology Presentation Rubric (for Project Extension)

	1 SIGNIFICANT REVISION NEEDED	2 SOME REVISION NEEDED	3 PROFICIENT	4 EXCEEDS EXPECTATIONS
Creativity and Design	• Not an original or creative product • Lacks use of color and space • Theme is inconsistent • Not neat and unprofessional looking • No visual appeal to the audience • Information or content being presented does not support research or pictures	• Somewhat original and creative product • Lacks use of color and space • Theme is inconsistent • Somewhat neat and professional looking • Lacks visual appeal to the audience • Information or content being presented somewhat supports research and pictures	• Original and creative product • Good use of color and space • Same theme carried throughout product • Neat and professional looking • Mostly visually appealing to the audience • Information or content being presented mostly supports research and pictures	• Original and creative product • Excellent use of color and space • Same theme carried throughout product • Neat and professional looking • Visually appealing to the audience • Information or content being presented supports research and pictures
Organization and Grammar	• Not accurate • Missing parts and not neat or unorganized • Six-plus grammatical errors	• Not accurate • Detailed, neat, or organized • Three to five grammatical errors	• Has accurate information • Detailed, neat, and organized • One or two grammatical errors	• Has accurate information • Detailed, neat, and organized • No grammatical errors
Use of Technology Features	• Many technical problems • Very inconsistent navigation • Two or fewer graphics and pictures • No use of advanced features such as video, transitions, sounds, or animations	• Some technical problems • Inconsistent navigation • Three or four graphics and pictures • Use of only one advanced feature such as video, transitions, sounds, or animations	• Few technical problems • Consistent navigation • Five to six graphics and pictures • Use of two to three advanced features such as video, transitions, sounds, or animations	• No technical problems • Easily navigated • Seven or more graphics and pictures • Use of four advanced features such as video, transitions, sounds, or animations
Content	• Includes little valuable information and only one or two facts	• Includes some important information with three to five facts	• Includes important information that is mostly clear, correct, and relevant to the audience • Grabs the audience's attention	• Covers content in great detail, leaving out no important information • Has information that is clear, correct, and relevant to the purpose and audience; grabs the audience's attention

page 9 of 9

Sample Student Work

Following are samples of completed student work done throughout this project. These are models of what student work should look like across various steps. A student-created survey is included, which was made by using Google Forms. There is a narrative writing example based on a completed student survey. Also included is a link to a completed StoryJumper product based on the narrative.

Student-Created Survey

Visit http://goo.gl/forms/RjcQ9tVtRs for a sample student-created survey.

Interest Survey

What is your favorite color?

What type of animals do you like?

What kind of books do you like to read?

What is your favorite thing to do?

What is your favorite food to eat?

Do you have any hobbies?

Submit

Narrative Writing Example

The following is an example of a narrative based on the interest survey. Because the patient mentioned traveling, this student wrote a narrative about one of her vacations. The student also incorporated elements of the patient's interests into the narrative.

There I was, saying good-bye to all my friends as I left to get on the plane. I was very excited but also a little scared because I didn't know what to expect. This would be my first time going out of the country and my first time going on a cruise. I was so ready to explore a new place!

When we got to Miami, Florida, I remember it being so hot and humid. After the boat left the dock and we started heading seaward, I was starting to take everything in. The boat was awesome. It had twelve floors and included an arcade, a candy shop, a huge pool, and a bunch of waterslides. I was thinking in my head, "I never want to leave!"

The first night was movie night on the lido deck. Before the movie started, we went to go get food from the buffet, and at that time, my obsession was white rice and hot chocolate. I know it's a weird combination. As we were walking back to where the movie was being played, my sister was walking a little too fast, so I tried to catch up. While doing so, I managed to slip and fall and spill rice and hot chocolate all over me! It was the most embarrassing thing ever! My sister had a mad expression on her face as she was helping me up. I asked her, "Why are you so mad? You're not the one who fell in front of everybody." And she replied, "I know, but I really wanted to watch this movie, and now you've just ruined my chance to see it!"

The next day, my sister and I were walking around the ship to find something to do. After we did a little shopping in the candy shop, we were headed to the arcade. Instead of taking the elevator, we used the stairs, and it was about three flights until we got to the arcade. At the time my sister and I were very excited to play, so we were running. My shoe was untied, and I tripped over my laces so I stopped to tie it. The next thing I knew, my sister was gone. I started to freak out because I didn't know where the arcade was! That's when panic mode kicked in. I searched everywhere, the candy shop, the main deck, and even those rooms with big noisy machines that money came out of. After almost an hour of roaming around, trying to find someone I knew, my aunt saw me. I never felt more relieved in my entire life.

The rest of the cruise was smooth sailing! We went to Jamaica, and I bought lots of souvenirs. There was a stop at the Cayman Islands that was a very relaxing and pretty beach. Luckily for the rest of the trip, there were no more silly accidents. My first cruise was a great experience, and I loved every second of it. This cruise will always be one of my favorite memories.

StoryJumper Example

The following is a sample page.

Visit http://bit.ly/1R33uf1 for a full example.

Create Excellence Framework Rating

CREATE ANALYSIS		
CREATE COMPONENT	**LEVEL**	**JUSTIFICATION**
Real-World Learning	4: Integrating	Students' learning in this project is focused on and impacts critically ill children in the community at a local hospital. There are connections to social studies through the students' analyses of news articles read at the beginning of the project and in the fact that students are modeling good citizenship. Integration of other subject areas is evident.
Cognitive Complexity	4: Integrating	The project is student generated at Bloom's Create level starting with the student-created survey. The project remains at the Create level as students write their own narrative based on survey results.
Student Engagement	4: Integrating	In this project, both students and the teacher are defining what the content, process, and product look like. Student inquiry is evident in the student-created survey and interactions they have with their focus child. Collaboration among students occurs during the writing process and the StoryJumper creation.
Technology Integration	4: Integrating	The technology in this project is essential for its completion, especially with the StoryJumper technology. Students are able to turn their narrative into a comfort book, which can then be published. This is a large part of the standards and project objectives. The technology used allows for collaboration in the writing process. The technology used is essential for students to solve the problem of how to comfort the critically ill children who are the focus of this project.

WHICH BAND MEMBER HAD THE MOST SUCCESSFUL SOLO CAREER?

Source: Adapted from Meghan Rhoads. Used with permission.

Content: English language arts

Learning Objectives:

1. Students will define success in their own words.
2. Students will judge a band member's solo career according to their personal definition of success and justify their response.

Standards:

Common Core English language arts—

- L.5.4.C Consult reference materials (e.g., dictionaries, glossaries, thesauruses), both print and digital, to find the pronunciation and determine or clarify the precise meaning of key words and phrases (NGA & CCSSO, 2010a).
- W.5.6 With some guidance and support from adults, use technology, including the Internet, to produce and publish writing as well as to interact and collaborate with others; demonstrate sufficient command of keyboarding skills to type a minimum of two pages in a single sitting (NGA & CCSSO, 2010a).
- W.5.7 Conduct short research projects that use several sources to build knowledge through investigation of different aspects of a topic (NGA & CCSSO, 2010a).

Project Options: Groups could create an interactive time line using HSTRY (www.hstry.co) or Dipity (www.dipity.com) that encompasses the solo career of their band member.

Resources Needed: Computer with Internet access to use HSTRY and iMovie. You also need the following resources for post-band music artists' solo careers.

- DeGroot, J. (2014, July 13). *7 bands that spawned multiple prominent solo careers: Genesis, Wu-Tang Clan, and more*. Accessed at www.musictimes.com/articles/7542/20140713/7-bands-that-spawned-multiple-prominent-solo-careers-genesis-wu-tang-clan-and-more.htm on June 29, 2016.
- Ginocchio, M. (2014, March 24). *10 artists who left amazing bands to create something better*. Accessed at http://whatculture.com/music/10-artists-left-amazing-bands-create-something-better.php on June 29, 2016.
- *Rolling Stone*. (2012, May 2). Readers poll: Ten best post-band solo artists. Accessed at www.rollingstone.com/music/pictures/readers-poll-ten-best-post-band-solo-artists-20120502 on June 29, 2016.

Which Band Member Had the Most Successful Solo Career?

Do you like music? What kind of music? Think about your favorite band. After the band broke up, did any of the members go on to have successful solo careers? Your group will research band members and decide which one achieved success.

Project Tasks

1. On your "Band Member Solo Career Worksheet," write your own original meaning of *success*. Then we will have a class discussion about definitions of success. You may add to your definition if you like during the discussion.

2. We will have a class brainstorming session about music bands, which ones broke up, and who went on to solo careers.

3. Your teacher will divide you into groups. Decide on a band name for yourselves. Work with your group to identify five band members who then had solo careers. Discuss these band members among yourselves. Your group must choose three to further research.

   ◆ Research each of the three band members' solo careers, and write down your findings on your worksheet. Make sure to include major accomplishments and philanthropies (or humanitarian work).

   ◆ In your groups, decide which band member's solo career was the most successful according to your definition of success, and justify your answer.

   ◆ When your "Band Member Solo Career Worksheet" is finished, bring it to your teacher for approval.

4. Now it's time to decide if you want to go solo or stay with your band. Do you want to create your presentation solo or with your band (group)?

5. Pretend to be your selected music artist, and tell your digital story. Be sure to tell why you are successful using your definition of success. We will have a class discussion about digital story tools and how to create a storyboard for your project. Please use the following resources to help you create your digital story.

   ◆ Kaffel, N. (2007, November). *Digital storytelling*: *How to create a digital story*. Accessed at http://bit.ly/YxN3jQ on June 29, 2016.

   ◆ Levine, A. (2014, February 5). *StoryTools*: *The fifty tools*. Accessed at http://bit.ly/2bvlvlU on June 29, 2016.

6. Finally, your group will present its digital stories to the class. You or your group will define your idea of success for the class. The class will make notes about whether each presentation did or did not match its solo artist to its definition of success. The class will vote on which group did the best job in matching the solo artist with its definition of success.

Band Member Solo Career Worksheet

Group members: _____ Date: _____

1. Define your meaning of success.

2. Brainstorm five different band members who have had solo careers.

   _____

   _____

   _____

   _____

   _____

3. Your group needs to narrow down your list to three and then record each artist's major accomplishments.

   a. First artist's name: _____

   Major accomplishments:

   _____

   _____

   b. Second artist's name: _____

   Major accomplishments:

   _____

   _____

   c. Third artist's name: _____

   Major accomplishments:

   _____

   _____

4. Which band member's solo career matches up with your definition of success? Support your opinion with three reasons.

   _____

   _____

   _____

5. Explain why your definition of success matches up with this band member's solo career.

Scoring Rubric

	1 SIGNIFICANT REVISION NEEDED	2 SOME REVISION NEEDED	3 PROFICIENT	4 EXCEEDS EXPECTATIONS
Objective 1: Students will define success in their own words.	This group provides a dictionary definition of success or no definition at all.	This group provides a basic definition of success.	This group provides an adequate definition of success.	This group provides an original definition of success.
Objective 2: Students will judge a band member's solo career according to their personal definition of success and justify their response.	There is a lack of or no effort put into research on all three of the band members' solo careers. Selection of the most successful band member's solo career does not match the group's original definition of success. The product, art and photos, color, and space are not original and do not carry the theme, tone, or concept. The product has an unprofessional look; the overall graphical theme does not appeal to the audience, does not complement the information, and is not based on logical conclusions and sound research. There are six or more grammatical errors.	Research on all three of the band members' solo careers is missing key information. Selection of the most successful band member's solo career matches the group's original definition of success but is missing details. There are some original, unique features in the product. Art and photos, color, and space are not original and do not carry the theme, tone, or concept. The product has an unprofessional look; the overall graphical theme does not appeal to the audience, does not complement the information, and is not based on logical conclusions and sound research. There are three to five grammatical errors.	Research on all three of the band members' solo careers is adequate. Selection of the most successful band member's solo career matches the group's original definition of success. The product is original and unique. Art and photos, color, and space are used in original ways that mostly carry the theme, tone, and concept. The product has a professional look with an overall graphical theme that mostly appeals to the audience, complements the information, and is based on logical conclusions and sound research. There are one or two grammatical errors.	Research on all three of the band members' solo careers is comprehensive. Selection of the most successful band member's solo career clearly and logically matches the group's original definition of success. The product is excellent, original, and unique. The overall graphical theme appeals to the audience, complements the information, and is based on logical conclusions and sound research. There are no grammatical errors.

Sample Student Work

Band Member Solo Career Worksheet

Group members: <u>Soraya, Gilbert, Hansel</u>   Date: <u>October 3</u>

1. **Define your meaning of success:** Success means to be accomplished and/or skilled at a certain task. If you are a successful person, that means that you try hard at everything you do and you almost always do well. It could mean that you are the first to do something in your field.

2. **Brainstorm five different band members who have had solo careers:** George Harrison, John Lennon, Ringo Starr, Michael Jackson, and Dave Grohl.

3. **Your group needs to narrow down your list to three and then record each artist's major accomplishments:** (1) George Harrison, (2) John Lennon, and (3) Ringo Starr

   * **Research on the first artist—**
   On December 26, 1970, George released his first single, "My Sweet Lord." It reached number one in the United States, making him the first Beatle to achieve this as a solo artist.

   On August 1, 1971, George started the first ever benefit concert, called the Concert for Bangladesh. It was put on to fund relief efforts for refugees from East Pakistan.

   In 1988, George Harrison formed his own band called the Traveling Wilburys.

   On November 29, 2001, George Harrison passed away from lung cancer.

   * **Research on the second artist—**
   In 1970, John released his first proper solo album, Back to the Basics. It included hit songs such as "Mother" and "Working Class Hero."

   The second solo album that he released was Imagine, which was very popular in sales. It was released on September 1, 1971.

   In 1975, John released his sixth solo album called Rock 'n' Roll. This album gave John legal battles and marked his five-year break from the music business.

   In 1980, John went back to the music industry, releasing a joint project with his wife Yoko Ono called <u>Double Fantasy</u>.

   On December 8, 1980, John Lennon was murdered outside his apartment in New York City.

   * **Research on the third artist—**
   In 1971, Ringo was the first Beatle to score seven consecutive top ten singles, one of them being "Back Off Boogaloo."

   From 1985 to present day, Ringo participates in his band that he formed called Ringo Starr and His All-Starr Band.

   In 1981, Ringo starred in the movie <u>Caveman</u>.

   From 1984 to 1986, Ringo was the narrator of the series <u>Thomas and Friends</u>.

   In 1985, he acted as the mock turtle in <u>Alice in Wonderland</u>.

4. **Which band member's solo career matches up with your definition of success? Support your opinion with three reasons.**

    George Harrison released many successful solo albums, he started his own band, and he was the first Beatle to hold a benefit concert to help others.

5. **Explain why your definition of success matches up with this band member's solo career.**

    My definition of success matches best with George Harrison's solo career because he was accomplished and extremely skilled at all his endeavors. Musically speaking, he released many successful solo albums, he started his own band, and he was the first Beatle to hold a benefit concert to help others. Unfortunately, George died of lung cancer in 2001.

Visit https://youtu.be/69nQTz1pNk0 (Rhoads, 2016) for an example of a digital story for a student's definition of success on George Harrison. Visit www.hstry.co/timelines/ringo-starr-s-solo-career for an example of an optional time line about the solo career of Ringo Starr.

Create Excellence Framework Rating

CREATE ANALYSIS		
CREATE COMPONENT	**LEVEL**	**JUSTIFICATION**
Real-World Learning	3: Investigating	Students simulate the role of a successful music artist in his or her solo career.
Cognitive Complexity	3: Investigating	Students analyze and evaluate which band member had the most successful solo career according to their own definition of success. Students also think at the attributing level because they are role-playing one of the successful band members.
Student Engagement	3: Investigating	Students have a choice for the tasks, content (selection of any band members to research), and product (choice of technology options) to differentiate tasks.
Technology Integration	3: Investigating	Students use technology for analyzing and evaluating tasks; however, the technology is an add-on.

WEBSITE OR APPS CRITIC

Source: Adapted from Marge Maxwell and Rebecca Stobaugh. Edited by Savannah Denning. Used with permission.

Content: Mathematics

Learning Objectives:

1. Students will demonstrate grade-level knowledge of fractions by successfully completing several applications (apps) about fractions.
2. Students will create a real-world writing piece critiquing fraction websites or apps.

Standards:

Common Core mathematics—

- 3.NF.A.1 Understand a fraction 1/b as the quantity formed by 1 part when a whole is partitioned into *b* equal parts; understand a fraction a/b as the quantity formed by *a* parts of size 1/b (NGA & CCSSO, 2010b).
- 3.NF.A.2 Understand a fraction as a number on the number line; represent fractions on a number line diagram (NGA & CCSSO, 2010b).
- 3.NF.A.3 Explain equivalence of fractions in special cases, and compare fractions by reasoning about their size (NGA & CCSSO, 2010b).

Project Options:

- Students may develop their own ideas to publish their work other than on the classroom website or blog; students may have knowledge of a publishing app or website that would allow them to publish their work adequately.
- Allow advanced students, as individuals or in a group, to design their own app or website.
- Students may present their reviews to other classes and other students either face to face or with video-chat programs.

Resources Needed: Students will need Internet access and devices to access fraction games. (Many games require Flash Player; therefore, some programs may not work properly on tablets.) Students will also need a word processing program to create their writing piece.

Website or Apps Critic

You will find and investigate five apps or websites that you think could help you and your classmates practice and understand the concept of fractions. You will then review the apps or websites you researched and rank the top five programs. To share your thoughts, you will publish a review of the five best apps for learning fractions in our classroom newsletter and on our class website. After the newsletter is published, the class will choose the top five apps or websites of those collected and critiqued to use for the next month to practice fractions.

Project Tasks

1. In a group discussion, determine the criteria you will use to evaluate the fraction apps or websites. Apps are applications or programs on a computer, tablet, or smartphone.

    Criteria might include *is fun to play*, *matches the fraction skills we are learning*, *has little or no cost*, and so on.

2. Investigate all the apps and websites dealing with fractions that look like they would meet the criteria your group identifies.

3. Develop your skills and knowledge about fractions as you play with the apps and websites. Turn in evidence of your score from the practice to your teacher.

4. As a group, select the best five apps or websites on fractions.

5. As a group, write a review of the best apps or websites for our parent newsletter and to post on our website. Be sure to include:

    *   An introduction to your article
    *   A chart including a summary of each app or website and an explanation of why the app or website received a one, two, three, four, or five ranking (five being a high ranking)
    *   A summary paragraph

6. From these reviews, as a class, choose the top five apps and websites that the class will use over the next month to practice fraction skills.

Scoring Rubric

	1 SIGNIFICANT REVISION NEEDED	2 SOME REVISION NEEDED	3 PROFICIENT	4 EXCEEDS EXPECTATIONS
Objective 1: Students will demonstrate grade-level knowledge of fractions by successfully completing several applications (apps) about fractions.	Students examine one or two apps or websites related to fractions.	Students examine a few apps or websites related to fractions.	Students examine five apps or websites related to fractions.	Students thoroughly examine six or more apps or websites related to fractions.
Objective 2: Students will create a real-world writing piece critiquing fraction websites or apps.	Students minimally evaluate fraction websites or apps.	Students write an article evaluating a few fraction websites or apps.	Students write an article evaluating five fraction websites or apps.	Students write a very detailed article evaluating all components of five fraction websites or apps.

Sample Student Work

Do you want your child to practice fractions? Well, I have some games they are going to have to try. I looked at many of the fraction apps available to find ones that practice fraction skills, are fun, and are free. Following are my favorite fraction apps.

APP	RANKING	REVIEW
Pizza Factory	1	I loved the Pizza Factory app. This app is a game where students determine the fraction of pizza. The game also gets harder the more you play it, so it challenges you. The sound effects and cute cartoon chef make this one fun to play.
Fraction Kitchen Lite	2	With this app, the chef is trying to start a nice restaurant. His arch-nemesis, La Cucaracha, gets in his way, though, which makes it fun. In the game, students help the chef create his recipes. The free version is a lite version, so the full features of the game are unavailable.
Freddy's Fractions	3	With the Freddy's Fractions game, you get to help an alien get home by using fractions. While this is fun, there are parts of this game that used decimals and percentages, which we haven't talked about yet.
enVisionMATH: Understanding Fractions	4	These are videos that are helpful in understanding fractions. They also have little quizzes to make sure you understand what they are saying. It isn't a game, which makes it not as fun as some of the other apps.
Oh No Fractions!	5	This website is a little tougher. It helps you compare fractions. I ranked this number five because it was a little difficult for me. But my brother, who is older, played it and enjoyed it. He said it helped him understand how to compare two fractions because it showed pictures of the fractions.

I hope you will have fun exploring these free apps. If you use these apps, I think you will find that your child will enjoy practicing fractions while learning and having fun.

Create Excellence Framework Rating

CREATE ANALYSIS		
CREATE COMPONENT	**LEVEL**	**JUSTIFICATION**
Real-World Learning	4: Integrating	To clearly connect to the real world, this instructional task has connections with writing to a real-world audience of parents through a newsletter-sharing website and apps critiques. The class of students chooses the apps or websites to use for the next month. The project is interdisciplinary with writing and mathematics.
Cognitive Complexity	3: Investigating	With this task, students are thinking at the highest cognitive levels by applying, analyzing, and evaluating. Students are evaluating as they rank the apps and websites for the criteria they identified.
Student Engagement	3: Investigating	In this project, the goal is for students to be focused and engaged in the learning. Students are encouraged to collaborate with others to complete this task. Students are able to investigate the ways they might want to learn fractions.
Technology Integration	4: Integrating	In this task, students are required to explore the fraction apps and websites.

ART SHOW!

Source: Adapted from Rebecca Stobaugh and Marge Maxwell. Edited by Savannah Denning. Used with permission.

Content: Mathematics

Learning Objectives:

1. Students will create a piece of art that incorporates geometric shapes to represent a familiar object or living thing.
2. Students will analyze classmates' work to identify geometric shapes included in the artwork.

Standard:

Common Core mathematics—

- 1.GA.A.2 Compose two-dimensional shapes (rectangles, squares, trapezoids, triangles, half-circles, and quarter-circles) or three-dimensional shapes (cubes, right rectangular prisms, right circular cones, and right circular cylinders) to create a composite shape, and compose new shapes from the composite shape (NGA & CCSSO, 2010b).

Project Options:

- Students may use various apps or programs to complete this project; they are not limited to Microsoft Word.
- Students may create a video presentation to share their artwork. The video presentations can stream during the gallery walk for students who are not in the class to watch them. These videos may also be shared via social media with parents' permission.
- To allow students more autonomy over their learning process and preferences, the teacher may allow students to choose from a wider range of media to create their artwork. Some students prefer pencil-and-paper tasks, and some students prefer to use technology. It is also an option to allow students to use other materials (such as household items, clay, LEGOs, building blocks, and so on).
- Students may self-assess their work or peer-assess their classmates' work using the chart provided. Students may provide feedback to their classmates to help them improve their work. Students will need opportunities to create multiple drafts of this project if the teacher chooses this option.
- The art show can be shared with parents during a parent night or another after-school activity to broaden the audience for students completing this project.

Resources Needed: Computer with Microsoft Word or Internet access to another web-drawing program

Art Show!

Our class will be hosting an art show for the school. We will showcase what we know about geometry! You will create a special project for the art show and give a short presentation about your artwork. Many other students from our school will do a gallery walk to view your artwork.

Project Tasks

1. Use Microsoft Word's drawing program or another program you know how to use to design a picture of a familiar object or living thing that incorporates at least three different two-dimensional shapes (rectangles, squares, trapezoids, triangles, half-circles, or quarter-circles).

2. After your teacher prints and posts your artwork and your classmates' artwork around the room on the walls, look at each posted picture. Use the recording chart that follows to record each artist's name, circle the shapes used in the picture, and guess the object or living thing.

3. You will take a turn standing beside your project while your classmates share their guesses about the living thing or object in your artwork. You will then explain the shapes you used and share the living thing or object you created.

STUDENT'S NAME	CIRCLE THE SHAPES				GUESS THE DRAWING
	rectangle half-circle	square quarter-circle	trapezoid	triangle	
	rectangle half-circle	square quarter-circle	trapezoid	triangle	
	rectangle half-circle	square quarter-circle	trapezoid	triangle	

Scoring Rubric

	1 SIGNIFICANT REVISION NEEDED	2 SOME REVISION NEEDED	3 PROFICIENT	4 EXCEEDS EXPECTATIONS
Objective 1: Students will create a piece of art that incorporates geometric shapes to represent a familiar object or living thing.	The student does not use geometric shapes accurately and logically in his or her drawing.	The students uses one or two geometric shapes accurately and logically in his or her drawing.	The student uses three geometric shapes accurately and logically in his or her drawing.	The student uses three or more geometric shapes accurately and logically in his or drawing.
Objective 2: Students will analyze classmates' work to identify geometric shapes included in the artwork.	The student is not able to identify geometric shapes included in classmates' work.	The student correctly identifies classmates' shapes with less than 75 percent accuracy.	The student correctly identifies classmates' shapes with 76 to 89 percent accuracy.	The student correctly identifies classmates' shapes with 90 percent or more accuracy.

Create Excellence Framework Rating

CREATE ANALYSIS		
CREATE COMPONENT	**LEVEL**	**JUSTIFICATION**
Real-World Learning	3: Investigating	This project simulates a real-world scenario (an art show) where students have an audience broader than their classmates.
Cognitive Complexity	3: Investigating	The teacher directs students' interaction with the core content standard. The Bloom's level of this task is the Analyze level. Students analyze which geometric shapes are needed to represent their own object or living thing. They then must analyze and recreate their classmates' scenarios with the geometric shapes.
Student Engagement	3: Investigating	Students have choice about which shapes they use to represent an object or living thing, as well as the technology they use to create the product. Because this is an open-ended task, students can produce projects that are influenced by their ability and interests.
Technology Integration	3: Investigating	Technology in this project is required for completion but is an alternative for traditional pencil-and-paper completion. Students use technology for the Analyze level of Bloom's taxonomy.

Sample Student Work

This student sample illustrates how one student organized his thinking in order to clearly communicate to the audience and demonstrate skill mastery.

STUDENT'S NAME	CIRCLE THE SHAPES	GUESS THE DRAWING
Sandra	(rectangle) square (trapezoid) (triangle) half-circle quarter-circle	hat
Marissa	(rectangle) (square) trapezoid triangle (half-circle) quarter-circle	bat and ball
Jevone	(rectangle) (square) trapezoid (triangle) half-circle quarter-circle	slide

Jevone's Presentation

I used a rectangle, triangle, and square in my picture. My picture is a slide.

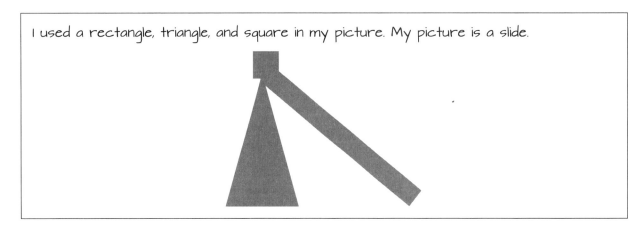

YIKES! FIVE HUNDRED PEOPLE ARE COMING TO DINNER!

Source: Adapted from Marge Maxwell and Rebecca Stobaugh. Edited by Savannah Denning. Used with permission.

Content: Mathematics

Learning Objectives:

1. Students will create a spreadsheet with formulas to calculate a scale-up of a recipe to feed five hundred people.
2. Students will evaluate each other's spreadsheets for accuracy and logic.

Standards:

Common Core mathematics—

- 5.NBT.B.7 Add, subtract, multiply, and divide decimals to hundredths, using concrete models or drawings and strategies based on place value, properties of operations, and/or the relationship between addition and subtraction; relate the strategy to a written method and explain the reasoning used (NGA & CCSSO, 2010b).
- 5.MD.A.1 Convert among different-sized standard measurement units within a given measurement system (e.g., convert 5 cm to 0.05 m), and use these conversions in solving multi-step, real-world problems (NGA & CCSSO, 2010b).

Project Options:

- Calculate each recipe's nutritional value.
- Extend calculations to nutritional value for each serving.

Resources Needed: Students will need access to devices to create a spreadsheet for this project. Students may need to access tutorials to use spreadsheets via online instructional videos for Google Apps Learning Center's Sheets (http://bit.ly/1TDvl8J).

Yikes! Five Hundred People Are Coming to Dinner!

Your class is in charge of the fall festival dinner. Last year, five hundred people attended and purchased a dinner. Most people who cook know how to double or triple a recipe. But how would you make a recipe for five hundred people? In this project, you will take your favorite recipe and adjust it so that you are able to feed five hundred people. Also, you will calculate the ingredients' cost for this gigantic meal. The teacher will divide you into small groups. Each group should work on the calculations for one recipe for the dinner. For example, one group can work on a chili recipe, one group can work on a cornbread recipe, and one group can work on a dessert recipe.

Project Tasks

1. Choose your favorite recipes from any cookbook, or find them on the Internet. It is recommended that you choose a recipe that can act as the main meal, like spaghetti, lasagna, chili, pancakes, and so on. Then you can just add bread and a dessert.

2. Print each recipe, and note the number of servings for each.

3. Divide 500 by the number of each recipe's servings. This result is the scale-up (or multiplier) factor.

4. Now multiply each ingredient by this scale-up factor, and record the new amounts of each ingredient in a spreadsheet on your computer or iPad. Fractions and mixed numbers can be easily multiplied if they are converted into decimals first.

5. Fill in the spreadsheet with your ingredients and amounts needed. To demonstrate the calculations, a sample is provided using 700 people. For example, your recipe makes 4 servings: 700 ÷ 4 = 175, so your scale-up factor is 175, and you must multiply each ingredient by 175. If your recipe for 4 calls for 1.5 teaspoons of salt, the recipe for 700 should use 1.5 × 175 = 262.5 teaspoons of salt.

6. Convert each unit of measure to the type of unit used to purchase the ingredient. For example, 262.5 teaspoons of salt may be required, but you purchase salt in ounces.

   ◆ Since 3 teaspoons = 1 tablespoon, 262.5 ÷ 3 = 87.5 tablespoons.
   ◆ Since 16 tablespoons = 1 cup, 87.5 ÷ 16 = 5.47 cups, which is slightly less than 5.5 or 5½ cups.
   ◆ Since 1 cup = 8 ounces, 5.5 × 8 = 44 ounces.

Note: Add comments to cells in your spreadsheet explaining your conversions to make it easier for others to understand your spreadsheet.

You may use the following conversions.

For dry measure:

- *3 teaspoons (t) = 1 tablespoon (T)*
- *8 tablespoons (T) = ½ cup (c)*
- *16 tablespoons (T) = 1 cup (c)*

For liquid measure:

- *8 ounces (oz) = 1 cup (c)*
- *16 ounces (oz) = 1 pint (pt)*
- *2 cups (c) = 1 pint (pt)*
- *2 pints (pt) = 1 quart (qt)*
- *4 quarts (qt) = 1 gallon (gal)*

For weight:

- *16 ounces (oz) = 1 pound (lb)*

Do the following to calculate the approximate cost of the ingredients for this dinner.

1. Write each ingredient amount in terms of the amount you would purchase. You will have to estimate for some of the ingredients. Fill in these amounts in the table provided. For example, if we continue the scenario of 700 people, 5.5 cups of salt are needed for a recipe for 700 people. Salt is sold in 26-ounce boxes, so we need to convert to ounces.

    - Since 1 cup = 8 ounces, 5.5 × 8 = 44 ounces.
    - Since 26 ounces = 1 box of salt, 44 ÷ 26 = 1.69 boxes. However, you cannot purchase part of a box of salt, so you need to purchase 2 boxes.
    - Salt costs $0.49 per box, so our cost will be 2 × 0.49 = $0.98.

2. Calculate each ingredient's cost. You may have to make a trip to the grocery store or check online sales advertisements to obtain the prices. Record these costs in your spreadsheet.

3. Calculate the cost per person. Divide the total cost of the dinner by the number of people.

After completing a spreadsheet for the recipe, switch spreadsheets, recipes, and ingredient lists with another group to see if its calculations and formulas are accurate and logical. Consider:

- Are there ingredients that really may not be necessary? Justify your answer.
- Are there alternative ingredients that could be substituted to save money?

After all groups have completed their recipe spreadsheets and had them checked, you and your classmates will determine the best price to charge each guest for the dinner.

1. On the class computer with a projector, the teacher will show a new spreadsheet to complete this calculation.

2. One member from your group should go up and type his or her recipe and cost per person in a row.

3. You or any classmate can volunteer to create the formula to add up all recipe costs.

4. Discuss the following questions with your classmates to determine how much money you all want to make from this dinner.

    - What will we use the money for?
    - Should we double or triple the cost of the meal to decide on how much guests will pay for the meal? What is a fair price?
    - What is the difference in gross profit and net profit?

Scoring Rubric

	1 SIGNIFICANT REVISION NEEDED	2 SOME REVISION NEEDED	3 PROFICIENT	4 EXCEEDS EXPECTATIONS
Objective 1: Students will create a spreadsheet with formulas to calculate a scale-up of a recipe to feed five hundred people.	Most formulas and calculations are not correct even with assistance from the teacher. No comments are placed in cells that needed explanations of unit conversions.	Some formulas and calculations are not correct even with assistance from the teacher. Many comments are missing in cells that needed explanations of unit conversions.	All formulas and calculations are correct with some assistance from the teacher. Comments are placed in cells that needed explanations of unit conversions.	All formulas and calculations are correct on the first attempt with no assistance. Comments are clearly placed in cells that needed explanations of unit conversions.
Objective 2: Students will evaluate each other's spreadsheets for accuracy and logic.	Groups do not check another group's spreadsheet to see if calculations and formulas are accurate and logical. Groups do not evaluate whether there are ingredients that really may not be necessary or do not justify their answers. Groups do not identify any alternative ingredients that could be substituted to save money.	Groups incorrectly check another group's spreadsheet to see if calculations and formulas are accurate and logical. Groups incorrectly evaluate whether there are ingredients that really may not be necessary or do not adequately justify their answers. Groups incorrectly identify alternative ingredients that could be substituted to save money.	Groups check another group's spreadsheet to see if calculations and formulas are accurate and logical. Groups evaluate whether there are ingredients that really may not be necessary and justify their answers. Groups identify alternative ingredients that could be substituted to save money.	Groups accurately check another group's spreadsheet to see if calculations and formulas are accurate and logical. Groups accurately evaluate whether there are ingredients that really may not be necessary and fully justify their answers. Groups accurately identify alternative ingredients that could be substituted to save money.

Real-World Learning Framework for Elementary Schools © 2017 Solution Tree Press • SolutionTree.com
Visit **go.SolutionTree.com/instruction** to download this free reproducible.

Sample Student Work

Yikes! Five Hundred People for Dinner

Here is a sample of student work to show calculations for 500 people.

CHILI							
Serves	6						
Number of people	500						
Scale-up factor	83.333333						
INGREDIENTS OF CHILI	AMOUNT	RECIPE UNIT	CONVERT TO PURCHASE UNIT	AMOUNT SCALED UP	IN WHAT UNITS AND AMOUNTS INGREDIENTS ARE PURCHASED		AMOUNT FOR FIVE HUNDRED PEOPLE	COST PER INGREDIENT
Ground beef	1	lb		83.33	5 lbs	$10.58	17	$176.33
Bay leaf	1			83.33	0.12 oz	$2.38	6	$14.28
Garlic, minced	0.5	t	0.083333333	6.94	8 oz	$2.24	1	$2.24
Chili powder	2	T	1	83.33	2.5 oz	$2.14	33	$71.33
Salt	1	t	0.166666667	13.89	26 oz	$1.98	1	$1.98
Onion	0.5	c	0.25	20.83	3 lbs (7 onions)	$3.48	7	$24.17
Cumin, ground	0.5	t	0.083333333	6.94	2 oz	$1.24	3	$4.31
Tomatoes, diced	1	29-oz can		83.33	1 29-oz can	$1.24	83	$102.92
Tomato paste	1	6-oz can		83.33	1 6-oz can	$0.56	83	$46.48
Kidney beans, red	1	16-oz can		83.33	1 16-oz can	$0.92	83	$76.36
Pepper	0.5	t	0.083333333	6.94	8 oz	$4.98	1	$4.98
Mozzarella cheese, shredded	6	T	3	250.00	8 oz	$2.18	31	$68.13
Jalapeno peppers, chopped	6	T	3	250.00	1 16-oz can	$1.78	16	$27.81

Continued →

Cost per person: $1.24

Recipe Directions

1. In a large saucepan over medium-high heat, combine the ground beef and onion. Sauté for about five minutes, or until beef is browned. Drain excess fat.

2. Add the chili powder, garlic, bay leaf, cumin, tomatoes, tomato paste, and salt and pepper to taste. Bring to a boil and reduce heat to low. Cover and simmer for 1½ hours, stirring occasionally. Stir in the kidney beans and heat through.

3. Put shredded mozzarella cheese and chopped jalapeno peppers in separate bowls for guests to add to their bowls of chili.

Spreadsheet With Formulas

The following spreadsheet includes formulas that the spreadsheet program will use to calculate the mathematics for the student groups. An alternative method is to provide students with a blank spreadsheet (either paper or electronic) and have students add data to the spreadsheet after they have completed the accurate calculations.

CHILI

Serves	6
Number of people	500
Scale-up factor	=B5/B4

INGREDIENTS OF CHILI	AMOUNT	RECIPE UNIT	CONVERT TO PURCHASE UNIT	AMOUNT SCALED UP	IN WHAT UNITS AND AMOUNTS INGREDIENTS ARE PURCHASED		AMOUNT FOR FIVE HUNDRED PEOPLE	COST PER INGREDIENT
Ground beef	1	lb		=B10*B$6	5 lbs	$10.58	=E10/5	=G10*H10
Bay leaf	1			=B11*B$6	0.12 oz	$2.38	6	=G11*H11
Garlic, minced	0.5	t	=B12/3/16*8	=D12*B$6	8 oz	$2.24	1	=G12*H12
Chili powder	2	T	=B13/16*8	=D13*B$6	2.5 oz	$2.14	=E13/2.5	=G13*H13
Salt	1	t	=B14/3/16*8	=D14*B$6	26 oz	$1.98	1	=G14*H14
Onion	0.5	c	=B15*8/16	=D15*B$6	3 lbs (7 onions)	$3.48	=E15/3	=G15*H15
Cumin, ground	0.5	t	=B16/3/16*8	=D16*B$6	2 oz	$1.24	=E16/2	=G16*H16
Tomatoes, diced	1	29-oz can		=B17*B$6	1 29-oz can	$1.24	83	=G17*H17
Tomato paste	1	6-oz can		=B18*B$6	1 6-oz can	$0.56	83	=G18*H18

Kidney beans, red	1	16-oz can		=B19*B$6	1 16-oz can	$0.92	83	=G19*H19
Pepper	0.5	t	=B20/3/16*8	=D20*B$6	8 oz	$4.98	1	=G20*H20
Mozzarella cheese, shredded	6	T	=B21/16*8	=D21*B$6	8 oz	$2.18	=E21/8	=G21*H21
Jalapeno peppers, chopped	6	T	=B22/16*8	=D22*B$6	1 16-oz can	$1.78	=E22/16	=G22*H22
Cost per person	=124/B5						Total Cost	=SUM (110:123)

Recipe Directions

1. In a large saucepan over medium-high heat, combine the ground beef and onion. Sauté for about five minutes, or until beef is browned. Drain excess fat.

2. Add the chili powder, garlic, bay leaf, cumin, tomatoes, tomato paste, and salt and pepper to taste. Bring to a boil and reduce heat to low. Cover and simmer for 1½ hours, stirring occasionally. Stir in the kidney beans and heat through.

3. Put shredded mozzarella cheese and chopped jalapeno peppers in separate bowls for guests to add to their bowls of chili.

Mathematics Projects

Spreadsheet With Comments

CHILI

Serves	6
Number of people	500
Scale-up factor	

INGREDIENTS OF CHILI		CONVERT TO PURCHASE UNIT				AMOUNT FOR FIVE HUNDRED PEOPLE	COST PER INGREDIENT
Ground beef	1		lb / 5 lbs	$10.58	=B10*B$6	=E10/5	=G10*H10
Bay leaf	1		0.12 oz	$2.38	=B11*B$6	6	=G11*H11
Garlic, minced		=B12/3/16*8	8 oz	$2.24	=D12*B$6	1	=G12*H12
Chili powder		=B13/16*8	2.5 oz	$2.14	=D13*B$6	=E13/2.5	=G13*H13
Salt		=B14/3/16*8	26 oz	$1.98	=D14*B$6	1	=G14*H14
Onion		=B15*8/16	3 lbs (7 onions)	$3.48	=D15*B$6	=E15/3	=G15*H15
Cumin, ground	0.5	=B16/3/16*8	2 oz	$1.24	=D16*B$6	=E16	
Tomatoes, diced	1		1 29-oz can	$1.24	=B17*B$6	83	
Tomato paste	1			.56	=B18*B$6	83	
Kidney beans, red	1		lb-oz can	.92	=B19*B$6	83	
Pepper	0.5	=B20/... *6*8	8 oz	$4.98	=D20*B$6	1	
Mozzarella cheese, shredded	6	=B21...	18		=D21*B$6	=E21	
Jalapeno peppers, chopped	6	=B22/16*8	.78		=D22*B$6	=E22	

Comment boxes:
- convert teaspoons to Tablespoons to cups to ounces
- convert Tablespoons to cups to ounces
- ground beef is sold in 5-pound tubes
- 1 medium onion = 1 c chopped onion; convert cups to ounces to pounds
- convert teaspoons to Tablespoons to cups to ounces
- convert Tablespoons to cups to ounces
- convert teaspoons to Tablespoons to cups to ounces
- approximately 130 bay leaves per ounce; multiply 130 by .12 and you get about 15 bay leaves in one container; since 84 bay leaves are needed, divide 84 by 15 and you need 6 boxes

Class Activity Calculating the Price to Charge Guests

CALCULATING WHAT TO CHARGE PER GUEST			
Number of people	500		
RECIPE	**COST PER PERSON**	**COST FOR FIVE HUNDRED**	
Chili	$1.24	$620.00	
Cornbread	$0.44	$220.00	
Dessert	$1.06	$530.00	
Tea/coffee	$0.21	$105.00	
Total	$2.95	$1,475.00	
WHAT IF . . .		**GROSS PROFIT**	**NET PROFIT**
Double	$5.90	$2,950.00	$1,475.00
Triple	$8.85	$4,425.00	$2,950.00

Create Excellence Framework Rating

Mathematics Projects

CREATE ANALYSIS		
CREATE COMPONENT	**LEVEL**	**JUSTIFICATION**
Real-World Learning	3: Investigating	Students simulate a real-life event and work through a relevant problem. Actually requiring students to carry out their project and prepare food for a significant number of people for a real event can easily take the project to level 4.
Cognitive Complexity	3: Investigating	The teacher directs student interaction with content and standards at an Analyze level (differentiating, organizing, attributing), Evaluate level (checking, critiquing), or Create level (generating, planning, producing). The teacher directs this task, and students are required to engage in higher-order thinking to analyze a recipe and transform the information to create a new recipe to meet the needs of feeding a large group.
Student Engagement	3: Investigating	Students have choice in the recipes they choose to analyze and adapt. Students also have choice in the methods and strategies they use to convert recipe measurements.
Technology Integration	3: Investigating	Technology makes this project and group work more efficient and relevant to real-world and workforce tasks.

A STICKY SITUATION: BUILDING A SWEET BRIDGE

Source: Adapted from Jessica Nissen Bauer, Lydia Renfro, and Savannah Denning. Used with permission.

Content: Mathematics

Learning Objectives:

1. Students will become engineers by designing and building a model of the strongest bridge possible.
2. Students will analyze cost efficiency by calculating the amount of materials used and finding the final cost of building their bridge.

Standards:

Common Core mathematics—

- 3.NBT.A.2 Fluently add and subtract within 1000 using strategies and algorithms based on place value, properties of operations, and/or the relationship between addition and subtraction (NGA & CCSSO, 2010b).
- 3.MD.A.2 Measure and estimate liquid volumes and masses of objects using standard units of grams (g), kilograms (kg), and liters (l). Add, subtract, multiply, or divide to solve one-step word problems involving masses or volumes that are given in the same units, e.g., by using drawings (such as a beaker with a measurement scale) to represent the problem (NGA & CCSSO, 2010b).
- 3.MD.B.3 Draw a scaled picture graph and a scaled bar graph to represent a data set with several categories. Solve one- and two-step "how many more" and "how many less" problems using information presented in scaled bar graphs. *For example, draw a bar graph in which each square in the bar graph might represent 5 pets* (NGA & CCSSO, 2010b).

Next Generation Science Standards—

- 3–5-ETS1–1 Define a simple design problem reflecting a need or a want that includes specified criteria for success and constraints on materials, time, or cost (Achieve, 2013).

Project Options: Students take their idea from step five and build another bridge. At this point, they may need to gather different supplies than those noted in the supply list.

Resources Needed:

- Toothpicks (student cost—$1)
- Large marshmallows (student cost—$4)
- Small marshmallows (student cost—$2)
- Glue containers (student cost—$2)
- Pipe cleaners (student cost—$3)
- Large Popsicle sticks (student cost—$4)
- Yarn or string (student cost—$5 per foot)
- Item graphic organizers
- Pencils
- Desks
- Buckets
- Computers (with Microsoft Excel or Google Sheets, and Microsoft Word)
- Cameras

A Sticky Situation: Building a Sweet Bridge

You are part of a civil-engineering team that has been called on by a local engineering company to build the strongest bridge while spending the least amount of money. The problem is you are not the only team that the company asked to take part in this task. The company will pick the best engineering team's model as the official bridge that it will build over the Ohio River. The company will consider two aspects to choose the winner—(1) what is strongest and (2) what is cheapest. You will need to use the given materials to build the sturdiest and strongest bridge.

You are only allowed to use toothpicks and marshmallows plus one other material of your choice (pipe cleaners, Popsicle sticks, or something similar).

Project Tasks

1. Build a bridge using as many marshmallows and toothpicks as needed plus one other material of your team's choice. Use the table "Bridge Building Price List" to represent parts of the bridge. Be sure that your bridge is four by eight inches long (measured with area squares).

2. Remember to keep track of how many materials you use to build the bridge. Determine how much money you spent building the bridge based on the given price sheet. Complete the "Sticky Situation Project Organizer."

3. Test your bridge. Be sure the desks are separated by five inches when testing weight. Complete the "Testing the Bridge and Analysis Worksheet" (page 204). Critique the overall effectiveness of your bridge design. Could you have made improvements?

4. Examine other designs. Complete the "Comparison Chart" worksheet (page 204) by comparing and contrasting data (price versus weight in grams). Create two bar graphs in Microsoft Excel displaying the data.

5. Think about the impact of gravity on the bridge. Complete the "Gravitational Force Conclusion" worksheet (page 205).

6. Review the section "Criteria for Success" (page 205), and design a persuasive Prezi or Glogster presentation to prove why your design is the best.

Bridge-Building Price List

ITEM	PRICE	REPRESENTATION
Toothpick	$1	Small steel beam
Small marshmallow	$2	Small joint or bracket
Large marshmallow	$4	Large joint or bracket
Popsicle stick	$4	Large steel beam
Glue container	$2	Cement or concrete
Pipe cleaner	$3	Cable
String or yarn	$5 per foot	Steel cable

Sticky Situation Project Organizer

> Use the following area to sketch your ideas for building a model bridge.
>
>
>
>
>
> Use the chart to document how many materials you use to create the model. Calculate the total cost. Transfer the data from your recording sheet to Google Sheets or Microsoft Excel. Choose Insert and Chart, and then choose the Double Bar Graph option.

Team number:

Team name:

ITEM	AMOUNT NEEDED	PRICE OF ITEM	TOTAL COST
Total cost:			

Testing the Bridge and Analysis Worksheet

Use this chart to record the number of area tiles your model can hold. Each tile represents 1 gram. Each gram in the model would equal 1,000 pounds.

RESULTS	
Number of Area Tiles (Tallies)	
Pounds the Bridge Can Hold	

After you have tested your bridge, write an analysis of your experiment. Think about ways that you could decrease the pressure of gravity on your bridge. Reflect on the positive aspects of your bridge and areas for improvement. Record your explanation here.

Comparison Chart

Use this chart to compare and contrast the groups' spending and bridge strength.

GROUP NUMBER	AMOUNT SPENT	AMOUNT OF WEIGHT BEFORE COLLAPSING (IN GRAMS)	OVERALL PLACE: STRENGTH	OVERALL PLACE: COST
1				
2				
3				
4				
5				

Compare and contrast every group's data to your own data. (How much money did each group spend in comparison to how much weight total its bridge was able to hold? Look for connections and such.) Use this information to create a bar graph using Google Sheets or Microsoft Excel.

Use the following directions.

1. Create a bar graph that shows each group's cost compared to the strength of its bridge.

2. Transfer the data from your recording sheet to Google Sheets or Microsoft Excel.

3. In Excel or Sheets, choose Insert and Chart. Choose the Double Bar Graph option.

Gravitational Force Conclusion

Use your observations to write a paragraph about the effects of gravity on your bridge and ways that you could decrease the pressure of gravity on the suspended bridge.

As you write, be sure to include:

- Scientific information you have learned about the effects of gravity
- How that information relates to your bridge project
- Examples from your project that support the scientific ideas about gravity
- Correct grammar, capitalization, and punctuation

Criteria for Success

When you complete a task, check it off the list. Use this tool as a guide to make sure you have successfully completed each step of the project.

COMPLETED	TASK
	Take pictures throughout the whole project!
	Use only small marshmallows, large marshmallows, and toothpicks.
	The bridge is four by eight inches long (measured with area squares).
	Desks are separated by five inches when testing weight.
	The amount of material and total cost are tracked on "Sticky Situation Project Organizer."
	The total amount of weight the bridge held is on the tally sheet.
	"Comparison Chart" is completed.
	A bar graph is created using Microsoft Excel or Google Sheets. • The bar graph is labeled correctly (title, x-axis, y-axis, numbers). • The bar graph number interval is realistic (if your bridge cost $400 and held 250 area squares, you don't have an interval of 2).
	An analysis is typed using Microsoft Word. • The analysis is free of grammatical errors. • The analysis uses correct punctuation and capitalization. • The analysis correlates with the bar graph that was created.
	A Prezi or Glogster presentation is created. • It includes progressive photographs from building and testing the bridge. • It has at least three captions on the photographs added to the presentation. • It includes a bar graph. • It includes an analysis. • It includes an explanation of the bridge model construction. The explanation can be created with an app or program like Blabberize (http://blabberize.com), PowToon (www.powtoon.com), Toontastic (https://toontastic.withgoogle.com), and such. • It uses correct grammar, capitalization, and punctuation.
	The gravitational force conclusion is written.

Scoring Rubric

	1 SIGNIFICANT REVISION NEEDED	2 SOME REVISION NEEDED	3 PROFICIENT	4 EXCEEDS EXPECTATIONS
Objective 1: Students will become engineers by designing and building a model of the strongest bridge possible.	Plan sketch is missing or irrelevant.	Plan sketch is included with several mistakes or omissions.	Plan sketch is included, complete, and accurate.	Plan sketch is completed and accurate with creative design elements.
	Model does not meet requirements on criteria for success.	Model meets some requirements on criteria for success.	Model meets all requirements on criteria for success.	Model meets all requirements on criteria for success and shows creative thinking.
	Model omits a type of required material, or other items are included.	Model does not omit a type of required material but may include items not listed.	Model utilizes all correct materials.	Materials are correctly and creatively used.
	Bridge is not tested, or bridge is tested with incorrect materials. Recording chart is missing or incomplete.	Bridge is tested with the correct materials. Recording chart is complete with errors.	Bridge is correctly tested. Recording chart is complete with few, minor errors.	Bridge is correctly tested. Recording chart is complete with no errors.
	Presentation (Prezi, Glogster) is missing, incomplete, or irrelevant. Presentation does not meet the requirements on criteria for success.	Presentation (Prezi, Glogster) is complete and included. Presentation meets some of the requirements on criteria for success.	Presentation (Prezi, Glogster) is complete and included. Presentation meets all the requirements on criteria for success, with very few errors.	Presentation (Prezi, Glogster) is complete and shows creativity. Presentation meets all the requirements on criteria for success, with no errors.
	Gravitational force conclusion is missing or incomplete. No scientific ideas are used to support student's thinking.	Gravitational force conclusion is complete. Few scientific ideas are used to support student's thinking. Conclusion does not include direct connections to bridge project.	Gravitational force conclusion is complete. Scientific ideas are used to accurately support student's thinking. Conclusion includes some connection to bridge project.	Gravitational force conclusion is complete and organized. Scientific ideas are clearly used to accurately support student's thinking. Conclusion includes direct ties to and examples of bridge project.

Real-World Learning Framework for Elementary Schools © 2017 Solution Tree Press • SolutionTree.com
Visit **go.SolutionTree.com/instruction** to download this free reproducible.

	1 **SIGNIFICANT REVISION NEEDED**	**2** **SOME REVISION NEEDED**	**3** **PROFICIENT**	**4** **EXCEEDS EXPECTATIONS**
Objective 2: Students will analyze cost efficiency by calculating the amount of materials used and finding the final cost of building their bridge.	Calculation chart is missing or included with many errors. Group comparison chart is missing or included with many errors.	Calculation chart is included with several errors. Group comparison chart is included with few errors.	Calculation chart is included with only minor errors. Group comparison chart is included with no errors.	Calculation chart is included with no errors. Group comparison chart is included with no errors.
	Bar graph is missing or completely incorrect. Written analysis is missing or irrelevant.	Bar graph is included with many errors. Written analysis is included with some support from the data in the comparison chart.	Bar graph is included with only minor errors. Written analysis is included with adequate support from the data in the comparison chart.	Bar graph is included with no errors. Written analysis is included with clear support from the data in the comparison chart.

Sample Student Work

Visit http://bit.ly/2bWjq6G (jnisse1, n.d.) for an example of student work.

Sticky Situation Project Organizer

Use the following area to sketch your ideas for building a model bridge.

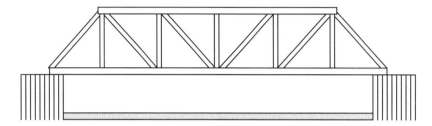

Use the chart to document how many materials you use to create the model. Calculate the total cost.

Team number:	3	Team name:	Dolphins
ITEM	**AMOUNT NEEDED**	**PRICE OF ITEM**	**TOTAL COST**
Large marshmallows	18	x $4	$72
Small marshmallows	18	x $2	$36
Toothpicks	50	x $1	$50
Glue container	1	x $2	$2
Popsicle sticks	5	x $4	$20
Total cost:			$180

Testing the Bridge and Analysis Worksheet

Objective: Students will test the bridge to see how much weight their bridge is able to hold before breaking.

Use this chart to record the number of area tiles your model can hold.

RESULTS	
Number of Area Tiles (Tallies)	卌 卌 卌 卌
Pounds the Bridge Can Hold	

After you have tested your bridge, write an analysis of your experiment. Think about ways that you could decrease the pressure of gravity on your bridge. Reflect on the positive aspects of your bridge and areas for improvement. Record your explanation here.

Comparison Chart

Use this chart to compare and contrast the groups' spending and bridge strength.

GROUP NUMBER	AMOUNT SPENT	AMOUNT OF WEIGHT BEFORE COLLAPSING (IN GRAMS)	OVERALL PLACE: STRENGTH	OVERALL PLACE: COST
1	$150	100	2	2
2	$135	75	4	4
3	$140	86	3	3
4	$164	138	1	1
5	$82	33	5	5

Compare and contrast every group's data to your own data. (How much money did each group spend in comparison to how much weight total its bridge was able to hold? Look for connections and such.) Use this information to create a bar graph using Google Sheets or Microsoft Excel.

Use the following directions:

1. Create a bar graph that shows each group's cost compared to the strength of its bridge.
2. Transfer the data from your recording sheet to Google Sheets or Microsoft Excel.
3. In Excel or Sheets, choose Insert and Chart. Choose the Double Bar Graph option.

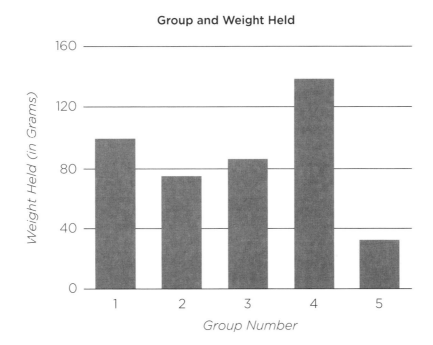

Mathematics Projects

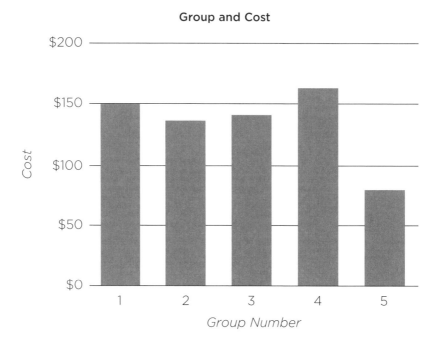

Create Excellence Framework Rating

CREATE ANALYSIS		
CREATE COMPONENT	**LEVEL**	**JUSTIFICATION**
Real-World Learning	3: Investigating	Students assume the role of a civil engineer.
Cognitive Complexity	4: Integrating	Students have to design and build a bridge that they feel will support the most weight. They ask guiding questions within their engineering team to help lead their group to the best bridge model. At the end, they critique their bridge construction.
Student Engagement	3: Investigating	Each team has the choice of what materials it will use to build its bridge. Students are working in teams to design their bridge.
Technology Integration	3: Investigating	The technology is an add-on; however, they are using several types within the project. They create a Prezi or Glogster presentation to showcase the information.

AUCTION YOUR ITEMS!

Source: Adapted from Rebecca Stobaugh and Marge Maxwell. Edited by Savannah Denning. Used with permission.

Content: Mathematics

Learning Objectives:

1. Students will use subtraction to make purchases during a classroom auction.
2. Students will examine the principles of supply and demand in action.

Standards:

Common Core mathematics—

- 2.OA.B.2 Fluently add and subtract within 20 using mental strategies. By end of Grade 2, know from memory all sums of two one-digit numbers (NGA & CCSSO, 2010b).
- 2.MD.C.8 Solve word problems involving dollar bills, quarters, dimes, nickels, and pennies, using $ and ¢ symbols appropriately. Example: If you have 2 dimes and 3 pennies, how many cents do you have (NGA & CCSSO, 2010b)?

C3 Framework for Social Studies State Standards—

- D2.Eco.2.K–2 Identify the benefits and costs of making various personal decisions (NCSS, 2013).

Project Options: A teacher could provide objects for the auction instead of students bringing them.

Resources Needed: Devices for small-group use, computer with Internet access and online spreadsheet in Google Sheets or Microsoft Excel, $20 in classroom money, note cards, paper, writing utensils, and items to auction. Possible items to auction include school supplies, food treats, and reward coupons (like for extra recess and homework passes).

Auction Your Items!

Grab your prized possessions and get ready to make some money! It is time to participate in an auction! Be sure to stay on your toes and watch for opportunities to outbid the people around you. Being alert is the key to getting a good deal at an auction.

Project Tasks

1. Bring two objects to sell in the auction.

2. Each person will be given $20 in classroom money. You will have ten minutes to view the items that will be up for auction. You will be able to buy up to two items. Each student will be given a note card with a number to raise when he or she would like to bid.

3. During the auction, I (the teacher) will show the item for purchase. I will start the bidding at $1. I then will continually raise the price a dollar until there are no more buyers. If no one else raises his or her hand for the next-higher price, then the student who bid the highest price will get the item. If the price goes to $20, the first card up when the price is called will receive the object for sale.

4. After each purchase, the buyer will pay me. Classmates should record in their chart the student's name, the item, and the subtraction equation, and complete the column showing the money left on the "Auction Calculation Chart."

5. In small groups, students will use the chart to graph the price of the items the classmates sold by using the National Center for Education Statistics bar graph—http://bit.ly/2emEVQf.

   ◆ On the website, select Bar Graph.
   ◆ Select the Data tab; give the graph the title "Auction Price." Label the x-axis as "Item" and the y-axis as "Price." Count up the number of items sold. Enter that number in the Data Set drop-down menu Items box.

6. Next, type in the name of the items sold under the Item Label heading. Under the Value column, list each item's price. In the Min-Value box, put 0; in the Max-Value box, put 20.

   ◆ Select the Preview tab, and review your work.
   ◆ On the Print/Save tab, print your bar graph.

7. Groups will answer the following questions.

   ◆ What are two or more factors that caused you to buy the item?
   ◆ How did you set the price of your item?
   ◆ What items sold for a low price? Why do you think that happened?
   ◆ What items sold for a high price? Why do you think that happened?

Real-World Learning Framework for Elementary Schools © 2017 Solution Tree Press • SolutionTree.com
Visit **go.SolutionTree.com/instruction** to download this free reproducible.

Auction Calculation Chart

STUDENT'S NAME	ITEM PURCHASE 1	EQUATION	MONEY LEFT	ITEM PURCHASE 2	EQUATION	MONEY LEFT

Mastery Checklist

LEARNING OBJECTIVE	MASTERY CHECKLIST
Students will use subtraction to make purchases during a classroom auction.	☐ Correctly completes the chart applying their subtraction skills
Students will examine the principles of supply and demand in action.	☐ Draws logical conclusions about how supply and demand impacted the price

Scoring Rubric

	1 SIGNIFICANT REVISION NEEDED	2 SOME REVISION NEEDED	3 PROFICIENT	4 EXCEEDS EXPECTATIONS
Objective 1: Students will use subtraction to make purchases during a classroom auction.	Students are not able to use subtraction to make purchases during a classroom auction.	Students make many errors as they use subtraction to make purchases during a classroom auction.	Students make very few errors as they use subtraction to make purchases during a classroom auction.	Students are able to use subtraction, error-free, to make purchases during a classroom auction.
Objective 2: Students will examine the principles of supply and demand in action.	Students are not able to discuss the principles of supply and demand.	Students are somewhat able to discuss the principles of supply and demand.	Students adequately discuss the principles of supply and demand.	Students clearly and accurately discuss the principles of supply and demand.

page 2 of 2

Sample Student Work

The following chart shows calculations for the students in a sample class.

Auction Calculation Chart

STUDENT'S NAME	ITEM PURCHASE 1	EQUATION	MONEY LEFT	ITEM PURCHASE 2	EQUATION	MONEY LEFT
Ainsley	$15	20 − 15 = 5	$5	$3	5 − 3 = 2	$2
Sarai	$20	20 − 20 = 0	$0	n/a	n/a	$0
Parker	$2	20 − 2 = 18	$18	$5	18 − 5 = 13	$13
Alex	$16	20 − 16 = 4	$4	$4	4 − 4 = 0	$0
Frederick	$18	20 − 18 = 2	$2	$2	2 − 2 = 0	$0
David	$19	20 − 19 = 1	$1	$1	1 − 1 = 0	$0
Patty	$8	20 − 8 = 12	$12	$11	12 − 11 = 1	$1
Suni	$10	20 − 10 = 10	$10	$8	10 − 8 = 2	$2
Jerome	$7	20 − 7 = 13	$13	$10	13 − 10 = 3	$3

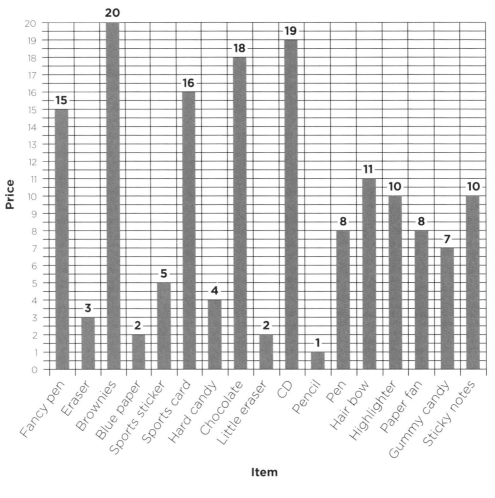

Auction Price

The following sample of student work matches the questions from the seventh step of the project.

- **What are two or more factors that caused you to buy the item?** We each bought things that we liked. If the starting price was low, then we were more likely to bid on an item.
- **How did you set the price of your item?** We set a low price on our items so everyone could bid on them.
- **What items sold for a low price? Why do you think that happened?** The pencil sold for $1. We all have pencils, so not many people wanted to bid on that item.
- **What items sold for a high price? Why do you think that happened?** The pan of brownies was sold for $20. It was right before lunch, and we were all hungry. Also, they had sprinkles on them. They looked very yummy.

Create Excellence Framework Rating

CREATE ANALYSIS		
CREATE COMPONENT	**LEVEL**	**JUSTIFICATION**
Real-World Learning	3: Investigating	This task is at the Investigating level. The learning simulates a real-world event, as students are participating in a live auction.
Cognitive Complexity	3: Investigating	The teacher directs student interaction with the content or standard. Students are working at high levels of thinking, at Bloom's Analyze level.
Student Engagement	3: Investigating	Students have choice in this task in the items they bring to auction and the items they purchase. Students' buying choices are their interests' influence.
Technology Integration	3: Investigating	Students must use technology to complete this project after the live auction is complete. Students use technology to create a visual model of the auction and analyze and evaluate the auction's trends and patterns.

WHAT IS YOUR OPINION?

Source: Adapted from Marge Maxwell and Rebecca Stobaugh. Edited by Savannah Denning. Used with permission.

Content: Mathematics

Learning Objectives:

1. Students will analyze student opinions about a school issue.
2. Students will use digital tools to create and administer a survey, incorporating fraction concepts.

Standards:

Common Core mathematics—

- 4.NF.C.5 Express a fraction with a denominator 10 as an equivalent fraction with denominator 100, and use this technique to add two fractions with respective denominators 10 and 100 (NGA & CCSSO, 2010b).
- 4.NF.C.7 Compare two decimals to hundredths by reasoning about their size. Recognize that comparisons are valid only when the two decimals refer to the same whole. Record the results of comparisons with symbols >, =, or <, and justify the conclusions (NGA & CCSSO, 2010b).

Project Options:

- Students will replicate the survey process while investigating a community issue.
- Have each student group review another group's survey and calculations. Ask, "How accurate do you think its results and analyses are? Explain. What recommendations would you have for this group?"
- Have the class repeat the survey but gather data from another class at your grade level. Let the students determine if the results are the same and explain them.

Resources Needed: Portable tablets with Internet access; Google Forms

What Is Your Opinion?

Have you ever wondered how polls are done? How do they calculate that 70 percent of Americans like a certain food or type of car? Do they ask every single person in America? No, they use a polling percentage or a sample (part of the population). Groups of students in your class will create their own poll, ask students around your classroom about their opinion on a specific school issue, and then predict the percentage of student opinions about that issue at your school.

Project Tasks

Decide on a school issue to gather data about.

1. I (your teacher) will divide the class into small groups of two to four students.

2. Your group will discuss issues around your school for which you would like to get opinions from your classmates. Possible school issues could include a new club for your school, a new enrichment class, new playground equipment, what new technology you would like, or new classroom materials your classmates would like.

3. Your group will create a survey in Google Forms (www.google.com/forms). You will have ten students in your class answer your survey. Record the issue that your group decided to poll on the following line.

_____

4. Discuss this issue in your group. Decide on a question and possible choices for this issue, and record them. You should record four to seven choices. Consider the following example about the purchase of iPad apps. The sample group has a $25 iTunes card that was donated to it.

    Question: What iPad apps do you think we should purchase with our $25? Select your top three choices.

    a. Explain Everything—$4.99
    b. Docs to Go—$14.95
    c. Explore Hawaii Volcanoes—$2.99
    d. iBiology4Kids—$4.99
    e. World Atlas HD—$1.99
    f. Quick Graph+—$1.99
    g. GarageBand—$4.99

5. Fill in the "Student Issue Worksheet" (page 220) to create your own question.

6. Show these questions and choice options to me for approval or possible revision.

Now use Google Forms to create your survey.

1. View one of the following tutorials to learn more about Google Forms.

    ◆ Google Forms tutorial (Gilbert, 2009): www.youtube.com/watch?v=WMXgutYKMgk

    ◆ Google Forms for the classroom (O'Byrne, 2011): www.youtube.com/watch?v =AeiDxeLVvuQ

2. I can log in to Google Drive (www.google.com/drive) for you. Your group will create a new form for your survey.

3. Now you can look at your trial results.

4. Decide how you will have classmates take the survey.

    ◆ The easiest way would be to open the survey on an iPad, an iPod Touch, or any other tablet device that is connected to the Internet. Your group will only need one device. It will only take a few seconds for each of ten of your classmates to answer your survey question. Click "Submit another response" before you give the device to another student.

    ◆ You could print ten copies of your survey question to give to ten other students. But if you do this, your group will have to type all ten responses into Google Forms.

Now you are ready to launch your survey! In other words, have classmates complete your survey.

1. Go give the survey to ten of your classmates. Have fun with it!

2. Check your responses in the Google spreadsheet.

Print the results from your survey spreadsheet and the summary graphs. Each group will meet and write its responses to the following questions.

1. How accurate do you think your survey results are? In other words, do you think the survey results really represent or explain what students in your class think about your school issue? Explain.

2. Calculate the mean, median, and mode for your question.

3. How could your group have improved your survey question? Explain.

4. What conclusions can you draw from your survey results?

5. To represent the data in fractions, put your answers in the "Survey Results Chart" (page 220).

    ◆ Take the result for each option of your survey question and write it as a fraction. For example, if 5 people selected option 1 and 10 classmates took your survey, then your fraction is $\frac{5}{10}$.

    ◆ Now, create an equivalent fraction with a denominator of 100. For example, $\frac{5}{10}$ is equivalent to $\frac{50}{100}$.

6. Put your answers in the "Survey Results Chart" (page 220) to represent the data as decimals. Take each fraction that has the denominator of 100 and convert it to a decimal. For example, $\frac{50}{100}$ equals 0.50.

Student Issue Worksheet

Names of group members: _____

School or class issue: _____

1. List the survey question you will ask: _____

2. Record six answers the survey takers will choose from.

    a. _____

    b. _____

    c. _____

    d. _____

    e. _____

    f. _____

Survey Results Chart

SURVEY QUESTION OPTIONS	RESULTS	FRACTION WITH 10 AS DENOMINATOR	FRACTION WITH 100 AS DENOMINATOR	DECIMAL

Scoring Rubric

	1 SIGNIFICANT REVISION NEEDED	2 SOME REVISION NEEDED	3 PROFICIENT	4 EXCEEDS EXPECTATIONS
Objective 1: Students will analyze opinions about a school issue.	Analysis of student opinions was incomplete. Responses are not connected to survey results.	Analysis of student opinions was incomplete or illogical. There is a weak connection between conclusions and results.	Analysis of student opinions was adequate and logical. There is a connection between conclusions and results.	Analysis of student opinions was comprehensive and logical. There is a clear connection between conclusions and results.
Objective 2: Students will use digital tools to create and administer a survey, incorporating fraction concepts.	Survey questions and options are missing or unrelated to the assigned school issue. Very few students took the survey. Students accurately used fraction concepts to analyze survey data with several mistakes.	Survey questions and options are missing some important elements. Surveys were given to a few other students. Students used fraction concepts to analyze survey data with some minor mistakes.	Students put thought and insight into deciding on the school issue with some assistance from the teacher. Survey questions and options are adequate. All students in the group gave surveys to other students. Students accurately used fraction concepts to analyze survey data.	Students put considerable thought and insight into deciding on the school issue with no assistance from the teacher. Survey questions and options are comprehensive and perceptive. All students in the group gave surveys to other students. Students accurately used fraction concepts to analyze survey data.

Sources: Gilbert, 2009; O'Byrne, 2011.

Sample Student Work

The following is the completed "Student Issue Worksheet" from the sample group first introduced in the project task.

Student Issue Worksheet

Names of group members: <u>Sam, Devi, Jordan, Kosal</u>

School or class issue: <u>"iPad Apps We Should Purchase" (Our class had a $25 iTunes card donation.)</u>

1. List the survey question you will ask: <u>What iPad apps do you think we should purchase with our $25? Select your top three choices.</u>

2. Record six answers the survey takers will choose from.

   a. <u>Explain Everything-$4.99</u>

   b. <u>Docs to Go-$14.95</u>

   c. <u>Explore Hawaii Volcanoes-$2.99</u>

   d. <u>iBiology4Kids-$4.99</u>

   e. <u>World Atlas HD-$1.99</u>

   f. <u>Quick Graph+-$1.99</u>

   g. <u>GarageBand-$4.99</u>

Survey Results

1. Print the results from your survey spreadsheet and the summary graphs.

Survey Respondent	Time Stamp	What iPad apps do you think we should purchase with our $25? Select your top three choices.
1	10/30/2012 14:55:27	1. Explain Everything—$4.99; 4. iBiology4Kids—$4.99; 7. GarageBand—$4.99
2	10/30/2012 14:55:42	2. Docs to Go—$14.95; 5. World Atlas HD—$1.99; 6. Quick Graph+—$1.99
3	10/30/2012 14:55:52	1. Explain Everything—$4.99; 5. World Atlas HD—$1.99; 7. GarageBand—$4.99
4	10/30/2012 14:56:05	4. iBiology4Kids—$4.99; 5. World Atlas HD—$1.99; 6. Quick Graph+—$1.99
5	10/30/2012 14:56:16	1. Explain Everything—$4.99; 2. Docs to Go—$14.95; 3. Explore Hawaii Volcanoes—$2.99

6	10/30/2012 14:56:26	5. World Atlas HD—$1.99; 6. Quick Graph+—$1.99; 7. GarageBand—$4.99
7	10/30/2012 14:56:38	1. Explain Everything—$4.99; 5. World Atlas HD—$1.99; 7. GarageBand—$4.99
8	10/30/2012 14:57:22	1. Explain Everything—$4.99; 4. iBiology4Kids—$4.99; 7. GarageBand—$4.99
9	10/30/2012 14:59:44	1. Explain Everything—$4.99; 3. Explore Hawaii Volcanoes—$2.99; 7. GarageBand—$4.99

Summary: See complete responses.

What iPad apps do you think we should purchase with our $25?

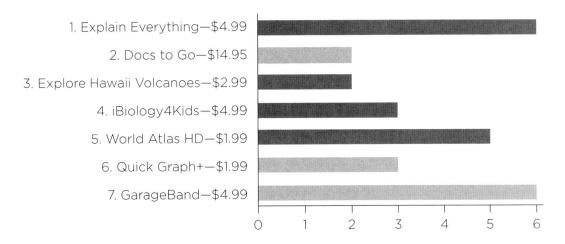

1. Explain Everything—$4.99	**6**	67%
2. Docs to Go—$14.95	**2**	22%
3. Explore Hawaii Volcanoes—$2.99	**2**	22%
4. iBiology4Kids—$4.99	**3**	33%
5. World Atlas HD—$1.99	**5**	58%
6. Quick Graph+—$1.99	**3**	33%
7. GarageBand—$4.99	**6**	67%
People may select more than one checkbox, so percentages may add up to more than 100%.		

Mathematics Projects

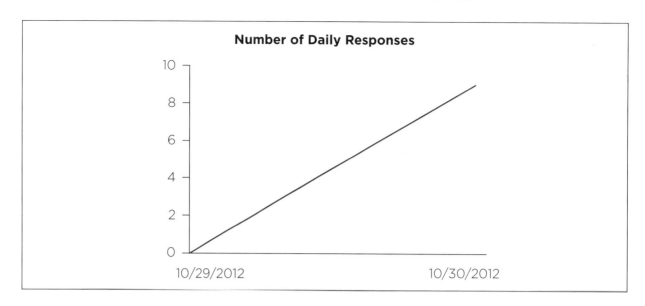

2. How accurate do you think your survey results are? In other words, do you think the survey results really represent or explain what students in your class think about your school issue? Explain.

I think that the results of our survey question are good. I think it shows what people think in our class.

3. Calculate the mean, median, and mode for your question.

Mean = 3.9; median = 3; mode is a tie between 2, 3, and 6.

4. How could your group have improved your survey question? Explain.

We could have looked up on the Internet what apps most other fourth-grade students like. We could have asked other people in our class what apps they like. We could have asked our librarian and other fourth-grade teachers what apps they like. Then we could have made better choices of apps to put in our question.

5. What conclusions can you draw from your survey results?

The three most popular apps were Explain Everything, GarageBand, and World Atlas HD.

Survey Results Chart

SURVEY QUESTION OPTIONS	RESULTS	FRACTION WITH 10 AS DENOMINATOR	FRACTION WITH 100 AS DENOMINATOR	DECIMAL
1. Explain Everything—$4.99	6	$6/10$	$60/100$	0.60
2. Docs to Go—$14.95	2	$2/10$	$20/100$	0.20
3. Explore Hawaii Volcanoes—$2.99	2	$2/10$	$20/100$	0.20
4. iBiology4Kids—$4.99	3	$3/10$	$30/100$	0.30
5. World Atlas HD—$1.99	5	$5/10$	$50/100$	0.50
6. Quick Graph+—$1.99	3	$3/10$	$30/100$	0.30
7. GarageBand—$4.99	6	$6/10$	$60/100$	0.60

Create Excellence Framework Rating

CREATE ANALYSIS		
CREATE COMPONENT	**LEVEL**	**JUSTIFICATION**
Real-World Learning	4: Integrating	In this project, learning impacts the classroom, school, and community as students solve an issue for the classroom. Learning is integrated across many subject areas.
Cognitive Complexity	4: Integrating	Students generate their own questions or issues to solve or work with during this project. Students are analyzing data, making evaluations, critiquing their own work, and creating surveys to address schoolwide issues.
Student Engagement	3: Investigating	Students have choice in this project, as they make decisions about schoolwide issues they would like to address. The task is differentiated based on student interests.
Technology Integration	4: Integrating	Student technology use is embedded in content and essential to project completion. The use of digital tools makes collaboration among students and teacher possible. Technology in this project also allows students to tackle issues that they could not have effectively addressed without digital tools. Students use high levels of thinking to solve these authentic issues.

Mathematics Projects

START YOUR OWN BUSINESS!

Source: Adapted from Lena White and Kelli Ralston. Used with permission.

Content: Social studies

Learning Objectives:

1. Students will create a business plan for their own business for the school fair.
2. Students will use web 2.0 tools to create a multimedia presentation advertising their business and product.

Standards:

C3 Framework for Social Studies State Standards—

- D2.Eco.2.K–2 Identify the benefits and costs of making various personal decisions (NCSS, 2013).
- D2.Eco.3.K–2 Describe the skills and knowledge required to produce certain goods and services (NCSS, 2013).

Project Options: Students will be able to use web tools that appeal to them. For instance, students who are more visually oriented may choose to use Animoto over Prezi. They may opt to use many different web 2.0 tools that work best with their choice of business. There is also opportunity to do the plan and project as a group, not just individually.

Resources Needed: This is an extensive list of options; not all are necessary to the project.

- Google Docs—Students can use this to work on their business template. Teachers and students can use Google Docs to comment, edit, and track changes of the business plan.
- Web 2.0 tools, such as Prezi, Animoto, or PowToon—These tools allow you to create your own movie or slide show using graphics, video, pictures, and text.
- Classroom Clipart—This is a great source for adding pictures to your presentation.
- Pics4Learning—This is another great source for photographs to use. The photos are listed by categories.
- Biz Kid$'s (n.d.) "Guide to Writing a Business Plan" (http://bizkids.com/wp/wp-content/uploads/Kids-Business-Plan.pdf)—This is a fantastic template for your business. Easy and simple, it will help you remember to include all the important steps!

Start Your Own Business!

After reading *Amelia Bedelia Means Business* (Parish, 2013) and discussing her efforts to raise money to buy a bike, we will brainstorm potential businesses for all the students in our class. It will be your task to create a business that can be successful and make money! After setting up your business, we will have a fair set up where you will get to advertise and sell items you make!

Project Tasks

1. Brainstorm! Discuss possible things you could sell with your partner. Remember to keep your costs low so the profit will be high. This should be completed and approved before you begin your project. Complete the "Business Plan Template" for step-by-step directions on creating your business plan.

2. Advertise! Once you have created a business plan that explains how you can be successful, you will advertise your product in a multimedia presentation using technology tools (web 2.0 tools, video, or a blog). Check out the resource list for ideas on tools that you can use. We will show your advertisements to our entire grade. Checklist for advertisement:

   ☐ One catchy quote or slogan that describes what you are selling
   ☐ A creative business name that is large and colorful
   ☐ At least four images
   ☐ Plenty of color
   ☐ The price
   ☐ Two reasons why someone should buy your item
   ☐ Information that makes people want to buy what you are selling

3. Produce! Make your product. You will need to decide how much of the product to make.

4. Set up! Gather items to decorate your table informing customers of your product and its price.

5. Sell! As students enter the classroom, you will need to be prepared to sell. The more you sell, the more money you will make.

6. Win! Whoever has the most profit wins.

7. Follow the guidelines! Use the rubric as you complete each step of your assignment. It gives details about your business plan as well as how to format the presentation. This will allow you to get the most points possible.

Business Plan Template

In order to increase collaboration among students and the teacher, this template can be copied into Google Docs, where students can then work to complete it with increased collaboration and immediate feedback from the teacher and peers.

Business name: Be creative, and make it grab people's attention!

1. The big idea: What is your business idea? What are you going to sell?

_____

_____

_____

_____

2. Skills and knowledge: List at least three skills that you must have or three things that you must know to create and sell your item.

_____

_____

_____

3. Marketing:

   ▲ Who is going to buy your product or service?

   ▲ How will you advertise (spread the word about) your business?

   ▲ What will you include in your presentation to grab people's attention and make them want to buy your item?

4. Costs and benefits: Businesses are started to make profit. Profit is the amount of money you earn from a business, after all its expenses are paid.

   ▲ Start-up costs: In order to begin your business, what amount of money will you need, and what will you spend that money on?

   ▲ Cost per unit: How much money will it cost for each item that you are making?

Real-World Learning Framework for Elementary Schools © 2017 Solution Tree Press • SolutionTree.com
Visit **go.SolutionTree.com/instruction** to download this free reproducible.

▲ Price per unit: How much money will you charge someone for buying your item? You will want to make this amount bigger than the cost per unit so that you make a profit.

▲ Profit: How much money will you make for each item sold? Subtract the cost per unit from the price per unit to find your profit.

5. Potential for success: In one complete paragraph (three to five sentences), explain why you think this business will be successful. Explain why your item will sell the most.

_____

_____

_____

_____

_____

Scoring Rubric

Acceptable student performance is level 3 or higher.

Objective 1: Students will create a business plan for their own business for the school fair.				
	1 **SIGNIFICANT REVISION NEEDED**	**2** **SOME REVISION NEEDED**	**3** **PROFICIENT**	**4** **EXCEEDS EXPECTATIONS**
Content	Provides a short, illogical plan Describes illogical coherence of the business plan's elements Contains six or more grammatical errors	Includes a brief analysis of the pieces of the business plan; many elements missing Describes poor coherence from one section of the business plan to another Some parts of the plan are not logical and do not fit Contains three to five grammatical errors	Has a logical analysis of most of the business plan's elements Includes an adequate description of the business idea, skills and knowledge, marketing, costs and benefits, and the business's potential for success Demonstrates understanding of most elements of a successful business plan Contains one or two grammatical errors	Has a logical, detailed analysis of all the business plan's elements Includes a detailed description of the business idea, skills and knowledge, marketing, costs and benefits, and the business's potential for success Demonstrates coherent, logical description of all elements of the business plan and how to be successful Contains no grammatical errors

Objective 2: Students will use web 2.0 tools to create a multimedia presentation advertising their business and product.

	1 SIGNIFICANT REVISION NEEDED	2 SOME REVISION NEEDED	3 PROFICIENT	4 EXCEEDS EXPECTATIONS
Advertisement or Presentation	Gives short, illogical advertisement	Has a brief advertisement; doesn't clearly explain the business	Has a persuasive advertisement; advertisement covers the entire business and explains it clearly Answers questions readily during the fair	Has a persuasive advertisement; advertisement covers the entire business and explains it clearly and completely Answers questions from peers during the fair

Sources: Biz Kid$, n.d.; Parish, 2013.

Sample Student Work

Prior to creating their multimedia presentation, the students will need to turn in a business plan template to ensure that all the elements of a plan are included. The teacher will be looking to see that it is a reasonable plan, they have found at least one person in their field who can give them guidance, and they have a projected future with possibility of a profit. Following is a sample of a completed template that is expected.

Business Plan Template

Business name: Krazy Kreations

1. The big idea: What is your business idea? What are you going to sell?

   My friend and I received kits at Christmas for knitting. We think we could make cool hats, scarves, and other knitted items to sell. We have surveyed fellow students, and the majority of the students we asked were interested in buying products like these if they are good quality and affordable. We know someone who is excellent at knitting, and she has agreed to help us and show us how to use patterns so that we can make interesting items.

2. Skills and knowledge: List at least three skills that you must have or three things that you must know to create and sell your item.

   a. We must learn how to knit different items; my aunt will help us do this.

   b. We must figure out how to advertise our products.

   c. We must learn how to divide up work evenly among the team.

3. Marketing:

   ◆ Who is going to buy your product or service?

   We can sell to friends at school or even teachers and parents.

   ◆ How will you advertise (spread the word about) your business?

   We will make flyers and hang them around school; we can ask our teachers to put it in the class newsletters; we can even ask if we can tell about our business on the morning announcements. There are many web 2.0 tools that we can use to create unique brochures and ads. We could use Animoto to create a commercial. We will show the commercial during computer lab time and send a link to our commercial to other teachers and ask them to show their classes, as well. There are lots of tools that we can use to make colorful advertisements to hang up around the school. Venngage is a tool that we are using in English language arts, and we can use it to make a brochure showing examples of our products and costs. We could also include quotations from our first customers about how great our products are.

- What will you include in your presentation to grab people's attention and make them want to buy your item?

  <u>Lots of color and pictures of knitted scarves and hats. We will include information about the knitted items and how they are made. Persuasive words will be used. When people come around to our booth, we will allow them to feel the knitted items and try them on for themselves.</u>

4. Costs and benefits: Businesses are started to make profit. Profit is the amount of money you earn from a business, after all its expenses are paid.

   - Start-up costs: In order to begin your business, what amount of money will you need, and what will you spend that money on?

     <u>$0. Our parents gave us the kits and supplies as a gift.</u>

   - Cost per unit: How much money will it cost for each item that you are making?

     <u>This will vary depending on the item—between $2 and $5. Most of the yarn is inexpensive and we have enough to make at least ten products before we have to buy more. We could sell more expensive items with some of the fancier yarns that cost a little more. Since we have so much yarn, most of the cost in the beginning will only be our time. We will have to practice to get faster at making things so that we can make more money.</u>

   - Price per unit: How much money will you charge someone for buying your item? You will want to make this amount bigger than the cost per unit so that you make a profit.

     <u>We will sell the smaller items for $5 and the more expensive ones for $10. If we sell any made from more expensive yarn, we will add the additional cost of the yarn to each product. We think these will be popular because many of these will look trendy and people will pay more for them.</u>

   - Profit: How much money will you make for each item sold? Subtract the cost per unit from the price per unit to find your profit:

     <u>$10 or $5 minus $5 or $2 = between $3 and $5.</u>

5. Potential for success: In one complete paragraph (three to five sentences), explain why you think this business will be successful. Explain why your item will sell the most.

   <u>We believe that this can be a great business for us. We can use the profits to buy more supplies, and our aunt is going to help us learn how to knit really cool pieces. Our friends will love it, and we hope we can keep getting new customers from other classes or families.</u>

Visit http://bit.ly/2chzCPL (Ralston, 2016) to access an example related to the sample business plan.

Social Studies Projects

Create Excellence Framework Rating

CREATE ANALYSIS		
CREATE COMPONENT	**LEVEL**	**JUSTIFICATION**
Real-World Learning	4: Integrating	The students are creating a business to sell a product at their school fair.
Cognitive Complexity	4: Integrating	Students are choosing and creating original projects. They are responsible for evaluating their own business plan and planning and producing the final product. Because they are required to present a business plan that could work, students have to use a higher level of cognitive complexity to ensure that they have planned and evaluated each step of creating a business.
Student Engagement	3: Investigating	Students choose their business based on interest and ability. The task can be presented in multiple ways, which the students choose, so that it is able to be differentiated for each student.
Technology Integration	3: Investigating	Students could create a business plan without technology, so it is an add-on; they use technology at the Create level of Bloom's revised taxonomy.

JUNIOR ARCHAEOLOGISTS AT WORK

Source: Adapted from Stephanie Ross. Used with permission.

Content: Social studies

Learning Objectives:

1. After completing a role-playing activity on identifying and inferring the use of Mayan artifacts, students will critique another group's results using the principle of analogy as their criteria.
2. Students will create a video critiquing the results of another group based on the principle of analogy and watch it in class.

Standards:

C3 Framework for Social Studies State Standards—

*   D2.His.2.3–5 Compare life in specific historical time periods to life today (NCSS, 2013).
*   D2.His.11.3–5 Infer the intended audience and purpose of a historical source from information within the source itself (NCSS, 2013).

Common Core English language arts—

*   SL.3.1 Engage effectively in a range of collaborative discussions (one-on-one, in groups, and teacher-led) with diverse partners on grade 3 topics and text, building on other's ideas and expressing their own clearly (NGA & CCSSO, 2010a).
*   W.3.1 Write opinion pieces on topics or text, supporting a point of view with reasons (NGA & CCSSO, 2010a).

International Society for Technology in Education—

*   6c Students communicate complex ideas clearly and effectively by creating or using a variety of digital objects such as visualizations, models or simulations (ISTE, 2016).
*   6d Students publish or present content that customizes the message and medium for their intended audiences (ISTE, 2016).

Project Options: Students have the discretion to choose which role fits them best within their group collaboration. They can also choose the order in which they wish to identify and interpret the artifacts in each dig box. Students can decide how to portray themselves as junior archaeologists for their video critique. Students can be as creative as they want during the filming of their critique as long as all criteria are met with the project. Finally, students can edit the video to display their own originality and creativity.

Resources Needed:

*   Introduction to archaeology video—http://bit.ly/2cbfnQk (Ross, 2015a)
*   Mayan digital story—http://bit.ly/2cBFkJe (Ross, 2015b)
*   Handheld camcorder
*   Windows Movie Maker tutorial—www.youtube.com/watch?v=LYU2UjnVPV8&feature=youtu.be (Ross, 2016)
*   Classroom or laptop computers
*   Dig boxes with pictures of artifacts
*   Links to sample artifacts for the dig boxes:
    *   http://bit.ly/2chzGPn—A picture of an ancient Mayan calendar
    *   www.tumblr.com/search/mayan%20artifacts—A pre-Columbian terracotta cyclindrical vessel

- www.loc.gov/exhibits/exploring-the-early-americas/recording-history.html—A stone artifact with incised hieroglyphs that may have been used in a Mayan ballgame
- www.metmuseum.org/toah/works-of-art/1978.412.195—An ancient Mayan scepter used on top of a staff for symbolism of status
- http://bit.ly/2d3tmg6—A decorative utensil
- http://bit.ly/2cYwlrd—An ancient Mayan toy
- http://bit.ly/2cMlwrz—A mano and metate used to grind corn by Mayans
- http://bit.ly/2cqzx9T—A cacao pot used for storing liquids
- www.ancientresource.com/lots/precolumbian/mayan_artifacts.html—An ancient Mayan necklace made from ceramic beads
- www.authenticmaya.com/maya_warfare.htm—A Mayan ax head

Junior Archaeologists at Work

Today, you all get to become junior archaeologists! You will learn about who archaeologists are and what they do. Many of you may already know what artifacts are, but you will get to work in groups at your own dig sites and uncover artifacts. When archaeologists uncover an artifact, they have methods to identify the artifact and to infer the artifact's use within the culture it came from. You, as junior archaeologists, will be identifying and inferring the use of Mayan artifacts. As archaeologists, you will be presenting critiques of your fellow archaeologists' findings at a national archaeology convention that we will hold right here at our school!

Project Tasks

1. Decide on the roles for group members. Complete the "Roles for Group Work Form" (page 238).

   ◆ Each group will have a dig box with ten artifacts in it. The dig box will simulate a real-world experience similar to how archaeologists excavate artifacts. As junior archaeologists, you will choose five out of the ten artifacts to excavate. Look carefully at each artifact and discuss its features. Complete all sections of the "Identification and Inference of Use Worksheet" (page 238) as a group.

   ◆ When you are finished, trade your worksheet with another group. Critique the other group's modern-day example. Complete a "Critique Worksheet" (page 239). Please complete all sections of the worksheet as a group. See the "Word Bank and Vocabulary Sheet" (page 240) for your critique.

2. Practice recording your video. If needed, create a script that the actor can read. When recording your video, remember you are role-playing as an archaeologist presenting your critique at a national or provincial conference. Announce your group name and the group name of whom you are critiquing. Use the artifact pictures as props during your critique.

3. Transfer the video file to the computer. Use Windows Movie Maker to edit, add a title, and add a credits page. Visit www.youtube.com/watch?v=LYU2UjnVPV8&feature=youtu.be (Ross, 2016) to access a tutorial on Windows Movie Maker. (Visit **go.SolutionTree.com/instruction** to access live links to the websites mentioned in this book.)

4. Now it's time for our junior archaeologist convention. Let's set up the classroom for the video presentations. Bring out the popcorn.

5. After listening to your fellow archaeologists' presentations, prepare at least one question you have about the junior archaeologists' conclusions.

Roles for Group Work Form

Group name: _____

Writer: _____

Task manager: _____

Video speaker or actor: _____

Cameraperson: _____

Technology specialist: _____

Identification and Inference of Use Worksheet

Directions: Use this chart to identify and infer each artifact's use in your dig box.

ARTIFACT NUMBER	MATERIAL ARTIFACT IS MADE OF	ARTIFACT DESCRIPTION	ARTIFACT'S PURPOSE	MODERN EXAMPLE OF THIS TYPE OF ARTIFACT
1				
2				
3				
4				
5				

Critique Worksheet

Critique of _____ group by _____ group.

Directions: Use this chart to critique the results of another group using the principle of analogy as your criteria. Remember, the principle of analogy states that the identity of unknown items may be inferred from those that are known. In other words, you can infer the identity of an artifact by comparing it to a modern-day artifact that has very similar features (Ashmore & Sharer, 1993). In your critique, decide if the group's identification and inference of the Mayan tool is correct. Is it a logical conclusion or comparison of today's tools? Why, or why not?

ARTIFACT NUMBER	THE GROUP'S MODERN-DAY EXAMPLE	YOUR CRITIQUE
1		
2		
3		
4		
5		

Source: Ashmore & Sharer, 1993.

Word Bank and Vocabulary Sheet

The following are vocabulary words we'll learn and use in this project.

- *Identification:* to establish the identity of an object
- *Inferring:* to come to an understanding or conclusion based on observations
- *Critique:* an analysis or review of someone else's work
- *Analogy:* inferring the identity of a past artifact by comparing it to something very similar that we have today
- *Principle of analogy:* used in archaeology to correctly interpret the identity and use of an artifact
- *Artifact:* an object from the past that man either made or used (or both)
- *Archaeology:* the study of past human remains
- *Archaeologist:* the person who studies archaeology

The following is a word bank to use with the lesson.

WORD BANK TERMS		
identification	infer	culture
analogy	artifact	archaeologist
archaeology	junior	decoration
critique	carvings	spout
symbol	design	disagree
cylindrical	agree	

Your critique should begin with either "We agree that . . ." or "We disagree that . . ."

Scoring Rubric

Acceptable student performance is proficient or higher.

Objective 1: After completing a role-playing activity on identifying and inferring the use of Mayan artifacts, students will critique another group's results using the principle of analogy as their criteria.

1 SIGNIFICANT REVISION NEEDED	2 SOME REVISION NEEDED	3 PROFICIENT	4 EXCEEDS EXPECTATIONS
Group does not use the principle of analogy to critique another group's results. Missing three or more critiques on the "Critique Worksheet." Group gives one or fewer details for the description of the artifact section on the identification worksheet. Group does not complete four or more sections on the identification worksheet. Students does not work well together. They have many problems and behavioral issues during the activity.	Group critiques another group's work using the principle of analogy. Missing one or two artifact critiques on the "Critique Worksheet." Group gives one detail for the artifact section description on the identification worksheet. Group does not complete two or three sections on the identification worksheet. Students work together with several problems during the activity.	Group provides one sentence for each artifact critique using the principle of analogy. Group completes all the sections of the "Critique Worksheet." Group gives one or two details for the artifact section description on the identification worksheet. All sections are completed on the identification worksheet. Students work together with few to no problems during the entire activity.	Group provides two sentences for each artifact critique using the principle of analogy. Group completes all sections of the "Critique Worksheet." Group gives three or more details for the artifact section description on the identification worksheet. All sections are completed on the identification worksheet. Students work very well together during the entire activity. There are no problems.

Objective 2: Students will create a video critiquing the results of another group based on the principle of analogy and watch it in class.

1 SIGNIFICANT REVISION NEEDED	2 SOME REVISION NEEDED	3 PROFICIENT	4 EXCEEDS EXPECTATIONS
Video has four or more technical problems and is watched in class. Group provides critiques but does not use the principle of analogy. Group does not role-play as junior archaeologists and does not announce team names. Group uses zero or one artifact as visual props to create a visually enhanced critique.	Video has three or four technical problems and is watched in class. Group gives one detail for critique using the principle of analogy. Group only critiques three or four artifacts. Group is role-playing as junior archaeologists but forgets to either announce its team name or the group name of the team members critiquing. Group uses two or three artifacts as visual props to create a visually enhanced critique.	Video has one or two technical problems and is watched in class. Group gives one or two details for critique using the principle of analogy. Group gives critique for all five artifacts. Group is role-playing as junior archaeologists and announces its team name and the team name of the group members are critiquing. Group uses four artifacts as visual props to create a visually enhanced critique.	Video has no technical problems and is watched in class. Group gives three or more details for critique using the principle of analogy. Group gives critique for all five artifacts. Group does an excellent job role-playing as junior archaeologists and announces its team name and the team name of the group members are critiquing. Group uses all artifacts as visual props to create a visually enhanced critique.

Source: Ross, 2016.

Sample Student Work

The following example is from the high-scoring group—Kabil.

Roles for Group Work Form

Group name: Kabil

Writer: Cornelious

Task manager: Jeiry

Video speaker or actor: Declan

Cameraperson: Cornelious

Technology specialist: Christal

Identification and Inference of Use Worksheet

Use this chart to identify and infer each artifact's use in your dig box.

ARTIFACT NUMBER	MATERIAL ARTIFACT IS MADE OF	ARTIFACT DESCRIPTION	ARTIFACT'S PURPOSE	MODERN EXAMPLE OF THIS TYPE OF ARTIFACT
1	gold	· Lots of symbols · Face in the middle · Arrow points from the middle	to buy things	coin
2	flint	· Looks like an ax · Bumpy · Pointed ends	to dig	pickax
3	limestone copper	· Bunch of lines · Has a brown and white end with shapes coming out	for use in war	sword
4	clay	· Spout at top · Cracks on top · Shapes on bottom	to hold water	teapot
5	iron stone	· Looks like a table · Cucumber shape · White stuff on it	to flatten stuff	rolling pin

Critique Worksheet

Critique of __Ikal__ group by __Kabil__ group.

Directions: Use this chart to critique the results of another group using the principle of analogy as your criteria. Remember, the principle of analogy states that the identity of unknown items may be inferred from those that are known. In other words, you can infer the identity of an artifact by comparing it to a modern-day artifact that has very similar features (Ashmore & Sharer, 1993). In your critique, decide if the group's identification and inference of the Mayan tool is correct. Is it a logical conclusion or comparison of today's tools? Why, or why not?

ARTIFACT NUMBER	THE GROUP'S MODERN-DAY EXAMPLE	YOUR CRITIQUE
1	money	agree
2	pickax	agree
3	hunting tools	disagree
4	pitcher	disagree
5	rolling pin	agree

Supplemental Information on Critique

The following is our critique of Ikal.

1. We agree with them because we said it was a coin. Coins are a form of money. Also because it's made of gold and is valuable.
2. We agree because we both said the same things. Also because we said it is used to dig.
3. We disagree because we said it's a sword. Also because it has a place for your hand, so you can hold it.
4. We disagree because we think it is a teapot. Also because it has something to pour out of.
5. We agree because we thought it was used to roll something. Also because we thought it was made of stone.

Visit http://bit.ly/2cGeFND to access the technology-integration component (Ross, 2015c).

Social Studies Projects

Create Excellence Framework Rating

CREATE ANALYSIS		
CREATE COMPONENT	**LEVEL**	**JUSTIFICATION**
Real-World Learning	3: Investigating	Learning simulates the real world since students are role-playing as archaeologists and learning a real-world occupation and method. Students are pretending to be real archaeologists, and they are examining real (pictures of) artifacts.
Cognitive Complexity	3: Investigating	The teacher directs student interaction by assigning a specific archaeology activity to the students. Students are working at the Evaluate level by critiquing the results of other students using a set of criteria provided to them.
Student Engagement	2: Practicing	This activity involves group work using real-world simulated objects (artifacts) and a real-world simulated experience (excavation, identification, and inference of use).
Technology Integration	3: Investigating	The technology use is an add-on as a means of communicating the critique's results. Technology is not essential for task completion. Students could have written a report of the results. Students are using the technology to communicate evaluation and critiquing thinking tasks.

THREE MINUTES TO CHANGE THE WORLD

Source: Adapted from Angela Gunter. Used with permission.

Content: Social studies

Learning Objectives:

1. Students will identify community or world problems.
2. Students will propose solutions for their selected problems to businesses or service organizations related to their problem.

Standards:

C3 Framework for Social Studies State Standards—

- D2.Civ.6.3–5 Describe ways in which people benefit from and are challenged by working together, including through government, work places, voluntary organizations, and families (NCSS, 2013).
- D4.3.3–5 Present a summary of arguments and explain notions to others outside the classroom using print and oral technologies (e.g., posters, essays, letters, debates, speeches, and reports) and digital technologies (e.g., Internet, social media, and digital documentary; NCSS, 2013).
- D4.7.3–5 Explain different strategies and approaches students and others could take in working alone and together to address local, regional, and global problems, and predict possible results of their actions (NCSS, 2013).

Project Options: Students may choose to create an interactive infographic using ThingLink or, if their organization would rather have a handout or flyer, a traditional infographic using Canva, Easel.ly, Piktochart, or Venngage. Students may present their projects virtually using Zoom or Skype to community representatives who are unable or too far away to attend the school conference.

Resources Needed: Project proposal guide; computer and Internet access; online presentation tools including iMovie, Animoto, LifeLogger, or PowToon; "Three Minutes to Change the World Promo" video clip located at www.youtube.com/watch?v=C0MbMBHrgK4 (Biz Kid$, 2012); Spark!Lab at http://invention.si .edu/try/sparklab (for exploration); "Design and Discovery Implementation Examples" located at http:// tinyurl.com/gotbo9s (Intel, n.d.); the nine printed invention descriptions, cut apart so the teacher can distribute a different invention description to each group

Three Minutes to Change the World

Can students really change the world? How would our community be different if everyone determined what they were passionate about and used that passion to solve problems? Consider ways that you can make a difference in your community, and create a three-minute video or multimedia presentation proposing a solution. Contact a representative of an organization connected to your community issue, invite him or her to our student-led solutions conference, and offer your video or presentation for his or her organization to use.

Project Tasks

1. Begin by watching "Three Minutes to Change the World Promo" at www.youtube.com /watch?v=C0MbMBHrgK4 (Biz Kid$, 2012) as a class.

2. As a whole group, brainstorm a list of community and world problems. A student volunteer writes ideas on the board as students call them out.

3. Next, in small groups of three (or individually), log in to Spark!Lab (http://invention.si.edu /try/sparklab) and explore the featured inventions and stories about their inventors. You have ten minutes. Consider interesting inventions and topics, and note them on your "Project Proposal Guide."

4. Individually, create a list of your passions on your "Project Proposal Guide." What do you enjoy doing? What talents do you have? How do you like to spend your free time? Next, look at the board and your notes. Are there any problems listed that could be addressed with your passion? For example, say you like to read. Are there any people in our community who could benefit from having someone read to them?

5. The teachers will distribute a different description of a student solution from "Design and Discovery Implementation Examples" (Intel, n.d.) to each group. You have five minutes to read your solution and summarize the information to present to the rest of the class. While others are presenting, take note of the most interesting inventions they present on your "Project Proposal Guide."

6. Your group will now decide on a problem to address and formulate a plan to solve it. Consider how your passions connect to social problems. How could you make others' lives easier? Clearly explain your project, plan, or product and how it would be used. You may work on a project individually if you prefer since your passions and interests may not be the same as others' in your group. Use your "Project Proposal Guide" to design your project.

7. Research online to find an organization related to your project. Find contact information, list it on your "Project Proposal Guide," and ask your teacher to help you write an email.

8. Decide what type of presentation to prepare. Will your organization benefit from or use a three-minute video? Another type of multimedia presentation? An interactive infographic? Explain your choice on the "Project Proposal Guide."

Real-World Learning Framework for Elementary Schools © 2017 Solution Tree Press • SolutionTree.com
Visit **go.SolutionTree.com/instruction** to download this free reproducible.

Project Proposal Guide

PROBLEMS STUDENTS CAN ADDRESS	SPARK!LAB NOTES

DESIGN AND DISCOVERY EXAMPLES NOTES	YOUR PASSIONS

SELECTED PROBLEM
State the problem and why it is important to address it.

Real-World Learning Framework for Elementary Schools © 2017 Solution Tree Press • SolutionTree.com
Visit **go.SolutionTree.com/instruction** to download this free reproducible.

PROPOSED SOLUTION
What product or service would make life easier, more fun, or more efficient?

CONTACT INFORMATION FOR AN ORGANIZATION ASSOCIATED WITH THE PROBLEM
List the email, webpage, address, phone number, or all of these of the contact person.

MULTIMEDIA FORMAT AND RATIONALE
Select iMovie, Animoto, LifeLogger, PowToon, ThingLink, Canva, Easel.ly, Piktochart, Venngage, or some other tool.
Why this format? Who might use it? For what? Where?

Scoring Rubric

	1 SIGNIFICANT REVISION NEEDED	2 SOME REVISION NEEDED	3 PROFICIENT	4 EXCEEDS EXPECTATIONS
Objective 1: Students will identify community or world problems.	Problem is unclear. Solution is implausible, not matched to the problem, or not present.	Problem is defined, and its significance is stated. Solution is present but not in much detail.	Problem is well defined, and its significance is fully explained. Solution is creative, well designed, and detailed.	Problem is very clearly defined, and its significance is explained in great detail. Solution is innovative, expertly designed, and elaborately detailed.
Objective 2: Students will propose solutions for their selected problems to businesses or service organizations related to their problem.	Multimedia product or three-minute video incorporates poor-quality visuals and graphics that distract from the message. Choice of media or product is not related to the organization's needs.	Multimedia product or three-minute video incorporates visuals and graphics. Choice of media or product is loosely related to the organization's needs and is explained in some detail.	Multimedia product or three-minute video incorporates good-quality visuals and graphics. Choice of media or product is clearly related to the organization's needs and is explained in detail.	Multimedia product or three-minute video incorporates excellent visuals, graphics, fonts, and effects to enhance the presentation. Choice of media or product is insightful, related to the organization's needs, and explained in great detail.

Sources: Biz Kid$, 2012; Intel, n.d.

Sample Student Work

The following is sample student work.

Project Proposal Guide

PROBLEMS STUDENTS CAN ADDRESS	SPARK!LAB NOTES
Hunger—backpacks of food Loneliness—visit elderly Can't read or do math—help with homework Animal abuse—volunteer at animal shelter Pollution—cleanup committee at school Language—help kids learn English	Water bike hard to build but good purpose Wagon to help carry children—help with hunger—never connected wagon and hunger before Do we have a children's museum like the one on Spark!Lab I can ask my parents to take me to visit?

DESIGN AND DISCOVERY EXAMPLES NOTES	YOUR PASSIONS
Ice pack after mom's bike wreck—created dispenser Wheelchair ramp—Americans With Disabilities Act—scrap metal Way to store necklaces—what about bracelets or earrings? Chicken coop door—keep them safe—how can I keep my cat safe???—weight lock Fresh water for guinea pig—maybe make something for my cat??? Toys for dogs—could make cat toys??? Better folder for school—Velcro Brush with gel button—cat brush??	Playing apps and games Making bracelets with string Playing with my cat, Miss Kitty Cooking—but not good at it Coloring and painting Helping my uncle walk my grandparents' dog New hairstyles

SELECTED PROBLEM
State the problem and why it is important to address it.

Pets are important to society. For some people, pets are the only friends they have, and pets help teach young people responsibility. Since we all have pets that bring us joy every day, we want them to experience fun and happiness as well. Our project is called "Kitty City," a fun activity center for cats with all the things they like to do.

PROPOSED SOLUTION
What product or service would make life easier, more fun, or more efficient?

Kitty City will be a playground for cats housed in a bookcase-sized area so it will not take up too much space in a room. After researching types of activities that are good for cats, we included stairs, ladders, and a wheel so cats can get exercise. We have also included two areas for cats to sleep with soft, fluffy material. In one corner, we will include a port for an electrical cord and charger for an iPad to display cat apps such as CAT ALONE or Friskies® Cat Fishing. On the top will be a disco ball with lights that spin so the cats will have light to chase. There are two spots that have a spring attached, one with a ball and one with a small stuffed animal for cats to bat back and forth. There are also different types of materials, sizes, and shapes of the scratching posts and play areas because cats prefer a variety. We will also include an optional tunnel that leads to a cat door (if you have one).

CONTACT INFORMATION FOR AN ORGANIZATION ASSOCIATED WITH THE PROBLEM
List the email, webpage, address, phone number, or all of these of the contact person.

Local veterinarian: Paul Smith; 5 Veterinarian Rd., Vetville; paul.smith@vet.com

Pet shelter: Second Chance Animal Shelter; 12306 Main St., Georgetown; secondchanceshelter@animalrescue.com

Pet grooming services: Make That Kitty Pretty; 181 Grooming St., Groomtown; makethatkittypretty@petgrooming.com

MULTIMEDIA FORMAT AND RATIONALE
Select iMovie, Animoto, LifeLogger, PowToon, ThingLink, Canva, Easel.ly, Piktochart, Venngage, or some other tool.

Why this format? Who might use it? For what? Where?

We created a demonstration video using Animoto for the animal shelter to put on its webpage. An animated slide show to demonstrate this product is more important than an infographic or other presentation because people can see the animals actually using it. There are many different features, and a demonstration of cats enjoying the Kitty City will attract attention. Cute cat photos are very popular, and people will likely share it through social media.

Visit https://bit.ly/2mGY2V9 to view the presentation "Three Minutes to Change the World: Kitty City" (Gunter, 2016).

Social Studies
Projects

Create Excellence Framework Rating

CREATE ANALYSIS		
CREATE COMPONENT	**LEVEL**	**JUSTIFICATION**
Real-World Learning	4: Integrating	Student projects focus on a real-world problem in the community and are marketed to community organizations.
Cognitive Complexity	4: Integrating	Students study problems in society and create plans to address the problems. Students also must consider the format that would be most appropriate for organizations and provide rationales for their choices.
Student Engagement	4: Integrating	Students work with other students in formulating project ideas and collaborate on the process of creation of the multimedia product.
Technology Integration	4: Integrating	Students select from various technology formats and programs, determining which would be most effective for their selected audience, which is an actual organization in their community.

— WHY WOULD ANYONE WANT TO GO THERE? —

Source: Adapted from Sheriden Edwards. Used with permission.

Content: Social studies

Learning Objectives:

1. Students will evaluate the current use and location of a reservoir (or other open unused space) in the local residential area.

2. Students will propose a plan of improvement for the land that will provide further recreational use to a sector of the community and offer an environmentally sustainable option.

Standards:

C3 Framework for Social Studies State Standards—

*   D2.Geo.2.3.5 Use maps, satellite images, photographs, and other representations to explain relationships between the locations of places and regions and their environmental characteristics (NCSS, 2013).

*   D2.Geo.8.3–5 Explain how human settlements and movements relate to the locations and use of various natural resources (NCSS, 2013).

Common Core English language arts—

*   W.5.7 Conduct short research projects that use several sources to build knowledge through investigation of different aspects of a topic (NGA & CCSSO, 2010a).

*   W.5.2.a Introduce a topic clearly, provide a general observation and focus, and group related information logically; include formatting (e.g., headings), illustrations, and multimedia when useful to aiding comprehension (NGA & CCSSO, 2010a).

Project Options: This project can be conducted in any area close to the school and familiar to the students. An underdeveloped area is best with a sympathetic landowner who would be willing to participate in the project. Alternatively, government lands, parks, or city or town property could be used with appropriate permissions.

Optional extensions could include the following.

*   Students give questionnaires or conduct a range of interviews with community representatives from various sectors.

*   The landowner may already have a budget in mind for redevelopment, and students could use this as a goal, or they could complete the project without a budget to avoid the mathematical element.

*   Students could be given prepared sheets with costs and dimensions of items such as wooden picnic benches, recycled plastic picnic benches, visitor center log buildings, litter bins, bird hides, fishing platforms, and so on.

Resources Needed: Computer and Internet access, PowerPoint or a similar program, and a price list of recreational equipment (optional—could be used to focus the task; alternatively, students could search for equipment using a search engine)

Why Would Anyone Want to Go There?

Think of an area near your school that may not be very attractive now but could be transformed into a park or facility useful to the public. The class will discuss optional public lands and visit the area chosen to think about ways to improve the property. You will design a plan to transform the property into a useful facility for a particular group of the population. So let's get started!

Project Tasks

1. As a class, discuss public unused properties near the school (if possible) and ideas for ways that the public could use the properties. The class will select one public property to study for this project.

2. On a field trip to the selected property, take photographs and make a note of the locations of attractive features on your map that visitors may wish to enjoy. Also, map the locations of amenities such as litter bins, car parks, access roads, paths, toilets, and so on. Alternatively, students could also use a GPS tracker like MapMyRun on an iPhone or iPod to map out the property. Then, students could upload the map to a computer and manipulate the map and draw their additions to the map.

3. Your group (of two to four students assigned by the teacher) will select one of the following community sectors to focus on for the property's design.

   - Families with young children
   - Older generation
   - Disabled people
   - Sports enthusiasts

4. Students must discuss the needs of their selected sector of the community and decide what facilities they will need in order to access and enjoy the area (recorded using a thought shower or mind map). The "Facility Idea Task Sheet" could be used to collect ideas.

5. Develop a multimedia presentation (you might use Prezi [https://prezi.com], PhotoPeach [http://photopeach.com], or Animoto [https://animoto.com]) stating how your project will:

   - Benefit your community group
   - Impact the environment, with an explanation of how the developments are environmentally sustainable
   - Impact the local community

6. Be sure to create before-and-after maps. The presentation should contain hyperlinks to pertinent pages, photos your group took of the site, and a map showing before and after the development.

7. Present your proposals to the rest of the class; the class will vote for the best development plans. Also, show the proposals to the landowner or government representative, who can then provide feedback to the students on their proposals.

Facility Idea Task Sheet

Group members: Your selected sector of the community:
Why would this sector of the community need or want to use this area?
Does this sector need anything to keep it safe?
Does this sector need anything to help it get around?
Will this sector benefit from a visitor center, a café, or some other recreational facility?
Use a search engine to research other environmental areas that cater to visits from your community sector, such as public parks, nature trails, sculpture parks, arboretums, or lakeside trails. What areas are already available for your community sector?
Your group will decide on the changes or developments you want to plan for the property. You can draw these on paper or on your computer using Tinkercad (www.tinkercad.com) or AutoCAD (www.autocad 360.com). Draw and label all your proposed changes. Write a justification for each change.
Discuss the issue of sustainability and environmental factors when considering developments and the balance between the environment and development. How will your changes to the property impact the environment?
Record expected expenses for your project. You will have a budget and must decide what your priorities will be in developing the area for your community sector. Prepare a budget sheet using Microsoft Excel or similar technology, listing the expenses for your project.

Scoring Rubric

	1 SIGNIFICANT REVISION NEEDED	2 SOME REVISION NEEDED	3 PROFICIENT	4 EXCEEDS EXPECTATIONS
Objective 1: Students evaluate the current use and location of a reservoir (or other open unused space) in the local residential area.	With help, student creates a map of the area indicating current land use and urban links.	Student creates a map of the area indicating current land use and urban links. This could be developed further.	Student creates a comprehensive map of the area indicating current land use and urban links.	Student creates a comprehensive map of the area indicating current land use and urban links. Included is an explanation of current land use.
Objective 2: Students propose a plan of improvement for the land that will provide further recreational use to a sector of the community and offer an environmentally sustainable option.	The development does not accurately match the community sector's needs. Sustainability has not been considered.	The development has some features that accurately match the community sector's needs. Sustainability options are not well explained.	The development accurately matches the community sector's needs. Sustainability options are chosen and explained.	The development accurately matches the community sector's needs, and the project has excellent sustainability options, which are explained well, and reasons are given why other options have not been chosen.
	A multimedia presentation is used to present the development plan. A map and comprehensive budget information are missing.	A multimedia presentation is used to present the development plan. There is a simple map and budget information.	A multimedia presentation is used to present the development plan. A map and comprehensive budget information are present.	A multimedia presentation is used to present the development plan. A map and comprehensive budget information are present and offer clear explanations why more expensive options have been considered.

Sample Student Work

The following student work sample is from Denton Church of England Primary School in Denton, United Kingdom.

Facility Idea Task Sheet

Group members: Jane, Marcus, Sally, and David Your selected sector of the community: Older generation
Why would this sector of the community need or want to use this area? In this area, there are few resources for the older generation, who can become isolated within their community. This could be an ideal meeting place and recreational area.
Does this sector need anything to keep it safe? These people sometimes have mobility problems, so wide, smoothly surfaced footpaths and barriers with few steps would be advantageous. Older people may need to sit down more, so there would need to be benches and seats.
Does this sector need anything to help it get around? Older people may have mobility buggies and so these would need to be able to get around the site.
Will this sector benefit from a visitor center, a café, or some other recreational facility? This group will definitely benefit from a café where they can sit and rest and also make friends. They will need toilet facilities near to the café.
Use a search engine to research other environmental areas that cater to visits from your community sector, such as public parks, nature trails, sculpture parks, arboretums, or lakeside trails. What areas are already available for your community sector? Belton House (www.nationaltrust.org.uk/belton-house) is a stately home with plenty of outside walks, which are popular with older people as well as families.
Your group will decide on the changes or developments you want to plan for the property. You can draw these on paper or on your computer using Tinkercad (www.tinkercad.com) or AutoCAD (www.autocad360.com). Draw and label all your proposed changes. Write a justification for each change. On the map is a weir; this is a hazardous area for older people because there are steps over a footbridge and only a partial barrier. This would need developing with a ramp at each end of the bridge and a more substantial barrier. To the southeast of the reservoir is a flatter area that would be accessible from the main entrance. Here could be located a visitor center and seating areas; it also benefits from lovely views of the reservoir. Towards the north of the reservoir, there is a good fishing area, but this would need developing with a platform and barrier to make it safe for older people to fish near the steep banks of the reservoir.
Discuss the issue of sustainability and environmental factors when considering developments and the balance between the environment and development. How will your changes to the property impact the environment? Resurfacing footpaths and building the visitor center and fishing platform will have an impact on the environment because there will be more people visiting, which may scare away some wildlife. Good footpaths mean that people will not make their own way through the undergrowth and damage the reservoir banks, so this should protect some wildlife areas. The buildings could be made from sustainable sources such as softwood or recycled plastic. The benefit of recycled plastic for benches and platforms is that although more expensive, it requires very little long-term maintenance.

Record expected expenses for your project. You will have a budget and must decide what your priorities will be in developing the area for your community sector. Prepare a budget sheet using Microsoft Excel or similar technology, listing the expenses for your project.

Total budget allocation: $42,819.74

AMENITY	QUANTITY	COST PER ITEM	TOTAL COST
Locally sourced visitor kiosk and SOIL toilets with disabled access	1	$24,468.42	$24,468.42
Footpath two meters wide, recycled tire texture (per meter)	500	$18.35	$9,175.66
Litter bins, recycled plastic	4	$73.41	$293.62
Lake-view platform, recycled timber	2	$305.86	$611.71
Interpretive signs	6	$305.86	$1,835.13
Picnic benches, wheelchair access (recycled plastic, no maintenance)	5	$1,101.08	$5,505.40
Total project cost	$41,889.94		

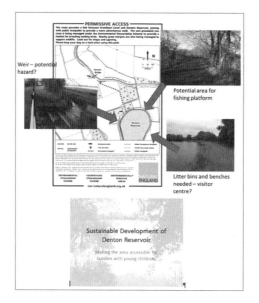

Visit http://slideroll.com/?s=hh3yqac1 to view the student presentation "Sustainable Development of Denton Reservoir" (Maxwell, 2016c).

Create Excellence Framework Rating

CREATE ANALYSIS		
CREATE COMPONENT	**LEVEL**	**JUSTIFICATION**
Real-World Learning	4: Integrating	Students look for ways to sustainably develop an area for a particular sector of their community. They present their ideas to landowners or government representatives and in doing so have an impact on their community. Students integrate skills from a variety of disciplines, including geography, writing, and mathematics.
Cognitive Complexity	4: Integrating	Students lead a development based on a community need that they have identified. Students are learning at the Create level of the revised Bloom's taxonomy since they are generating ideas and solutions for their community.
Student Engagement	4: Integrating	The project revolves around the students' application of their own research and implementation of their own idea. Students are initiating collaborations within the community.
Technology Integration	4: Integrating	Students are using technology throughout the project in order to refine their own ideas, create and present their plan, and provide links to community profiles and needs.

Social Studies Projects

MUSICIANS AND SOLDIERS: SUPPORTING EACH OTHER

Source: Adapted from Hayley Clayton. Used with permission.

Content: Social studies and music

Learning Objectives:

1. Students will analyze how musicians help soldiers stay emotionally stable.
2. Students will create multimedia presentations to express what they have learned about the relationship between soldiers and musicians.

Standards:

Common Core English language arts—

- RI.5.3 Explain the relationships or interactions between two or more individuals, events, ideas, or concepts in a historical, scientific, or technical text based on specific information in the text (NGA & CCSSO, 2010a).
- RI.5.5 Compare and contrast the overall structure (e.g., chronology, comparison, cause/effect, problem/solution) of events, ideas, concepts, or information in two or more texts (NGA & CCSSO, 2010a).
- SL.5.5 Include multimedia components (e.g., graphics, sound) and visual displays in presentations when appropriate to enhance the development of main ideas or themes (NGA & CCSSO, 2010a).

C3 Framework for Social Studies State Standards—

- D2.His.5.3–5 Explain connections among historical contexts and people's perspectives at the time (NCSS, 2013).

Project Options: Students will create a presentation with the technology of their choice. For example, one student could use iMovie and another could use Fakebook.

Resources Needed:

- Computers with Internet access for research and presenting
- Online tools such as YouTube, Prezi, PowerPoint, emaze, PlayPosit, iMovie, Fakebook, or other such tools
- Headphones or audio for listening to jazz music

Musicians and Soldiers: Supporting Each Other

Music can inspire people! Did you know that music impacts soldiers' lives? This project focuses on how musicians and soldiers benefit from each other during wartimes. You will analyze what kind of lifestyle musicians led and how music integration in the camps lifted soldiers' spirits.

Project Tasks

1. In groups of three or four, research online for information about famous musicians helping the war effort and problems soldiers during that era faced. Record your responses on the "Musicians and Soldiers Task Sheet." Then, submit your completed worksheet to me (your teacher) for approval.

2. Create a multimedia project that explains the relationship between soldiers and musicians in your war of choice. The following are options for your project.

    *   Create a video.
    *   Create some music of the war such as by playing or singing themes of victory or bravery.
    *   Design a simulation or role play of musicians and soldiers.
    *   Compose a sequence of emails or some kind of communication sent home describing the relationship between the soldier and musician.
    *   Make a cartoon animation using technology like PowToon (www.powtoon.com).

Musicians and Soldiers Task Sheet

Name: _____

Date: _____

War of choice: _____

Answer the following research questions.

1. Name three musicians of your choice who volunteered to entertain troops or keep up the spirits of Americans back home. Give two facts about each musician.

    a. _____

       _____

    b. _____

       _____

    c. _____

       _____

2. List three problems from your research that most soldiers faced in battle or while training.

a. _____

b. _____

c. _____

3. Use this information to make a Venn diagram recording the similarities and differences in the lives of the musicians and soldiers in your war.

4. What kind of lifestyle did the musicians live as traveling entertainers during your war of choice?

5. How did music lift soldiers' spirits in your war of choice?

6. How did musicians and soldiers influence each other in your war of choice? Think about how they complemented or connected with one another.

Scoring Rubric

	1 SIGNIFICANT REVISION NEEDED	2 SOME REVISION NEEDED	3 PROFICIENT	4 EXCEEDS EXPECTATIONS
Objective 1: Students will analyze how musicians help soldiers stay emotionally stable.	Product provides a short, illogical analysis of how musicians and soldiers complemented each other; many parts are missing. Product describes an illogical and irrelevant connection or no connection at all between the musicians and the soldiers. Answers to one or two questions from the worksheet are inadequate. Product is not unique or original; multimedia project does not appeal to the audience and is not based on logical conclusions and sound research. Product is inaccurate, missing components, or unorganized. Product has many technical problems, one to three graphics, and no clear connection between soldiers and musicians through the multimedia presentation.	Product provides a somewhat detailed and logical analysis of how musicians and soldiers complemented each other. Product describes a connection made between the musicians and soldiers that is somewhat clear; many parts are irrelevant or illogical. Product provides answers to three or four questions from the worksheet. There are some original, unique features in the product. Multimedia project does not appeal to the audience and is not based on logical conclusions and sound research. Product is not accurate, in-depth, neat, or organized. Product has some technical problems and four to six graphics from outside sources. The connection between the soldiers and musicians is somewhat clear through the multimedia presentation.	Product provides a detailed and logical analysis of how musicians and soldiers complemented each other. Product describes a connection made between the musicians and soldiers that is mostly clear, relevant, and logical. Product adequately answers four to five questions from the worksheet. Product is original and unique. Multimedia project has an acceptable look that appeals to the audience and complements the information and is based on logical conclusions and sound research. Product is accurate, neat, and organized. There are few technical problems and seven to nine graphics from outside sources. Multimedia presentation clearly presents the connection between the soldiers and musicians.	Product provides a unique, detailed, and logical analysis of how musicians and soldiers complemented each other. Product describes a connection made between the musicians and soldiers that is clear, relevant, and logical. Product answers all six questions in detail from the worksheet. Product is excellent, original, and unique. Multimedia project has an outstanding look that appeals to the audience and complements the information and is based on logical conclusions and sound research. Product is accurate, neat, and organized with thorough details and information. There are no technical problems and ten or more graphics from outside sources. Multimedia presentation clearly and in detail presents the connection between the soldiers and musicians. Product accomplishes the rubric criteria on the first attempt.

Sample Student Work

The following is a student sample using entertainers during World War II.

Musicians and Soldiers Task Sheet

Name: Katie

Date: 1/1/16

War of choice: World War II

Answer the following research questions.

1. Name three musicians of your choice who volunteered to entertain troops or keep up the spirits of Americans back at home. Give two facts about each musician.
    a. Glenn Miller: Glenn Miller and his orchestra traveled to England for the U.S. troops so they could hear music in the camps. Glenn Miller's plane was lost over the English Channel.
    b. Benny Goodman: Benny Goodman wrote songs about WWII. Some of his songs, such as "My Guy's Come Back," relate to the families waiting for loved ones at home.
    c. Andrews Sisters: The Andrews Sisters sang jazz tunes that encouraged the United States. Songs such as "Boogie Woogie Bugle Boy" tell the encouraging story of the U.S. soldiers so that the public can have hope.

2. List three problems from your research that most soldiers faced in battle or while training.
    a. Soldiers watched their fellow soldiers give their lives for their country.
    b. They faced rationing and air raids.
    c. They were away from their families for months at a time.

3. Use this information to make a Venn diagram recording the similarities and differences in the lives of the musicians and soldiers in your war.

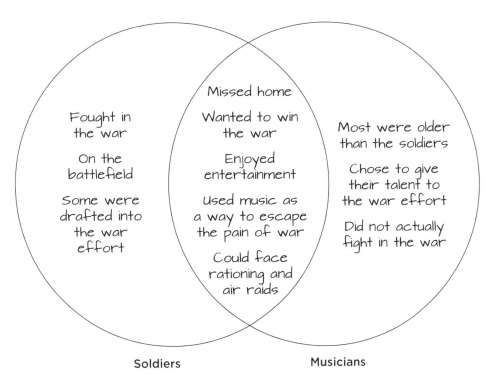

Soldiers

Fought in the war

On the battlefield

Some were drafted into the war effort

Missed home

Wanted to win the war

Enjoyed entertainment

Used music as a way to escape the pain of war

Could face rationing and air raids

Most were older than the soldiers

Chose to give their talent to the war effort

Did not actually fight in the war

Musicians

Social Studies Projects

4. What kind of lifestyle did the musicians live as traveling entertainers during your war of choice?

    The musicians were away from home for months at a time. They even had to hide in the underground to escape air raids in England. They shared their gifts with the soldiers to lift their spirits.

5. How did music lift soldiers' spirits in your war of choice?

    The music reminded the soldiers of home and that home was fighting for them. They were reminded that their fighting was not in vain. Music was an escape from the horrors of the war.

6. How did musicians and soldiers influence each other in your war of choice? Think about how they complemented or connected with one another.

    The musicians offered an escape from the war. They connected the soldiers to the culture at home, and they rallied the troops to fight with all they had for the war effort. They reminded the soldiers of home and the values of why they were fighting in the first place.

Final product examples:

- Jazz musicians and WWII iMovie (Clayton, 2015): https://youtu.be/ED8kSxEIV-E
- Emaze Presentation—Example of Student Work: https://app.emaze.com/@AWFZWZFO/untitled

Create Excellence Framework Rating

CREATE ANALYSIS		
CREATE COMPONENT	**LEVEL**	**JUSTIFICATION**
Real-World Learning	3: Investigating	Music in WWII is a real-world topic, and by researching both the musicians and soldiers, the students can empathize with the feelings of each side because the information they gather will give the students a glimpse of the hardships the musicians faced.
Cognitive Complexity	3: Investigating	The students analyze how music affects soldiers during the war. The students are differentiating different aspects of the musicians' lives and the soldiers' lives, and then organizing them to see if they complement each other. The prompt is still teacher directed.
Student Engagement	3: Investigating	Students are engaged in the task, and there are multiple solutions, but the question is still teacher directed. However, the students can choose which type of technology they want to use to create their presentation, so the product is differentiated.
Technology Integration	3: Investigating	Technology is an add-on to the lesson, but it is used for higher-level thinking. The students are using technology to analyze the lives of musicians and soldiers.

PLASTIC BAGS, BOTTLES, AND STRAWS, OH MY!

Source: Adapted from Cindy Hundley. Used with permission.

Content: Science

Learning Objectives:

1. Students will plan, implement, and discuss a service-learning project on ocean plastic pollution.
2. Students will create a website and blog that shares information on the content objective as well as evidence of the impact of their service-learning project.

Standards:

Next Generation Science Standards—

*   5-ESS3–1 Obtain and combine information about ways individual communities use science ideas to protect the Earth's resources and environment (NGSS Lead States, 2013).
*   3–5-ETS1–2 Generate and compare multiple possible solutions to a problem based on how well each is likely to meet the criteria and constraints of the problem (NGSS Lead States, 2013).

Common Core English language arts—

*   RI.5.3 Explain the relationships or interactions between two or more individuals, events, ideas, or concepts in a historical, scientific, or technical text based on specific information in the text (NGA & CCSSO, 2010a).
*   W.5.7 Conduct short research projects that use several sources to build knowledge through investigation of different aspects of a topic (NGA & CCSSO, 2010a).
*   SL.5.5 Include multimedia components (e.g., graphics, sound) and visual displays in presentations when appropriate to enhance the development of main ideas or themes (NGA & CCSSO, 2010a).

Common Core mathematics—

*   5.G.A.2 Represent real world and mathematical problems by graphing points in the first quadrant of the coordinate plane, and interpret coordinate values of points in the context of the situation (NGA & CCSSO, 2010b).

Project Options:

*   After completing the service-learning project, students could create a digital book describing the process they followed for their project. The book could contain their plan, their actions, and their results. This book could then be published as a hard copy to share with others within the school.
*   After implementing their plastic pollution project within the school, students could visit other schools in person or via Skype to share their story and successes. Students could offer tips for a more successful program and offer to collaborate when appropriate.
*   Students could continue to work together to attack another form of pollution. Students could communicate with local companies that pollute our environment with chemicals and dirt to create a letter-writing campaign to address air pollution. They could also organize a trash cleanup event to address the amount of litter on the local school grounds or in a community park.

Resources Needed: Computer with Internet access, link to TED-Ed flipped lesson "Tough Truths About Plastic Pollution"—http://ed.ted.com/on/Kyp6SEb5 (Hundley, n.d.)

Plastic Bags, Bottles, and Straws, Oh My!

Pollution is everywhere! What can we do about it? We have been studying the effects of plastic pollution on the marine animals that live in or near the ocean by reviewing texts, videos, and images from a variety of multimedia sources. Many of our daily practices are contributing to this problem. Let's take action by creating a service-learning project for our school. We will focus on reducing the amount of plastic used throughout the day.

Project Tasks

1. Complete the TED-Ed lesson "Dianna Cohen: Tough Truths About Plastic Pollution" at http://ed.ted.com/on/Kyp6SEb5 (Hundley, n.d.). The following image is what the lesson looks like online. Complete the sections Watch, Think, Dig Deeper, Discuss, and Finally.

Dianna Cohen: Tough Truths About Plastic Pollution

LESSON CREATED BY CINDY HUNDLEY USING TED-ED

VIDEO FROM TED-ED YOUTUBE CHANNEL

Let's Begin . . .

Dianna Cohen is a visual artist and co-founder of the Plastic Pollution Coalition. She describes the global issue of plastic pollution in our oceans as well as her initial solutions to the problem, which included using plastic in art as well as cleaning up the garbage gyres in the ocean. However, she ends her talk by describing a more realistic solution to the ocean plastic pollution crisis.

Watch

Think

Dig Deeper

Discuss

. . . And Finally

---

2. Your group of three or four will create a website and blog using one of the following web tools: Weebly (www.weebly.com), Kidblog (http://kidblog.org), PBworks (www.pbworks .com), or WordPress (https://wordpress.com). This webpage will be used as a collaborative tool for brainstorming, planning, sharing information, commenting, making announcements, and analyzing the impact of your project. There should be at least three pages on your website in addition to the home page. These pages should be labeled for your plan, any resources used, persuasive techniques to encourage action in others, and evidence of the work your group has accomplished (videos, comments, data, or pictures). (Visit https:// ithemes.com/tutorial/category/wordpress-101 [iThemes, n.d.] to find helpful tutorials on the creation of a website and blog using WordPress.)

3. After you have prepared the service-learning project plan, your group will work with your peers to implement the plan within the school community. Your group will have to adhere to the following guidelines to implement this plan.

    *   Complete the "Plan Task Sheet" for your project.
    *   Get permission from your homeroom teacher so that you may successfully and adequately complete your job in case you will be late to class, leave early, or use some of your class free time.
    *   Keep track of the work you do by jotting your actions down in a log. Include any numerical data you collect.
    *   Meet weekly with the group to discuss problems and successes, or to answer any questions that have arisen.
    *   Come to meetings prepared. If you are unable to complete your job, please discuss this with your group members and make sure someone can assist you in completing the task in your absence.
    *   Upon completion of the project, your group will discuss the results of the plan and include a blog post on its website so that others can be made aware of the impact of your hard work.

Plan Task Sheet

Name: _____

• What is the purpose of the project?

• What are your goals?

• Who will be involved?

• Who will be responsible for completing each job?

- When will the project take place (beginning and end dates)?

- What materials are needed to complete the project?

- What resources will be used?

- What experts will be contacted?

- How will your work be assessed?

Scoring Rubric

Objective 1: Students will plan, implement, and discuss a service-learning project on ocean plastic pollution.

	1 SIGNIFICANT REVISION NEEDED	2 SOME REVISION NEEDED	3 PROFICIENT	4 EXCEEDS EXPECTATIONS
Project Plan	• Project plan attempts to provide a service to the school but is not realistic in purpose. • Plan shows little evidence of organization. • Plan addresses some of the provided questions effectively. Others are not addressed or lack detail. • Plan includes some group members; a few members are doing all the assigned tasks. • Plan is posted on the website but is limited in its detail and description.	• Project plan provides a service to individual rooms in the school building. • Plan shows some evidence of organization, but some gaps are present. • Plan addresses most of the provided questions effectively. • Plan includes most group members; some members are assigned more tasks than others. • Plan is listed on the website but lacks detail.	• Project plan provides a service to the school related to the authentic topic of plastic pollution. • Plan is organized. • Plan addresses all provided questions effectively. • Plan is realistic. • Plan includes all group members equally. • Plan is recorded on the group website.	• Project plan provides a service to the school and community related to the authentic topic of plastic pollution. • Plan is well organized and includes detailed descriptions of each component. • Plan addresses all provided questions in addition to student-initiated questions. • Plan includes all group members and outside experts. • Plan is recorded in great detail on the group website in addition to another student-initiated web 2.0 tool.
Project Implementation	• Project is not fully implemented.	• Very few changes are made even if they would make the project more effective. • Most of the group members complete their assigned tasks effectively; some members fail to complete their tasks or do so ineffectively. • Project activities are recorded on the website with little detail or description.	• When necessary, changes are made to the plan to meet the intended purpose of the project. • All group members complete their assigned tasks effectively. • Project activities are recorded on the group website.	• When appropriate, additions and deletions are made to the plan in order to meet the intended purpose of the project. • All group members and additional volunteers complete their assigned tasks effectively and within the provided time frame. • Project activities are recorded on the group website in addition to another student-initiated web 2.0 tool.

Real-World Learning Framework for Elementary Schools © 2017 Solution Tree Press • SolutionTree.com
Visit **go.SolutionTree.com/instruction** to download this free reproducible.

Project Analysis	• Analysis is not complete.	• Students report some of the results of their project; some data may be missing or incomplete. • Data are represented in a visual form; the chosen form may not be the most appropriate. • Project analysis is listed on the website but lacks detail and description of some components.	• Students accurately report the results of their project. • Data are appropriately represented in a visual form. • Each component of the project is analyzed. • Project analysis is recorded on the group website.	• Students accurately report the results of their project, specifically noting individual actions. • Data are appropriately represented in more than one visual form. • Each component, as well as the overall project, is analyzed. • Project analysis is recorded on the group website in addition to another student-initiated web 2.0 tool.

Objective 2: Students will create a website and blog that shares information on the content objective as well as evidence of the impact of their service-learning project.

	1 **SIGNIFICANT REVISION NEEDED**	**2** **SOME REVISION NEEDED**	**3** **PROFICIENT**	**4** **EXCEEDS EXPECTATIONS**
Website Requirements	• Website is not complete.	• Website contains fewer than four pages including the home page. • The project plan is present, but viewers cannot easily find it. • Some activities completed throughout the project are listed but are not labeled to be easily found and may lack detail and description. • Some of the project's results are present but are not labeled to be easily found and may lack data, detail, and description. • Most group members contribute to the creation and maintenance of the website; some members do not participate in this task.	• Website contains four pages including the home page. • Viewers can find the project plan easily. • The activities performed throughout the project are described, are recorded, and can be easily found. • The project's results are recorded and can be easily found. • All group members contribute to the creation and maintenance of the website.	• Website contains more than four pages including the home page. All pages are related to the topic of ocean plastic pollution. • The project plan is clearly visible and includes a detailed description of the plan. • The activities performed throughout the project are clearly visible and include a detailed description of each task. • The project's results are clearly visible and include a detailed description of each analysis. • All group members and additional volunteers contribute to the creation and maintenance of the website.

| Collabora-tion | • Some students work together, but there are disruptions that impact the success of the project.

• Group work is not divided equally among all members; a few students do all the work.

• Group members do not attempt to hold one another accountable for their actions. Many members are allowed to neglect their assigned tasks with little or no consequence. | • Most students work together, but the group do not complete all assigned tasks.

• Group work is not divided equally among all members; some members do more of the work than others.

• Group members attempt to hold one another accountable for their actions. Some members are allowed to neglect their assigned tasks with little or no consequence. | • Students work together effectively, completing all assigned tasks.

• Group work is divided equally among members.

• Group members hold one another accountable for their actions respectfully. | • Students and additional volunteers work together effectively, completing all assigned and modified tasks.

• Group work is divided equally among members and volunteers.

• Group members hold one another accountable for their actions in a respectful and professional manner. |

Sources: Hundley, n.d.; iThemes, n.d.

Real-World Learning Framework for Elementary Schools © 2017 Solution Tree Press • SolutionTree.com
Visit **go.SolutionTree.com/instruction** to download this free reproducible.

Sample Student Work

Visit https://reduceoceanplasticpollution.wordpress.com to access the Wilkerson Traditional Elementary Ocean Plastic Pollution Project. This website demonstrates student work that includes student research, a detailed project plan, and project results.

Create Excellence Framework Rating

CREATE ANALYSIS		
CREATE COMPONENT	**LEVEL**	**JUSTIFICATION**
Real-World Learning	4: Integrating	The learning the students will be doing will impact their school community and has the potential to impact the global community. The website they create can additionally impact others as it raises awareness of the problem of ocean plastic pollution and provides others with a plan that could be duplicated in other schools and communities. Students will be communicating to an authentic audience for a real-world purpose.
Cognitive Complexity	4: Integrating	Students will be creating their own project based on the information they find in their research of ocean plastic pollution. They will additionally be asked to evaluate the information they find, generate a plan, implement the plan, and analyze the results. While the group topics will be based on the overarching topic of ocean plastic pollution, the route they take for their plan and website will be student generated.
Student Engagement	4: Integrating	Students will be provided with the general topic for their work (ocean plastic pollution) but will be given the opportunity to define the content they choose to focus on for their service-learning project. Students will have the opportunity to collaborate with their peers while planning, creating, implementing, and evaluating the service-learning project as well as in the creation and maintenance of the website and blog. While all students will be creating a website, blog, and service-learning project, each product will be different as it is guided by student choice and not teacher directed.
Technology Integration	3: Investigating	While students will be collaborating in order to create, implement, and analyze this project, the creation of the website is not essential to the completion of the service-learning project. Students will, however, use the technology component of the project to analyze their research, create the website, and evaluate the impact their work has on the ocean plastic pollution problem.

PICK THAT PET!

Source: Adapted from Savannah Denning. Used with permission.

Content: Science

Learning Objectives:

1. Students will investigate and analyze the features and habitats of potential class pets.
2. After viewing classmate presentations, students will make a decision about which class pet option would be the best fit for the classroom and construct an opinion writing piece to support their decision.

Standards:

Next Generation Science Standards—

- 2-LS4–1 Make observations of plants and animals to compare the diversity of life in different habitats (Achieve, 2013).
- 3-LS4–2 Use evidence to construct an explanation for how the variations in characteristics among individuals of the same species may provide advantages in surviving, finding mates, and reproducing (Achieve, 2013).

Common Core English language arts—

- W.2.1 Write opinion pieces in which they introduce the topic or book they are writing about, state an opinion, supply reasons that support the opinion, use linking words (e.g., *because, and, also*) to connect opinion and reasons, and provide a concluding statement or section (NGA & CCSSO, 2010a).
- W.2.2 Write informative/explanatory texts in which they introduce a topic, use facts and definitions to develop points, and provide a concluding statement or section (NGA & CCSSO, 2010a).
- W.2.6 With guidance and support from adults, use a variety of digital tools to produce and publish writing, including in collaboration with peers (NGA & CCSSO, 2010a).
- SL.2.1 Participate in collaborative conversations with diverse partners about *grade 2 topics and texts* with peers and adults in small and larger groups (NGA & CCSSO, 2010a).

Project Options:

- Students may prefer to work independently, in which case that preference can be taken into consideration during this project.
- Students may be included in the creation of the class survey when it is time to vote for a class pet using Google Forms to create the survey and in pushing it out to students via Google Classroom or a class blog.
- Students may also share their class pet policy projects with other schools to broaden their outreach and authentic communication. Using Google Drive and Google Apps for Education is strongly suggested to promote teacher and student collaboration and make providing detailed and meaningful feedback more effective and efficient.

Resources Needed: Students will need computers or devices with Internet access, a reliable search engine like KidRex, and several presentation tools, programs, or apps.

Pick That Pet!

Our class is ready to adopt a class pet! The pet we choose to adopt is going to be a class decision. You and your group mates will select three potential class pets that you will investigate to determine if they would be good fits for our classroom. You must take into consideration the conditions of our classroom and the animal's individual features. Your group will choose one class pet animal to present to your classmates. You will present your group's opinion about which class pet we should adopt, as well as evidence to support your idea. Our class will vote and adopt the pet!

Project Tasks

1. With your classmates, develop a list of three possible class pets that you would like to research.

2. Begin your research about each animal's unique features to determine which choice would be the best fit for our classroom environment. You may use any resources you prefer: Internet research resources (like KidRex [www.kidrex.org]), library books, animal videos (no longer than ten minutes), or professionals.

3. Complete an "Animal Features Page" for each animal in your group.

4. With your group, choose the best fit from your three possible selections. Prepare a presentation to share with your classmates that would convince them to choose your pet suggestion for our class pet. You may choose any presentation tool, program, or app you are familiar with, including Smore (www.smore.com), Prezi (https://prezi.com), Google Slides (www.google.com/slides), iMovie (www.apple.com/mac/imovie), Book Creator (http://bookcreator.com), Glogster (www.glogster.com), and ThingLink (www.thinglink.com). Use the "Presentation Planning Guide," and review the "Presentation Guidelines" (page 278).

5. After all presentations have been given, construct an opinion writing piece to explain which animal you will vote for and your thinking behind why that animal is a perfect fit. Then, the class will vote to determine which class pet we will adopt. Review the "Opinion Writing Guidelines" (page 278).

6. Finally, create a new class pet handbook or guide for other students and classes in our school. This can take many forms—use your imagination and your resources! Guides could be in the form of videos, commercials, presentations, brochures, or written reports. Review the "Pet Handbook Guidelines" (page 278).

7. Purchase the class pet!

Real-World Learning Framework for Elementary Schools © 2017 Solution Tree Press • SolutionTree.com
Visit **go.SolutionTree.com/instruction** to download this free reproducible.

Animal Features Page

Animal: _____

Sources: _____

Animal features:

Animal habitat:

Pros:	Cons:

Presentation Planning Guide

Animal choice:

Presentation tool, program, or app:

Animal features:

Animal habitat:

Pros:	Cons:

Presentation Guidelines

When you are creating your pet presentation, please be sure to include the following information.

☐ Pet choice

☐ Animal features

☐ Animal habitat requirements

☐ Pros (positives) for your pet choice

☐ Cons (negatives) for your pet choice

Opinion Writing Guidelines

When you are writing your opinion piece, please follow these guidelines.

☐ Include a sentence that introduces the topic you are writing about.

☐ Clearly state your opinion about your choice for a class pet.

☐ Support your opinion with at least three reasons that are directly connected to information about the animal's features or habitat.

☐ Include a conclusion statement that restates your opinion.

☐ Use correct grammar, capitalization, and punctuation throughout your writing piece.

Pet Handbook Guidelines

When you are creating your pet handbook, please be sure to include the following information.

☐ Schoolwide rules we should adopt to make choosing a class pet easier for classrooms

☐ Teachers' and students' responsibilities when adopting a class pet

☐ Suggestions for three top class pet options and the reasoning behind your choices

☐ Topics and rules for food, shelter, and exercise

Use the following table for organizing class pet ideas.

Presentation Listening Guide

Class pet suggestion:	
Pros:	Cons:
Animal features:	
Animal habitat:	

Use the following table to organize your thoughts when listening to presentations.

Group Presentation Feedback

POSITIVE FEEDBACK	POSITIVE FEEDBACK	AREA FOR GROWTH
My opinion:		

Real-World Learning Framework for Elementary Schools © 2017 Solution Tree Press • SolutionTree.com
Visit **go.SolutionTree.com/instruction** to download this free reproducible.

Scoring Rubric

	1 SIGNIFICANT REVISION NEEDED	2 SOME REVISION NEEDED	3 PROFICIENT	4 EXCEEDS EXPECTATIONS
Objective 1: Students will investigate and analyze the features and habitats of potential class pets.	Student research does not represent his or her own thinking or analysis. Much of the information is simply transferred from one source to another. Some animal features organizers are missing or irrelevant. Student does not utilize the "Presentation Planning Guide." Student presentation meets few of the requirements listed on the guidelines page. The presentation is incomplete or irrelevant.	Student research shows some individual thinking and analysis. Some of the information is simply transferred from one source to another, while there may be attempts to paraphrase. Animal features organizers are included for three animal choices but have missing parts. Student completes the presentation guide but does not use the guide to create a presentation. Student presentation meets some of the requirements listed on the guidelines page. The presentation is complete but unorganized.	Student research shows adequate individual thinking and analysis. Information is accurately paraphrased. Animal features organizers are complete and correct for three animal choices. Student adequately utilizes the planning guide to build a presentation around the initial plan. Student presentation meets all the requirements listed on the guidelines page. The presentation is organized and complete.	Student research shows remarkable individual thinking and analysis. Information is accurately paraphrased. Animal features organizers are complete and organized and show exceptional thoughtfulness. Student completes the planning guide with no flaws and uses the guide to build and organize a presentation. Student presentation meets all the requirements listed on the guidelines page and may include additional, but relevant, information. The presentation is organized and is creatively designed.

	1 SIGNIFICANT REVISION NEEDED	2 SOME REVISION NEEDED	3 PROFICIENT	4 EXCEEDS EXPECTATIONS
Objective 2: After viewing classmate presentations, students will make a decision about which class pet option would be the best fit for the classroom and construct an opinion writing piece to support their decision.	The class pet guide is poorly organized and does not communicate clear ideas. Student does not contribute to group efforts. Student does not include an introduction or conclusion statement. Student does not state an opinion. Student's opinion is not supported with adequate reasoning. Student does not show grade-level competency in language mechanics, even with support from the teacher.	The class pet guide is somewhat organized and may communicate some clear ideas. Student contributes somewhat to group efforts. Student includes either an introduction or conclusion statement. Student states an opinion that lacks clarity. Student's opinion is supported with very little reasoning. Student shows some competency in grade-level language mechanics. Student may require support from the teacher.	The class pet guide is well organized and communicates clear ideas. Student adequately contributes to group efforts. Student includes both an introduction and conclusion statement. Student adequately states a clear opinion. Student's opinion is supported with adequate reasoning. Student shows competency in grade-level language mechanics. Student requires little support from the teacher.	The class pet guide is exceptionally organized and communicates clear ideas. Student shows leadership in group research efforts. Student includes a creative introduction and conclusion statement. Student states a clear and strong opinion. Student's opinion is supported with exceptional reasoning. Student shows exceptional competency in grade-level language mechanics. Student requires very little support from the teacher.

Real-World Learning Framework for Elementary Schools © 2017 Solution Tree Press • SolutionTree.com
Visit **go.SolutionTree.com/instruction** to download this free reproducible.

Sample Student Work

Visit http://bit.ly/2g1ilxb for a sample feature class presentation.

Animal Features Page

Creature features: Axolotl

- Amphibians usually develop from an egg into a larval form and finally into an adult. But axolotls remain in their larval form throughout their life.
- Axolotls are completely aquatic. They do have lungs but breathe through their gills and also through their skin.
- Axolotls only need to be fed every two or three days.
- Axolotls are famous for their amazing healing abilities. They can regenerate almost any injured part of their body, including the limbs, the tail, the skin, and even major organs like the heart, liver, and kidney.
- The axolotl salamander looks young forever.
- Axolotls can live up to fifteen years on a diet of worms, insects, and small fish.
- Like all amphibians, it is poikilothermic (its body temperature is dependent on its surroundings).

Axolotl Care Sheet

- Most axolotls reach about ten inches total in length.
- A ten-gallon aquarium can accommodate a single adult axolotl, but due to the large amount of waste produced by these messy creatures, a twenty-gallon aquarium is a safer choice. Axolotls do not emerge from the water, so a land area would go unused. Fill the aquarium to the depth of your choice, but it will be easier to maintain good water parameters when the aquarium is filled, as you would for aquarium fish. A lid or aquarium hood should be kept in place at all times because axolotls have been known to jump out of their aquariums.

The following is a sample opinion piece.

I think our class should adopt an axolotl. One reason why I think this would be a perfect pet for our classroom is because our classroom temperature is pretty cool. Axolotls need cool temperatures between 60 and 75 degrees, and that is just right for our classroom. Also, I think that an axolotl would be a good pet because they only need to be fed every two to three days. We are out of school on the weekend, so this animal feature would be great for our classroom. We can feed the axolotl on Friday, and he or she will be okay until we come back to school. Another reason that an axolotl would be a good class pet for us is because they can regrow body parts. We would all be sad if our class pet got sick or hurt, but this type of animal can regrow body parts that are hurt and can heal and get better really easy. Finally, one last reason I think an axolotl would be a good pet is because they live in water all the time, in a tank. Axolotl do not like to be touched or handled, so they would be pretty easy to take care of. They don't need a lot of attention or special care, so we can enjoy the pet and still focus on our schoolwork. These are all reasons why I think our class should adopt an axolotl for our class pet.

Source: Josie, n.d.

Create Excellence Framework Rating

CREATE ANALYSIS		
CREATE COMPONENT	**LEVEL**	**JUSTIFICATION**
Real-World Learning	4: Integrating	Learning emphasizes and impacts the classroom and the school with the creation of a class pet adoption policy. Learning is integrated across all subjects, combining science, writing, and speaking and listening standards.
Cognitive Complexity	3: Investigating	The teacher directs student interaction with the standard; students are analyzing information, evaluating the best possible class pet option and supporting their choice, and creating products to aid other classrooms that are interested in adopting class pets.
Student Engagement	4: Integrating	Students partner with the teacher to determine the means of creating their products (class presentations and school policy products). There is an inquiry-based approach, and students are urged to use their creativity in the creation of products. Students must collaborate with others in order to adequately complete each portion of this project.
Technology Integration	4: Integrating	Student technology is embedded in content and essential to project completion. Technology promotes student and teacher collaboration (especially if students are using Google Drive tools for education). Technology empowers students to communicate with professionals outside of school.

A PENGUIN'S LIFE

Source: Adapted from Carolyn Crowe. Used with permission.

Content: Science

Learning Objectives:

1. Students will analyze the most important behaviors and physical attributes that penguins use for survival.
2. Students will create a multimedia presentation to demonstrate a day in the life of a penguin.

Standards:

Next Generation Science Standards—

- LS1.A Organisms have both internal and external macroscopic structures that allow for growth, survival, behavior, and reproduction (NGSS Lead States, 2013).

Common Core English language arts—

- W.2.7 Participate in shared research and projects (e.g., read a number of books on a single topic to produce a report; record science observations; NGA & CCSSO, 2010a).
- RI.2.9 Compare and contrast the most important points presented by texts on the same topic (NGA & CCSSO, 2010a).
- SL.2.4 Tell a story or recount an experience with appropriate facts and relevant, descriptive details (NGA & CCSSO, 2010a).

Project Options: Students could compare and contrast penguins' characteristics and behaviors with those of people.

Resources Needed: Computer with Internet access, web tools for a multimedia presentation (iMovie, emaze, PowToon), and books on penguins, including *National Geographic Readers: Penguins!* by Anne Schreiber (2009) and *Penguins!* by Gail Gibbons (1998)

Science
Projects

A Penguin's Life

What would it be like to be a penguin? What behaviors and physical attributes would you use to survive in arctic temperatures? You would definitely need a coat to live there! Just like people, penguins have many physical characteristics and behaviors that are essential to their survival.

Project Tasks

1. Individually, watch the PlayPosit video (https://www.playposit.com/share/170427/330037), and complete the check-in questions in the video.

2. In groups of four students, find information about penguin behaviors and physical characteristics that support its survival. Use at least two of the following resources, and complete the "Penguin Life Task Sheet."

   - *National Geographic Readers: Penguins!* by Anne Schreiber (2009)
   - *Penguins!* by Gail Gibbons (1998)
   - SeaWorld Parks and Entertainment's (n.d.b) "Penguin Physical Characteristics" (https://seaworld.org/en/animal-info/animal-infobooks/penguin/physical-characteristics)
   - SeaWorld Parks and Entertainment's (n.d.a) "Penguin Behavior" (https://seaworld.org/en/animal-info/animal-infobooks/penguin/behavior)

3. As a whole class, each group will share its most important behaviors and characteristics. You will get to vote on which group is the most convincing through the use of relevant details.

4. Pretend that you are a penguin.

   - Describe what a day in your life is like in a multimedia presentation.
   - Be sure to share the most essential behaviors or physical characteristics that you need for survival.
   - You may use PowToon, emaze, iMovie, or another tool your teacher approves to present this information.

page 1 of 4

Penguin Life Task Sheet

Group members' names: _____ Date: _____

Complete part one of the "Penguin Life Task Sheet."

Describe six penguin behaviors and six physical characteristics that help them survive. Draw a picture that represents each behavior or characteristic.	
Behaviors	1.
	2.
	3.
	4.
	5.
	6.
Physical Characteristics	1.
	2.
	3.
	4.
	5.
	6.

Review your ideas. What are the three most important behaviors or physical characteristics that penguins use for survival? Explain why without these the penguin couldn't survive.

Now complete part two of the "Penguin Life Task Sheet."

IMPORTANT BEHAVIORS OR PHYSICAL CHARACTERISTICS	EXPLANATION
1.	
2.	
3.	

Scoring Rubric

	1 SIGNIFICANT REVISION NEEDED	2 SOME REVISION NEEDED	3 PROFICIENT	4 EXCEEDS EXPECTATIONS
Objective 1: Students will analyze the most important behaviors and physical attributes that penguins use for survival.	Student lists only one or two penguin behaviors and characteristics. Student provides analysis of one penguin behavior and attribute.	Student lists three to five penguin behaviors and characteristics. Student provides analysis of one or two penguin behaviors and attributes; elements are missing.	Student lists six penguin behaviors and characteristics. Student provides adequate analysis of three essential penguin behaviors and attributes.	Student lists six-plus penguin behaviors and characteristics. Student provides thorough analysis of three essential penguin behaviors and attributes.

	1 SIGNIFICANT REVISION NEEDED	2 SOME REVISION NEEDED	3 PROFICIENT	4 EXCEEDS EXPECTATIONS
Objective 2: Students will create a multimedia presentation to demonstrate a day in the life of a penguin.	Multimedia presentation is incomplete. Information is missing or incorrect.	Multimedia presentation has some original elements. Description covers some of the penguin behaviors.	Multimedia presentation is original and appeals to the audience. Presentation describes penguin behaviors completely. Information is clear, appropriate, correct, and relevant to the materials researched.	Multimedia presentation is original and unique and appeals to the audience. Presentation describes penguin behaviors completely and in depth. Information is clear, appropriate, correct, and relevant to the materials researched.

Sources: Gibbons, 1998; Schreiber, 2009; SeaWorld Parks and Entertainment, n.d.a., n.d.b.

Sample Student Work

The following is sample student work.

Penguin Life Task Sheet

Group members' names: Muhammad, Beck, and Carolyn   Date: March 2

Complete part one of the "Penguin Life Task Sheet."

Describe six penguin behaviors and physical characteristics that help them survive.	
Behaviors	1. Preening-Cleaning their feathers
	2. Molting-When they lose old feathers to make way for new growth
	3. Bowing-To flirt with a boy or a girl penguin
	4. Diving-To catch fish
	5. Nesting-Make a nest to protect the babies
	6. Social-They like to be around other penguins
Physical Characteristics	1. Feathers-Short, closely spaced to keep water away from the skin and keep them warm
	2. Webbed feet-Legs and webbed feet are set far back on the body, which gives penguins their upright posture on land
	3. Flippers-Shaped like a paddle, which is perfect for swimming
	4. Coloration-Dark on the back and white on the belly; the dark side blends in with the dark ocean and belly looks like the color of the sea, which helps them avoid predators
	5. Body shape-Perfect for swimming with a big head and long body
	6. Tail-Short and wedge-shaped

Review your ideas. What are the three most important behaviors or physical characteristics that penguins use for survival? Explain why without these the penguin couldn't survive.

Now complete part two of the "Penguin Life Task Sheet."

IMPORTANT BEHAVIORS OR PHYSICAL CHARACTERISTICS	EXPLANATION
1. Preening	Penguins straighten and condition their feathers. They oil their feathers in order to help them swim and glide easily to catch food.
2. Nesting	Penguins only lay one or two eggs, and this helps ensure that their species will continue on.
3. Body shape	Penguins have long bodies, which help them to swim easily to catch food to eat.

Visit www.youtube.com/watch?v=9zrRIb1AuLM&rel=0 to access the PowToon presentation "Penguin Life" (Crowe, 2015). See "A Day in the Life of a Penguin" (http://bit.ly/2cApn9y; techn0teach, 2011) to access the SlideShare presentation.

Create Excellence Framework Rating

CREATE ANALYSIS		
CREATE COMPONENT	**LEVEL**	**JUSTIFICATION**
Real-World Learning	3: Investigating	Students are simulating real-world learning, as they are role-playing as a penguin. They are obtaining a better grasp on the world around them, even though their learning is not impacting their community.
Cognitive Complexity	3: Investigating	Students are summarizing a penguin's characteristics based on their readings. Students then have to select the most important characteristics that penguins need to survive. Finally, they assume a penguin's point of view and create a multimedia presentation describing the life of a penguin.
Student Engagement	3: Investigating	Students are able to choose the penguin behaviors that they want to focus on and can select the multimedia presentation or product that they want to use, based on their learning preferences.
Technology Integration	3: Investigating	Technology is an add-on for this project, and students are using a multimedia presentation to design their final product.

Science
Projects

"CH-CH-CH-CHANGES" IN LAND FORMATIONS!

Source: Adapted from Tara Cox, Lydia Renfro, and Savannah Denning. Used with permission.

Content: Science

Learning Objectives:

1. Students will complete and reflect on an experiment demonstrating water's role in the formation of caves.
2. Students will research land movements and create a model showing the effects water and wind have on land.
3. Students will present and explain a model showing the effects of water and wind on land and develop relevant questions to ask their audience.

Standards:

Next Generation Science Standards—

- 2-ESS2-b Develop models to investigate how wind and water can move Earth materials from one place to another and change the shape of the land quickly or slowly (NGSS Lead States, 2013).

Common Core English language arts—

- RI.2.1 Ask and answer such questions as *who, what, where, when, why,* and *how* to demonstrate understanding of key details in a text (NGA & CCSSO, 2010a).
- SL.2.2 Recount or describe key ideas or details from a text read aloud or information presented orally or through other media (NGA & CCSSO, 2010a).
- SL.2.5 Create audio recordings of stories or poems; add drawings or other visual displays to stories or recounts of experiences when appropriate to clarify ideas, thoughts, and feelings (NGA & CCSSO, 2010a).

Project Options: Predetermined groups of three or four students may choose which of the following land movements they would like to research. They will then, after investigation, create a model depicting how water and wind encourage that particular land movement. Suggestions include—

- Canyons
- Sinkholes
- Sand dunes
- Hurricanes' effect on land

After groups have presented to their first-grade audiences, their audience members can give them feedback on their presentation by writing comments on their Smore, Animoto, or other digital presentation. If technology isn't available, students can leave feedback on sticky notes or index cards.

Resources Needed:

- Video to show the students: Example—"ES1405: Observe an Animation of Cave Formation" (http://bit.ly/1iRDofJ; Wood, n.d.)
- Book to read about cave formation: Example—*Caves* by Larry Dane Brimner (2000), forty-eight pages, nonfiction, ages seven and up

- Website for cave formation: Example—"Cave Geology" (http://caveofthewinds.com/more-to-explore /kids-area/geology-for-kids; Cave of the Winds, n.d.)

After students conduct research, they should select from the following resources what the group believes it will need to create a replica of the land movement it has chosen to model. Students must think critically when choosing their resources, as many items are listed that are unnecessary in creating a specific final product. This is why it's important to research a topic prior to creating a model.

- Sand
- Drinking straw
- Rocks
- Graham crackers
- Sugar cubes
- Soil
- Water
- Two-liter bottle
- Colored lamp oil

All groups should have:

- Computer or tablet (You will research your land movement using at least one credible website and one credible book source.)
- 9 × 13 aluminum baking pan (This will hold your model.)

"Ch-Ch-Ch-Changes" in Land Formations!

Did you know that caves are like sugar? Really, they are! Caves are made up of limestone that is soluble. If something is soluble, it means that the substance dissolves in water. We have learned that sugar dissolves in things like sweet tea and drink mixes. Unlike tea, however, the formation that caves undergo is a much longer process.

Project Tasks

After researching water's role in cave formation, we will experience this process as a class, using clay, a clear cup of water, and sugar cubes. To prepare:

1. Use the "Shaping Landforms Checklist" (page 297) to help you understand this project.

2. Read a book or watch a video about how caves are formed. (See suggestions in Resources Needed.)

3. Collect the following tools for your group experiment.

    - One ball of clay
    - One clear cup of water (filled halfway)
    - Four sugar cubes
    - The "Predict, Observe, Explain Chart" (page 297)
    - A pencil
    - A computer or tablet computer

To conduct the experiment:

1. Flatten out the clay, and press the sugar cubes, in groups of two, into the clay, keeping the cubes close together. This should result in a 2 × 2 square of sugar cubes.

2. Wrap the clay around the sugar cubes, leaving one side of the cubes visible but firmly in the clay, creating the shape of a ball.

3. What do you think will happen if you place the ball into the water? Complete the predict portion of your "Predict, Observe, Explain Chart."

4. Place the ball into the water, making sure that the sugar cubes are visible from outside the clear cup, so that all group members may see the changes occurring.

5. During the experiment, complete the observe portion of your "Predict, Observe, Explain Chart."

6. Complete the explain portion of the experiment addressing each of the following questions.

    - What did the clay and sugar cubes represent in the experiment?
    - Why do you think the sugar cubes dissolved in the water?
    - What was the purpose of this experiment?

Now you will create your own and present your findings.

1. Each group should choose a different land change to learn about. Your group should develop three questions for your land change research and have your teacher approve them. Use the "Land Change Research Question Organizer" (page 298) and the "Research Question Organizer" (page 299) for this. Use your technology resources to answer your questions.

2. Design a model to showcase that land change. Complete the "Land Change Model Sketch" on page 299. You can select your own materials and decide how you want to demonstrate your land change. Review the checklist to help your group understand this task.

3. Collect the tools your group will use to create a model. Before you begin, obtain another "Predict, Observe, Explain Chart," and complete the predict section of the chart.

4. While creating your model, complete the observe portion of your "Predict, Observe, Explain Chart." Take pictures throughout the process to document your work.

5. As you finish your model, complete the explain portion of the experiment answering each of the following questions.

   • What effect does water and wind have on the land changes your group chose?
   • How do you believe the land would be different if water and wind were not present?
   • In what areas is your land change most common? Why do you think that is?

6. Choose a form of technology to help you share your observations and explanations with your assigned first-grade class group. Each group member must explain, within the presentation, his or her role in the product's creation. Share your observations and explanations with the first-grade class. You may create an Animoto (https://animoto.com), Piktochart (https://piktochart.com), or Smore (www.smore.com) for your presentation. Your presentation must have the following.

   • Pictures of the creation of the model
   • Research from at least two credible sources (one website, one book)
   • Your role in the group task

7. Each group member must also develop one question to ask the audience during the presentation. After the presentation, the first-grade students will provide feedback for your work.

Shaping Landforms Checklist

Every student is expected to complete each of the following steps on the checklist. Place a check mark next to the item as you finish each task.

CHECK WHEN COMPLETE	TASK
	I completed *each* written section of my "Predict, Observe, Explain Chart."
	I drew pictures to go along with my written predictions and observations on my worksheet.
	I helped my group choose three research questions. We used the "Land Change Research Question Organizer" and received teacher approval before we began research.
	I actively participated in my group's research, and we used: • The research organizer • One credible website • One credible book source
	I assisted my group in taking photographs of our model as it was being created.
	I helped the other members in my group use technology to create a presentation.
	My group explained the landform, using the pictures of our model, in our technology presentation.
	My group used the "Land Change Model Sketch" planner.
	My group demonstrated a real-life example of something that is soluble.
	I explained my role in the task during my group's presentation.

Predict, Observe, Explain Chart

My group chose to create a model of _____.

Directions: In the following boxes, you will write your predictions of what might happen when you use particular resources to create your model, what you observe while creating the model, and what you learned throughout your research and investigation.

PREDICT	OBSERVE	EXPLAIN

Directions: Under Predict and Observe, draw pictures that match what you wrote about.

PREDICT	OBSERVE

Land Change Research Question Organizer

Use this chart to plan your research questions for land change. Be sure to partner with your teacher for feedback on your planned questions.

Land change choice: _____

RESEARCH QUESTION	TEACHER APPROVAL
1.	
2.	
3.	

Land Change Model Sketch

Before you begin creating your model, make a plan.

What do you think your model should look like when you begin? What about in the middle of your demonstration? What should it look like when you are finished?

Beginning	
Middle	
End	

Research Question Organizer

Use this chart to help you organize your research.

RESEARCH QUESTION	NOTES	SOURCE
1.		
2.		
3.		

Scoring Rubric

	1 **SIGNIFICANT REVISION NEEDED**	**2** **SOME REVISION NEEDED**	**3** **PROFICIENT**	**4** **EXCEEDS EXPECTATIONS**
Objective 1: Students will complete and reflect on an experiment demonstrating water's role in the formation of caves.	Student does not successfully complete the experiment. Student fails to complete the "Predict, Observe, Explain Chart's" written section. Student's graphic section of the "Predict, Observe, Explain Chart" lacks pictures.	Student successfully completes the experiment with significant assistance from the teacher. Student completes the "Predict, Observe, Explain Chart's" written section. Pictures are not included within student's "Predict, Observe, Explain Chart."	Student adequately completes the experiment. Student completes the "Predict, Observe, Explain Chart's" written section, logically. Pictures are included within student's "Predict, Observe, Explain Chart."	Student completes the experiment and shows leadership skills. Student's chart shows well-thought-out predictions, detailed observations, and educated assumptions for explanations. Student includes detailed pictures within the "Predict, Observe, Explain Chart."
Objective 2: Students will research land movements and create a model showing the effects water and wind have on land.	Student does not develop three research questions and does not gain approval from the teacher. Student does not participate in research. Student does not participate in the creation of the final product.	Student develops two research questions and gains approval from the teacher. Student offers some participation in land movement research. Student offers some participation in the creation of the final product.	Student develops three thoughtful research questions and gains approval from the teacher. Student participates in land movement research. Student participates in the creation of the final product.	Student develops three challenging research questions and gains approval from the teacher. Student participates in land movement research and shows leadership in his or her group. Student participates in the creation of the final product and shows leadership in his or her group.

	1 SIGNIFICANT REVISION NEEDED	2 SOME REVISION NEEDED	3 PROFICIENT	4 EXCEEDS EXPECTATIONS
Objective 3: Students will present and explain a model showing the effects of water and wind on land and develop relevant questions to ask their audience.	Student does not explain his or her role in the group during the presentation. Technology presentation or flyer fails to provide the audience with information regarding how water and wind change the land. Student does not develop or ask the audience a question. The group does not include a real-life example of a soluble substance.	Student vaguely explains his or her role in the group during the presentation. Presentation or flyer is very vague in providing information on how the land is affected. Pictures are not present in the final product. Student may develop a question but does not ask the audience. The question may be unclear. The group includes a real-life example of a soluble substance but may not explain what the term means.	Student adequately explains his or her role in the group during the presentation. Student's group uses technology to explain how its model is a good representation of land changes due to water and wind. Students do use one credible website or one book to conduct their research. Student develops a clear and appropriate question and asks the audience. The group includes a real-life example of a soluble substance and explains the term.	Student explains his or her role in the group in detail during the presentation. Student's group presentation or flyer is authentic and clearly provides the audience with an understanding of the natural effects on the land chosen. Each student's role in creating the presentation is addressed, and two credible sources are used to complete research (one website, one book). Student develops a clear and challenging question and asks the audience. The group includes a real-life example of a soluble substance and thoroughly explains the term.

Sample Student Work

Visit www.smore.com/8amxc to access a link to the student sample work "How Canyons Are Made" (Denning, n.d.). Copies of each group's flyer or other technology would be shared with students from the first-grade classes. The second-grade students would act as experts in their field of study and teach what they have learned.

Predict, Observe, Explain Chart

My group chose to create a model of <u>cave formation.</u>

Directions: In the following boxes, you will write your predictions of what might happen when you use particular resources to create your model, what you observe while creating the model, and what you learned throughout your research and investigation.

PREDICT	OBSERVE	EXPLAIN
I think that the sugar will make the clay explode.	Pieces of the sugar cubes started breaking apart, and the water started bubbling. When the sugar disappeared, there was a big dent in the clay.	I learned that the base of a cave is made up of sandstone. The sandstone tries to protect the limestone. Limestone is soluble—that means it dissolves in liquid. When it rains, limestone breaks away and makes caves.

Directions: Under Predict and Observe, draw pictures that match what you wrote about.

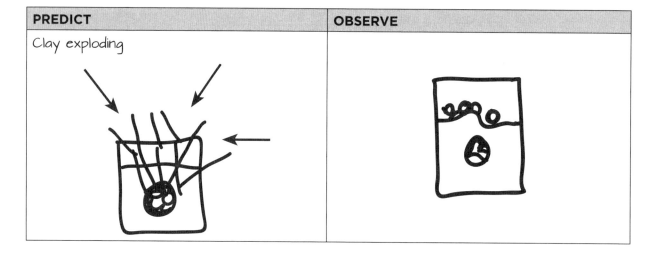

Create Excellence Framework Rating

CREATE ANALYSIS		
CREATE COMPONENT	**LEVEL**	**JUSTIFICATION**
Real-World Learning	3: Investigating	Students are simulating the role of scientists, and they conduct their own experiment. Upon experiencing the phenomenon and collecting research, they are assuming the experts' role and are responsible for describing the results of their findings to younger students.
Cognitive Complexity	4: Integrating	Students are working at the Analyze level of Bloom's taxonomy as they take part in the whole-group experiment. Students are also working at the Evaluate and Create levels as they research, perform, and present their own experiment related to land changes.
Student Engagement	4: Integrating	Every group has a choice in the land change it researches. Students also select which technology they will use for their presentation. It can meet the specific interests of the students because of the range of technology permitted within this assignment. For example, those who prefer explaining information through speech would probably enjoy creating an Animoto presentation. Any students who like informing others of related information in one clean product may wish to develop a Smore presentation, and students who would like to create posters to teach other students about the topic in specific details would probably choose to create a Piktochart.
Technology Integration	3: Investigating	Creating a technology product is necessary in completing this assignment. Students design a digital presentation to share with other students. Photography is also a requirement for the final product.

Science Projects

PULL-TOY PROJECT

Source: Adapted from Gabe VanCappellen and Sam Northern. Used with permission.

Content: Science, specifically automation and robotics

Learning Objectives:

1. Students will design and create an original pull-toy with a gear assembly for children.
2. Students will critique the design and engineering process classmates use to decide the most innovative pull-toy the engineering teams create.

Standards:

Next Generation Science Standards—

- 3–5-ETSI-2 Generate and compare multiple possible solutions to a problem based on how well each is likely to meet the criteria and constraints of the problem (NGSS Lead States, 2013).
- 3–5-ETSI-3 Plan and carry out fair tests in which variables are controlled and failure points are considered to identify aspects of a model or prototype that can be improved (NGSS Lead States, 2013).

Project Options: Students will design and create a prototype pull-toy for children. Teams will decide the age group for which they would like to market their pull-toy. The pull-toy will be built using VEX Robotics parts and must meet the following constraints: four-wheel chassis that can be pulled across a table or floor, use of a gear mechanism to simulate movement, and artwork to make the pull-toy look realistic.

Resources Needed: You'll need isometric graph paper, a computer with Internet access for research, an iPad to document the build, a pencil, and one VEX kit per group.

Pull-Toy Project

You have been studying forces and motion, types of movement, speed and rotation, and the way gears work. You will be divided into groups of three, and each group is to act as an engineering firm. The engineering firms have been asked to create a prototype pull-toy for children. A pull-toy is pulled along the ground and a movement is produced—for example, a head nods, a tail wags, or a figure bobs up and down. The pull-toy will be built using VEX Robotics parts and must include the following: four-wheel chassis that can be pulled across a table or floor, use of a gear mechanism to simulate movement, and artwork to make the pull-toy look realistic. At the conclusion of the builds, the engineering teams will review the other teams' pull-toy designs and decide on the best pull-toy design.

Project Tasks

1. With your knowledge of mechanisms, you and your partners will work as an engineering firm to design and build a mechanism that will meet the following criteria.

   ◆ The mechanism is to be built entirely from VEX parts provided in the lab.
   ◆ The mechanism is to be built on a small four-wheel chassis capable of being pulled across a tabletop surface. The movement of the wheels will set the toy in motion.
   ◆ A gear mechanism attached to the wheels will make another part of the pull-toy move.
   ◆ A printed illustration or photograph should be added to the pull-toy to interact with the working mechanism as the toy is moving.

2. To begin this process, use the templates to document your design process. First, complete the "Design Brief" template to define the problem. In the Design Statement section, describe the design of your pull-toy and how you tested it. Identify how you met the project's constraints in the appropriate section. After you test your prototype, explain how you made adjustments to your pull-toy in the Modifications section. In the Deliverables section, list the hardware, design documents, and other products your team created for your final prototype.

   Then, use isometric graph paper to create detailed sketches with metric measurements. All measurements must be listed.

3. Create a parts list. Keep a detailed list of the parts used to construct your pull-toy. Engineers do this to help with mass production. Be sure to include the measurement of each part used.

4. When all groups have completed their pull-toy, you will use the project rubric to review the pull-toys other groups built.

Note: Engineering firms use design briefs to communicate with each other as they may be working in different departments and not side by side. The document is used as a template for what is being created and also describes the constraints that must be followed to properly complete the task. For engineering firms, it can be difficult to meet the constraints, but this is a requirement for safety and customer happiness. This is helpful for organization while completing the project.

Design Brief

As a group, come up with a name for your engineering firm, and list that in the Designer row. The client should be the target audience you plan to market your toy to. Identify the problem you are seeking to resolve with your pull-toy prototype. Describe how your group designed, tested, and modified your pull-toy in accordance with the project's constraints. Prepare and list the deliverables that you will share with your client.

Client	
Designer	
Problem Statement	
Design Statement	
Constraints	
Modifications	
Deliverables	

Real-World Learning Framework for Elementary Schools © 2017 Solution Tree Press • SolutionTree.com
Visit **go.SolutionTree.com/instruction** to download this free reproducible.

Scoring Rubric

Objective 1: Students will design and create an original pull-toy with a gear assembly for children.				
	1 SIGNIFICANT REVISION NEEDED	**2 SOME REVISION NEEDED**	**3 PROFICIENT**	**4 EXCEEDS EXPECTATIONS**
Design Brief	Design brief is less than 50 percent complete.	Design brief is 50 percent complete.	Design brief is 80 percent complete.	Design brief is complete and includes all required information, including client, designer, problem statement, design statement, constraints, and deliverables.
Design Sketches	Sketches are not complete. Heading information is not complete and is inaccurate. Sketches are not created with pencil.	Sketches are missing more than half the identification of the components. More than half the heading information is not complete or is inaccurate. Most designs are completed in pencil.	One or two sketches are incomplete and are missing important information, such as measurements. Some heading information is incomplete or inaccurate. All designs are unique and are completed in pencil.	Three sketches are complete and annotated to show all important information. Heading information is complete and accurate. All designs are unique and are completed in pencil.
Research	There is no research other than what is available from the textbook or lecture notes.	Research is randomly completed with little or no documentation of sources.	Research is documented on some topics. One or two do not have proper citation information. Research is limited to two or three resources.	Research is documented with appropriate citations. Research shows a variety of resources and is not limited to two or three sources.
Test and Evaluate	Student tests and evaluates prototype. Modifications are not completed, and changes are not documented.	Student tests and evaluates prototype. Some modifications are completed, but changes are not documented.	Student tests and evaluates prototype. Student makes modifications if necessary, but changes are not documented.	Student tests and evaluates prototype, makes modifications if necessary, and thoroughly documents changes.
Prototypes	A significant difference exists between the final product and the final design. No apparent attempt was made to follow the design. Prototype is in poor working condition with frequent errors.	A significant difference exists between the final product and the final design, but an attempt was made to follow the design. Prototype is in adequate working condition with some errors.	A slight difference exists between the final product and the final design. Prototype is in working condition with few errors.	The final product exactly matches the final design. Prototype is in excellent working condition with no errors.

The student engineering firms will use the following rubric when critiquing the work of other students. All engineering firms had to follow the constraints while building the prototype of their pull-toy. Student input was used while creating this rubric.

Objective 2: Students will critique the design and engineering process classmates use to decide the most innovative pull-toy the engineering teams create.

	1 SIGNIFICANT REVISION NEEDED	**2 SOME REVISION NEEDED**	**3 PROFICIENT**	**4 EXCEEDS EXPECTATIONS**
Professionalism	Student does not act as a critic. Questions are off topic or inappropriate.	Student takes the role as a critic moderately seriously. Some questions are off topic. Student asks only one question about the group's prototype design.	Student takes the role as a critic seriously and judges the prototype with a professional approach. Student asks two questions about the group's prototype design.	Student takes the role as a critic seriously and judges the prototype with a professional approach. Student asks the group three or more questions about the group's prototype design.
Objectivity	Student shows bias while critiquing the work of other student groups and provides no positive feedback.	Student is somewhat objective and gives one example of positive feedback.	Student is objective and shows no bias to any other students' work. Student provides two examples of positive feedback while critiquing student work.	No bias is evident. Student takes the viewpoint of a consumer and provides three or more examples of positive feedback while critiquing student work.
Design Process Notes	The design process notes do not describe work done at each step of the design process.	Some design process notes are missing or incomplete.	The project design process notes do not explain all steps thoroughly.	The project includes a detailed step-by-step description of the design process.
Teamwork	Student does not listen to other team members, does not show respect for varying opinions, and does not effectively communicate ideas and opinions or engage in compromise. Student completes some of his or her portion of the project on time.	Student does not always effectively listen to team members or show respect for varying opinions. Student does not always communicate ideas and opinions or engage in compromise. Student completes most of his or her portion of the project on time.	Student generally listens to team members, respects varying opinions, communicates ideas and opinions effectively, and engages in compromise. Student completes his or her portion of the project on time.	Student consistently listens to all team members, respects varying opinions, communicates ideas and opinions effectively, and engages in compromise. Student completes his or her portion of the project on time.

Sample Student Work

In this example, a group of students designed a four-wheeled pull-toy that uses bevel gears and a chain drive to introduce children to gear systems and movement. The pull-toy makes the video game character Sonic the Hedgehog appear to be running. Students' deliverables include a detailed sketch of the pull-toy and a working prototype.

Design Brief

Client	Children five to eight years old
Designer	GVC Designs
Problem Statement	Is your child tired of playing with the same old boring toys? Our new pull-toy will keep your child entertained and also introduce him or her to gear systems and movement.
Design Statement	Design, model, and test a four-wheeled pull-toy that will use bevel gears and a chain drive to make video game characters appear to be running through a level on the Sonic the Hedgehog game.
Constraints	Four-wheel chassis
	Pulled by string
	Must use gear mechanism to simulate movement
	One week build time
	Use of VEX Robotics parts
Modifications	Adjust position of the bevel gears on the axles to improve movement of the chain drive
	Reposition the bevel gears for greater accuracy
Deliverables	Detailed sketch with measurements
	Working prototype complete with illustration

Parts List and Design Process Notes

The sample group of students created a detailed list of the parts used to construct their prototype pull-toy. The students describe how they planned, constructed, and modified their mechanism.

- Two axles, 30 centimeters (cm) long
- Two axles, 15 cm long
- Four wheels, 7 cm in diameter
- Four bracket plates, 20 cm long
- Twenty locking washers for axles and gears
- Twenty-two bolts, 8 millimeters (mm) long
- Twenty-two nuts
- Two support brackets, 19 cm long
- Twelve plastic axle supports
- Two flat plates, 18 cm long
- Four bevel gears (16 teeth)
- Four spur gears (8 teeth)

- Chain drive
- Fasteners

To complete the prototype of my pull-toy, I first sketched out the chassis. Prior to sketching, I had a general idea of the parts I wanted to use and measured those. Next, I brainstormed and decided that I wanted to use a bevel gear system that would be attached to the wheels and axles. I connected this to spur gears above the frame that would be joined together using a chain drive. I engineered the gear system to be a speed setup so the characters would look like they were moving faster. The input gears have sixteen teeth, and the output gears have eight teeth. This makes the output turn twice as fast as the input. While building, I did have to continually adjust the position of the bevel gears on the axles to improve movement of the chain drive. This was the most difficult part of the build, getting the position of the bevel gears correct. After assembling the chassis and testing the gear systems, I decided to illustrate a level from the Sonic the Hedgehog video game. I chose this because fifth-grade students are interested in video games and many of them are familiar with the characters I planned to use. After illustrating the world, I printed off pictures of two characters from the game: Sonic and Tails. Sonic is the blue male character, and Tails is the tan female character. To attach them to the chain drive, I used two-sided tape. Visit www.youtube.com/watch?v=2rAxQRMAXpU to see a video of the pull-toy, "VEX Pull-Toy for IDP Project LME 535" (VanCappellen, 2014).

The following is a hand sketch of pull-toy chassis with dimensions.

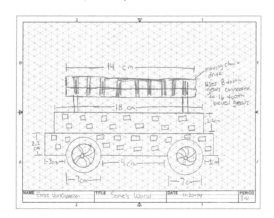

The side view of the pull-toy shows the illustration simulating a level in the Sonic the Hedgehog video game. You can also see the seven-centimeter-diameter wheels used on the chassis. The string used to pull the prototype is also visible.

The top view of the pull-toy shows the four spur gears used to make the chain drive operate.

On the undercarriage of the four-wheel chassis, you see the two bevel gear setups, one for each axle. The bevel gears are connected to the spur gears on the upper section and turn the chain drive when the pull-toy is pulled along a flat surface.

Create Excellence Framework Rating

CREATE ANALYSIS		
CREATE COMPONENT	**LEVEL**	**JUSTIFICATION**
Real-World Learning	3: Investigating	Students' creations simulate a real-world task. The students participate as an engineering firm. There are a variety of choices students must make when designing their pull-toy. Students must build on their prior knowledge of gear mechanisms to complete this task.
Cognitive Complexity	3: Investigating	The instructor gives students the task. Students plan and produce a pull-toy that must meet certain criteria. Student groups evaluate and critique the work of other engineering firms.
Student Engagement	3: Investigating	Students have a choice of the type of gear mechanism to complete the task. Students collaborate with others to form engineering firms. Students use mathematics and science skills to complete the project.
Technology Integration	4: Integrating	Students use technology to create the robotic pull-toy, and it is fully embedded in this lesson. As engineering firms, students design and create a unique pull-toy prototype to complete this lesson.

THE SCIENCE OF MAKING MUSIC

Source: Adapted from Anthony Paganelli and Andrea Paganelli. Used with permission.

Content: Science and music

Learning Objectives:

1. Students will create a musical instrument utilizing various items that can include wood or paper products, strings, and even technological items, such as cellular phones, apps, or electronic devices.
2. Students will design a musical performance.

Standards:

Next Generation Science Standards—

*   1-PS4–1 Plan and conduct investigations to provide evidence that vibrating materials can make sound and that sound can make materials vibrate (NGSS Lead States, 2013).

National Core Arts—

*   MU:Cr1.1.Ka With guidance explore and experience music concepts (NCCAS, n.d.).
*   MU:CR1.1.1b With limited guidance generate musical ideas in multiple tonalities and meter (NCCAS, n.d.).

Project Options: This assignment could be adjusted to any grade or skill level and is adaptable to multiple cross-curricular subjects. Use the Landfill Harmonic video at www.youtube.com/watch?v=UJrSUHK9Luw (jammer jhed, 2012) to extend the assignment. This video can be used to create real-world connections with conservation, geography, and social studies.

Resources Needed: iPad with Internet access, recording device, speaker, Dot and Dash coding robots, Dash's xylophone attachment and accompanying software application, and everyday items representing different tonalities

Essential Vocabulary: Students need to know the following terms.

*   *Vibration*—to move back and forth in a pattern
*   *Tonality*—the feel and type of sound
*   *Meter*—a pattern of sound
*   *Musical instrument*—anything that can make sound
*   *Musical performance*—everyone playing together in the same way

The Science of Making Music

Would you like to make music? Have you always wondered how this could be done? This project offers you the opportunity to create music and musical instruments using different tonalities (sounds) and meters (beats). The musical instrument creation and performance will allow you to collaborate and learn together. Anything goes for a scientist in a Maker Music environment!

Luigi Russolo, a composer, wrote *The Art of Noises* to say that all sounds are music. The sound of a drum is music, but so are the sounds of a blender, a rubber band, a piece of paper, a computer, a robot, tapping feet, and clapping hands.

We will be making musical instruments out of everyday objects. These musical instruments will be used to create a song and performance using the coding robots Dot and Dash, Dash's xylophone, and computer applications. This song will then become our class song!

Project Tasks

1. In groups of three to five people, choose five everyday materials, such as paper plates, kitchen utensils, tools, and so on. Explore these materials for tonalities or sound. Use your "Feel the Vibration" figure to record your findings.

2. Now, let's have a classroom discussion about this exploration.

   * Did the materials make sound?
   * What did you do to the material to produce the sound?
   * Could you hear differences in sounds between different materials?
   * Could you feel the sound?
   * Look at your rubber band, and make a sound vibration by stretching and plucking it. Can you feel the vibration?

3. In your group, use the same five everyday materials to try to create a pattern of sound or meter.

   * Create some patterns of sound that are fast.
   * Create some patterns of sound that are slow.

4. Demonstrate your group's slow and fast patterns of sound or meter. After each group's demonstration, we will repeat the pattern with your chosen instrument.

5. Now that you know about everyday materials' vibrations and tonalities, create an instrument that makes a sound.

6. Pair with a friend to use the iPad with the Xylo app to explore plotting tonalities or sounds to create meter. Each group will contribute their Xylo app meter of music to create the transition song for the class.

   You will be able to use the Xylo app to create meter by tapping your finger on the meter bars provided. Each tap of your finger will create a sound that will have different tonalities based on the color bars. Place sounds or tonalities in different spots on the Xylo app to create meter.

7. Share your Xylo app meter creation to contribute to the class song.

   - The group song will be created by opening an empty song and having each group enter its meter. This will create and play the class song to which you will play along.
   - Prepare to perform your song with Dash and the Xylo app. You will play along with your created instrument. Record your performance with other students using the recording device.

8. All songs will be played for the class. The class will decide each song's purpose. For example, one song may be the song to line up, one may be a transition to a different subject, or one may signal it's time to go to recess or another activity.

Note whether there is a vibration with the sound.

Feel the Vibration

MATERIAL NUMBER	NO	I DON'T KNOW	YES
1			
2			
3			
4			
5			

Scoring Rubric

QUESTIONS TO ASK	YES	NO
Does your instrument make vibrations and sound?		
Did you create a meter for your song?		
Did you place plot points on the Xylo app?		
Did you play your instrument during the performance?		

Sample Student Work

Visit www.youtube.com/watch?v=QeY5F8T3zWg to access "Makerspace Music for Presentation" (Paganelli, 2016) to listen to an example of a music makerspace that combines technology and handmade instruments to create a short composition.

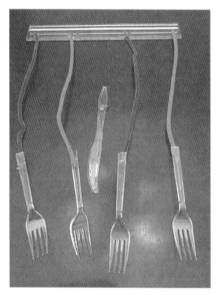

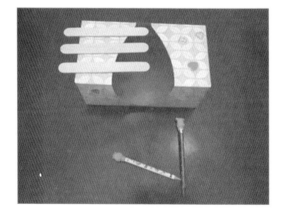

Create Excellence Framework Rating

CREATE ANALYSIS		
CREATE COMPONENT	**LEVEL**	**JUSTIFICATION**
Real-World Learning	4: Integrating	The student creation of a musical instrument engages students in authentic, cross-curricular learning about vibration and sound production. Student composition of a transition song for the class replicates real-world engagement in composition.
Cognitive Complexity	3: Investigating	The students plan and analyze components to create the musical instrument with a rudimentary understanding of vibration and sound. Students produce music through plotting points of tonality and sound to create the composition.
Student Engagement	4: Integrating	The students have choice, control, and collaboration in the process to create their musical instruments and composition. Allowing instruments and compositions to be more or less complex will address students' learning preferences.
Technology Integration	4: Integrating	All students have hands-on access to technology in the creation of the composition, which is essential to project completion. The students collaborate with each other and the teacher to create the musical performance.

References and Resources

Abrami, P. C., Lou, Y., Chambers, B., Poulsen, C., & Spence, J. C. (2000). Why should we group students within-class for learning? *Educational Research and Evaluation, 6*(2), 158–179.

Achieve. (2013). *Next Generation Science Standards.* Accessed at www.nextgenscience.org/sites/default/files/NGSS%20DCI% 20Combined%2011.6.13.pdf on January 26, 2015.

Anderson, L. W., & Krathwohl, D. R. (Eds.). (2001). *A taxonomy for learning, teaching, and assessing: A revision of Bloom's taxonomy of educational objectives* (Complete ed.). New York: Longman.

Antonetti, J. V., & Garver, J. R. (2015). *17,000 classroom visits can't be wrong: Strategies that engage students, promote active learning, and boost achievement.* Alexandria, VA: Association for Supervision and Curriculum Development.

Associated Press. (2015, December 11). *Teen honored by CNN for launching literacy program.* Accessed at http://tweentribune .com/article/junior/teen-honored-cnn-launching-literacy-program on January 29, 2016.

Associated Press. (2016, January 8). *Students gather blankets for Syrians.* Accessed at http://tweentribune.com/article/junior /students-gather-blankets-syrians on January 29, 2016.

Baron, K. (2010, March 15). *Six steps for planning a successful project.* Accessed at www.edutopia.org/stw-maine-project-based -learning-six-steps-planning on January 26, 2015.

Barton, K. C., & Smith, L. A. (2000). Themes or motifs?: Aiming for coherence through interdisciplinary outlines. *Reading Teacher, 54*(1), 54–63.

Berliner, D. C. (1990). What's all the fuss about instructional time? In M. Ben-Peretz & R. Bromme (Eds.), *The nature of time in schools: Theoretical concepts, practitioner perceptions* (pp. 3–35). New York: Teachers College Press.

Biz Kid$. (n.d.). *Guide to writing a business plan.* Accessed at http://bizkids.com/wp/wp-content/uploads/Kids-Business-Plan .pdf on June 29, 2016.

Biz Kid$. (2012, January 13). *Three minutes to change the world promo* [Video file]. Accessed at www.youtube.com /watch?v=C0MbMBHrgK4 on June 29, 2016.

Bloom, B. S. (Ed.). (1956). *Taxonomy of educational objectives: Book 1—Cognitive domain.* New York: Longman.

Blumenfeld, P. C., & Meece, J. L. (1988). Task factors, teacher behavior, and students' involvement and use of learning strategies in science. *Elementary School Journal, 88*(3), 235–250.

Brimner, L. D. (2000). *Caves.* New York: Children's Press.

Bronson, P., & Merryman, A. (2010, July 10). The creativity crisis. *Newsweek.* Accessed at www.newsweek.com/creativity -crisis-74665 on March 22, 2016.

Brookhart, S. M. (2013). Assessing creativity. *Educational Leadership, 70*(5), 28–34. Accessed at www.ascd.org/publications /educational-leadership/feb13/vol70/num05/Assessing-Creativity.aspx on June 3, 2015.

Bruner, J. (1960). *The process of education.* Cambridge, MA: Harvard University Press.

Buck Institute for Education. (n.d.). *What is project based learning (PBL)?* Accessed at http://bie.org/about/what_pbl on February 26, 2015.

Buck Institute for Education. (2013a). *Critical-thinking rubric for PBL (for grades k–2).* Accessed at https://bie.org/object /document/k_2_critical_thinking_rubric on June 3, 2015.

Buck Institute for Education. (2013b). *Critical-thinking rubric for PBL (for grades 3–5).* Accessed at https://bie.org/object /document/3_5_critical_thinking_rubric_non_CCSS on June 3, 2015.

Buck Institute for Education. (2013c). *Collaboration Rubric for PBL (for grades 3–5).* Accessed at https://bie.org/object /document/3_5_collaboration_rubric_CCSS_aligned on June 3, 2015.

Buck Institute for Education. (2013d). *Creativity Innovation Rubric for PBL (for grades k–2).* Accessed at https://bie.org/object /document/k_2_creativity_innovation_rubric on June 3, 2015.

Buck Institute for Education. (2013e). *Teamwork rubric for PBL (for grades k–2).* Accessed at https://bie.org/object/document / K_2_teamwork_rubric_for_PBL on June 3, 2015.

Buck Institute for Education. (2014). *Designing your project.* Accessed at www.bie.org/object/document/3_5_critical_ thinking _rubric_ccss_aligned on January 15, 2014.

Bulger, M., Mayer, R. E., & Almeroth, K. C. (2006, June). *Engaged by design: Using simulations to promote active learning.* Paper presented at the World Conference on Educational Media and Technology, Orlando, FL.

Cave of the Winds. (n.d.). *Just for kids.* Accessed at http://caveofthewinds.com/learning-center/just-for-kids on October 30, 2016.

Certo, J. L., Cauley, K. M., Moxley, K. D., & Chafin, C. (2008). An argument for authenticity: Adolescents' perspectives on standards-based reform. *High School Journal, 91*(4), 26–39.

Chao, E. L. (2001). *Report on the American workforce: Message from the secretary of labor.* Washington, DC: U.S. Department of Labor.

City, E. A., Elmore, R. F., Fiarman, S. E., & Teitel, L. (2009). *Instructional rounds in education: A network approach to improving teaching and learning.* Cambridge, MA: Harvard Education Press.

Clayton, H. (Hayley Clayton). (2015, November 23). *Jazz musicians in WWII* [Video file]. Accessed at www.youtube.com /watch?v=ED8kSxEIV-E&feature=youtu.be on September 15, 2016.

Common Cents New York. (2013). *About the penny harvest.* Accessed at http://pennyharvest.org/penny-harvest/about-penny -harvest on May 29, 2015.

Create Excellence. (n.d.). *Resources.* Accessed at http://create-excellence.com/resources on June 29, 2016.

Crie, M. (2005). *Inquiry-based approaches to learning.* New York: Glencoe. Accessed at www.glencoe.com/sec/teachingtoday /subject/inquiry_based.phtml on June 27, 2016.

Cronin, J. F. (1993). Four misconceptions about authentic learning. *Educational Leadership, 50*(7), 78–80.

Crowe, C. (Carolyn Crowe). (2015, December 6). *Penguin life* [Video file]. Accessed at www.youtube.com/watch ?v=9zrRIb1AuLM&rel=0 on June 29, 2016.

Danielson, C. (2014). *The framework for teaching: Evaluation instrument.* Princeton, NJ: Danielson Group. Accessed at www .danielsongroup.org/framework on October 30, 2016.

DeGroot, J. (2014, July 13). *7 bands that spawned multiple prominent solo careers: Genesis, Wu-Tang Clan, and more.* Accessed at www.musictimes.com/articles/7542/20140713/7-bands-that-spawned-multiple-prominent-solo-careers-genesis-wu -tang-clan-and-more.htm on June 29, 2016.

Denning, S. (n.d.). *How canyons are made.* Accessed at www.smore.com/8amxc on June 29, 2016.

Denton CE School Class 3. (2013). *The further adventures of the railway children.* Charleston, SC: CreateSpace.

Dewey, J. (1913). *Interest and effort in education.* Boston: Houghton Mifflin.

Dewey, J. (1938). *Experience and education.* New York: Macmillan.

Disney Channel (disneychannel). (2014, February 4). *Minga—Friends for change—Disney Channel official* [Video file]. Accessed at www.youtube.com/watch?v=NyeGqAxEMHE on June 29, 2016.

Dwyer, D. (2009, October 30). *End-user design: Creating schools for today and tomorrow (part V).* Accessed at http:// 21stcenturyscholar.org/2009/10/30/end-user-design-creating-schools-for-today-and-tomorrow-part-iv on January 26, 2015.

Edutopia. (2008, May 30). *Using today's technology tools to study yesterday's* [Video file]. Accessed at www.edutopia.org/ferryway -ironworks-integrated-studies-video on June 29, 2016.

Ennis, R. H. (1987). A taxonomy of critical thinking dispositions and abilities. In J. B. Baron & R. J. Sternberg (Eds.), *Teaching thinking skills: Theory and practice* (pp. 9–26). New York: Freeman.

European Commission (2013). *Survey of schools: ICT in Education.* Brussels, Belgium: European Schoolnet. Accessed at https:// ec.europa.eu/digital-single-market/news/survey-schools-ict-education on November 1, 2016.

Flores, E. (2016, March 24). *South Korea* [Animation]. Accessed at https://prezi.com/_xe0bfjvdbgu/south-korea on June 29, 2016.

Forkosh-Baruch, A., Mioduser, D., Nachmias, R., & Tubin, D. (2005). "Islands of innovation" and "school-wide implementations": Two patterns of ICT-based pedagogical innovations in schools. *Human Technology, 1*(2), 202–215.

Gabel, D. L. (Ed.). (1994). *Handbook of research on science teaching and learning.* New York: Macmillan.

Gavin, M. K., Casa, T., Adelson, J. L., Carroll, S. R., & Sheffield, L. J. (2009). The impact of advanced curriculum on the achievement of mathematically promising elementary students. *Gifted Child Quarterly, 53*(3), 188–202.

Gibbons, G. (1998). *Penguins!* New York: Holiday House.

Gilbert, R. (2009, August 9). *Google Form tutorial* [Video file]. Accessed at www.youtube.com/watch?v=WMXgutYKMgk on June 29, 2016.

Ginocchio, M. (2014, March 24). *10 artists who left amazing bands to create something better.* Accessed at http://whatculture .com/music/10-artists-left-amazing-bands-create-something-better.php on June 29, 2016.

Gordon, D. (2011). Return to sender: Schools continue to deliver new graduates into the workplace lacking the tech-based "soft skills" that businesses demand—Experts blame K–12's persistent failure to integrate technology. *Technological Horizons in Education Journal, 38*(3), 30–35.

Gray, L., Thomas, N., & Lewis, L. (2010, May). *Teachers' use of educational technology in U.S. public schools: 2009—First look* (NCES 2010–040). Washington, DC: National Center for Education Statistics.

Greaves, T. W., Hayes, J., Wilson, L., Gielniak, M., & Peterson, E. L. (2012). *Revolutionizing education through technology: The Project RED roadmap for transformation.* Eugene, OR: International Society for Technology in Education.

Greaves, T. W., Hayes, J., Wilson, L., Gielniak, M., & Peterson, R. (2010). *The technology factor: Nine keys to student achievement and cost-effectiveness.* Chicago: Market Data Retrieval.

Gregory, G. H., & Chapman, C. (2007). *Differentiated instructional strategies: One size doesn't fit all* (2nd ed.). Thousand Oaks, CA: Corwin Press.

Grow, G. O. (1991). Teaching learners to be self-directed. *Adult Education Quarterly, 41*(3), 125–149.

Gunter, A. (2016, March 5). *Three minutes to change the world: Kitty city* [Video file]. Accessed at https://animoto.com/play /nsAAZCKJnjd0iIdXlSu0cQ?autostart=1 on June 29, 2016.

Harlaxton CE School Year 6. (2014). *The further adventures of the railway children.* Charleston, SC: CreateSpace.

Harris, G. (2010, June 11). *A new model for inquiry in the school library program* [PowerPoint slides]. Accessed at www .slideshare.net/GregoryHarris/inquiry2010 on January 26, 2015.

Hart County School District. (2011). *Create task/project template.* Hart County, KY: Author.

Herrington, J., Oliver, R., & Reeves, T. C. (2003). Patterns of engagement in authentic online learning environments. *Australian Journal of Educational Technology, 19*(1), 59–71.

Hundley, C. (n.d.). *Dianna Cohen: Tough truths about plastic pollution* [Video file]. Accessed at http://ed.ted.com/on/Kyp6SEb5 on June 29, 2016.

Hung, D., Tan, S. C., & Koh, T. S. (2006). Engaged learning: Making learning an authentic experience. In D. Hung & M. S. Khine (Eds.), *Engaged learning with emerging technologies* (pp. 29–48). Dordrecht, the Netherlands: Springer.

Illinois Mathematics and Science Academy. (2011). *IMSA's PBL teaching and learning template*. Accessed at http://pbln.imsa .edu/model/template on January 26, 2015.

Intel. (n.d.). *Implementation examples: Experiencing engineering through design*. Accessed at http://tinyurl.com/gotbo9s on June 29, 2016.

International Society for Technology in Education. (2007). *The ISTE standards for students*. Accessed at www.iste.org/standards /standards/standards-for-students on June 29, 2016.

International Society for Technology in Education. (2008). *ISTE NETS-T standards: Advancing digital age teaching*. Eugene, OR: Author. Accessed at www.iste.org/standards/standards/standards-for-teachers on October 30, 2016.

International Society for Technology in Education (2016). *2016 ISTE standards for students*. Accessed at www.iste.org/standards /standards/for-students-2016 on November 10, 2016.

International Society for Technology in Education, Partnership for 21st Century Skills, & State Educational Technology Directors Association. (2007). *Maximizing the impact: The pivotal role of technology in a 21st century education system*. Washington, DC: Authors. Accessed at www.p21.org/storage/documents/p21setdaistepaper.pdf on January 26, 2015.

iThemes. (n.d.). *WordPress 101: What is WordPress?* Accessed at https://ithemes.com/tutorial/category/wordpress-101 on June 29, 2016.

Jacobs, H. H. (Ed.). (2010). *Curriculum 21: Essential education for a changing world*. Alexandria, VA: Association for Supervision and Curriculum Development.

jammer jhed. (2012, December 13). *The landfill harmonic orchestra* [Video file]. Accessed at www.youtube.com/watch ?v=UJrSUHK9Luw on June 29, 2016.

Jenkins, H. (2009). *Confronting the challenges of participatory culture: Media education for the 21st century*. Cambridge, MA: MIT Press.

jnisse1. (n.d.). *A sticky situation: Building a sweet bridge*. Accessed at http://jnisse1.edu.glogster.com/a-sticky-situation-building -a-sweet-bridge on June 29, 2016.

Jones, B. F., Valdez, G., Nowakowski, J., & Rasmussen, C. (1995). *Plugging in: Choosing and using educational technology*. Oak Brook, IL: North Central Regional Educational Laboratory.

Josie. (n.d.). *Class pet opinion piece*. Accessed at http://bit.ly/2cqewfL on September 6, 2016.

Jukes, I., McCain, T., & Crockett, L. (2010). *Understanding the digital generation: Teaching and learning in the new digital landscape*. Thousand Oaks, CA: Corwin Press.

Kaffel, N. (2007, November). *Digital storytelling: How to create a digital story*. Accessed at http://courseweb.lis.illinois .edu/~jevogel2/lis506/howto.html on June 29, 2016.

Keyek-Franssen, D. (2010, December 15). Clickers and CATs: Using learner response systems for formative assessments in the classroom. *Educause Review*. Accessed at www.educause.edu/ero/article/clickers-and-cats-using-learner-response-systems -formative-assessments-classroom on January 26, 2015.

Krathwohl, D. R. (2002). A revision of Bloom's taxonomy: An overview. *Theory Into Practice, 41*(4), 212–218.

Kwit, H. C. (2012, November 1). *Making the Common Core come alive!: Supporting educators in the implementation of the Common Core* [e-newsletter]. Accessed at www.prweb.com/releases/2012/11/prweb10080978.htm on January 26, 2015.

Lemke, C., Coughlin, E., & Reifsneider, D. (2009). *Technology in schools: What the research says—A 2009 update*. Culver City, CA: Cisco.

Levine, A. (2014, February 5). *StoryTools: The fifty tools*. Accessed at http://cogdogroo.wikispaces.com/StoryTools on June 29, 2016.

Licensed Geriatric Resources for Education and Learning. (n.d.). *What's new with Let's Get Real?* Accessed at www.lgreal.org/index .shtml on February 19, 2015.

Lin, L. (2006). Cultural dimensions of authenticity in teaching. *New Directions for Adult and Continuing Education, 111*, 63–72.

Lombardi, M. M. (2007, May). *Authentic learning for the 21st century: An overview* (ELI Paper No. 1). Washington, DC: Educause Learning Initiative. Accessed at https://net.educause.edu/ir/library/pdf/ELI3009.pdf on January 26, 2015.

Martinez, M. (2014). *Deeper learning: The new normal.* Accessed at www.advanc-ed.org/source/deeper-learning-new-normal on January 26, 2015.

Marzano, R. J. (2007). *The art and science of teaching: A comprehensive framework for effective instruction.* Alexandria, VA: Association for Supervision and Curriculum Development.

Maxim, G. W. (2014). *Dynamic social studies for constructivist classrooms: Inspiring tomorrow's social scientists* (10th ed.). Boston: Pearson.

Maxwell, M. (2012). *Designing instruction using revised Bloom's taxonomy.* Accessed at http://margemaxwell.com/wp-content /uploads/2013/08/Bloom-Taxonomy-Assignment.pdf on August 17, 2015.

Maxwell, M. (Marge Maxwell). (2016a, March 23). *Alex painting aura* [Video file]. Accessed at https://youtu.be/ERON _2dcpUQ on June 29, 2016.

Maxwell, M. (Marge Maxwell). (2016b, March 23). *Sofia painting aura* [Video file]. Accessed at https://youtu.be/8incmYBBo9E on June 29, 2016.

Maxwell, M. (2016c, March 9). *Sustainable development of Denton Reservoir: Making the area accessible for families with young children* [PowerPoint slides]. Accessed at www.slideroll.com/show.php?s=hh3yqac1 on September 19, 2016.

Maxwell, M., Constant, M., Stobaugh, R., & Tassell, J. L. (2011). Developing a HEAT framework for assessing and improving instruction. In C. Maddux (Ed.), *Research highlights in technology and teacher education 2011* (pp. 13–20). Chesapeake, VA: Society for Information Technology and Teacher Education.

Maxwell, M., Stobaugh, R., & Tassell, J. L. (2011). Analyzing HEAT of lesson plans in pre-service and advanced teacher education. *Journal of the Research Center for Educational Technology, 7*(1), 16–29.

McGinnis, J. O. (2006). Age of the empirical. *Policy Review, 137,* 47–58.

Meece, J. L., Blumenfeld, P. C., & Hoyle, R. H. (1988). Students' goal orientations and cognitive engagement in classroom activities. *Journal of Educational Psychology, 80*(4), 514–523.

Miller, A. (2011, June 28). *Assessing the Common Core standards: Real life mathematics* [Blog post]. Accessed at www.edutopia .org/blog/assessing-common-core-standards-real-life-mathematics on January 26, 2015.

Moersch, C. (2002). Measures of success: Six instruments to assess teachers' use of technology. *Learning and Leading With Technology, 30*(3), 10–13, 24–27.

Morrisey, B. (2016, May 19). *A kids' guide to composting.* Accessed at www.ecofriendlykids.co.uk/composting.html on June 29, 2016.

National Coalition for Core Arts Standards. (n.d.). *National Core Arts Standards.* Accessed at www.nationalartsstandards.org on June 29, 2016.

National Council for the Social Studies. (2013). *College, career, and civic life: C3 Framework for social studies state standards— Guidance for enhancing the rigor of K–12 civics, economics, geography, and history.* Silver Spring, MD: Author. Accessed at www.socialstudies.org/system/files/c3/C3-Framework-for-Social-Studies.pdf on June 11, 2015.

National Governors Association Center for Best Practices & Council of Chief State School Officers. (2010a). *Common Core State Standards for English language arts and literacy in history/social studies, science, and technical subjects.* Washington, DC: Authors. Accessed at www.corestandards.org/assets/CCSSI_ELA%20Standards.pdf on June 27, 2016.

National Governors Association Center for Best Practices & Council of Chief State School Officers. (2010b). *Common Core State Standards for mathematics.* Washington, DC: Authors. Accessed at www.corestandards.org/assets/CCSSI_Math% 20Standards.pdf on June 27, 2016.

National Governors Association Center for Best Practices & Council of Chief State School Officers. (2012). *Common Core State Standards initiative: Preparing America's students for college and career.* Washington, DC: Authors.

National Research Council. (1996). *National Science Education Standards: Observe, interact, change, learn.* Washington, DC: National Academy Press.

National Research Council. (2012). *A framework for K–12 science education: Practices, crosscutting concepts, and core ideas.* Washington, DC: The National Academies Press.

National Service-Learning Clearinghouse. (2007, June). *Why districts, schools, and classrooms should practice service-learning.* Denver: RMC Research. Accessed at www.communityschools.org/assets/1/AssetManager/A7_Howard_Why%20Districts .pdf on January 26, 2015.

NGSS Lead States. (2013.) *Next Generation Science Standards: For states, by states*. Washington, DC: The National Academies Press.

Northern, S. (Samuel Northern). (2016, January 18). *Playground safety and appearance* [Video file]. Accessed at https://youtu .be/MzO5T2UcKYQ on June 29, 2016.

November, A. (2012). *Who owns the learning?: Preparing students for success in the digital age*. Bloomington, IN: Solution Tree Press.

Oblinger, D. (2003). Boomers, gen-Xers, and millennials: Understanding the "new students." *Educause Review, 38*(4), 36–45.

O'Byrne, I. (Ian O'Byrne). (2011, August 13). *Google Forms tutorial* [Video file]. Accessed at www.youtube.com/watch ?v=AeiDxeLVvuQ on June 29, 2016.

Office of Educational Technology. (2016, January). *Future ready learning: Reimagining the role of technology in education*. Washington, DC: U.S. Department of Education. Accessed at http://tech.ed.gov/files/2015/12/NETP16.pdf on June 27, 2016.

Ohler, J. (2013). The uncommon core. *Educational Leadership, 70*(5), 42–46.

Paganelli, A. (Anthony Paganelli). (2016, January 15). *Makerspace music for presentation* [Video file]. Accessed at www.youtube .com/watch?v=QeY5F8T3zWg on June 29, 2016.

Parish, H. (2013). *Amelia Bedelia means business*. New York: Greenwillow Books.

Partnership for 21st Century Skills. (2009). *Curriculum and instruction: A 21st century skills implementation guide*. Tucson, AZ: Author. Accessed at www.p21.org/storage/documents/p21-stateimp_curriculuminstruction.pdf on January 26, 2015.

Partnership for 21st Century Skills. (2011). *Framework for 21st century learning*. Accessed at www.p21.org/our-work/p21 -framework on January 26, 2015.

Pence, H. E., & McIntosh, S. (2010). Refocusing the vision: The future of instructional technology. *Journal of Educational Technology Systems, 39*(2), 173–179.

Pink, D. H. (2005). *A whole new mind: Moving from the information age to the conceptual age*. New York: Riverhead Books.

Pink, D. H. (2009). *Drive: The surprising truth about what motivates us*. New York: Riverhead Books.

Postman, N., & Weingartner, C. (1969). *Teaching as a subversive activity*. New York: Delacorte Press.

Prensky, M. (2001). Digital natives, digital immigrants. *On the Horizon, 9*(5), 1–6.

Prensky, M. (2010). *Teaching digital natives: Partnering for real learning*. Thousand Oaks, CA: Corwin Press.

Ralston, K. (2016, February 19). *Student example*. Accessed at www.powtoon.com/online-presentation/b0zvhBcAzAz/student -example on June 29, 2016.

Raphael, L. M., Pressley, M., & Mohan, L. (2008). Engaging instruction in middle school classrooms: An observational study of nine teachers. *Elementary School Journal, 109*(1), 61–81.

Rasicot, J. (2006, March 2). Learning in the classroom by reaching out to others. *Washington Post*. Accessed at www .washingtonpost.com/wp-dyn/content/article/2006/03/01/AR2006030101181.html on January 27, 2015.

Raths, J. (2002). Improving instruction. *Theory Into Practice, 41*(4), 233–237.

Ray, B. (2012, January 3). *Design thinking: Lessons for the classroom* [Blog post]. Accessed at www.edutopia.org/blog/design -thinking-betty-ray on January 26, 2015.

Reeves, T. C. (2006). How do you know they are learning?: The importance of alignment in higher education. *International Journal of Learning Technology, 2*(4), 294–309.

Renzulli, J. S., Gentry, M., & Reis, S. M. (2004). A time and a place for authentic learning. *Educational Leadership, 62*(1), 73–77.

Rhoads, M. (Meghan Rhoads). (2016, January 3). *George Harrison and success* [Video file]. Accessed at https://youtu.be /69nQTz1pNk0 on June 29, 2016.

Richardson, W. (2013). Students first, not stuff. *Educational Leadership, 70*(6), 10–14.

Richardson, W., & Mancabelli, R. (2011). *Personal learning networks: Using the power of connections to transform education*. Bloomington, IN: Solution Tree Press.

Richter, R. (n.d.). *Composting for kids!* Accessed at http://aggie-horticulture.tamu.edu/kindergarden/kidscompost/CompostingForKids.pdf on June 29, 2016.

Roberts, J. L., & Inman, T. F. (2009). *Strategies for differentiating instruction: Best practices for the classroom* (2nd ed.). Waco, TX: Prufrock Press.

Robinson, K. (2009). *The element: How finding your passion changes everything*. New York: Penguin.

Robinson, K., & Aronica, L. (2015). *Creative schools: The grassroots revolution that's transforming education*. New York: Penguin.

Rolling Stone. (2012, May 2). Readers poll: Ten best post-band solo artists. Accessed at www.rollingstone.com/music/pictures/readers-poll-ten-best-post-band-solo-artists-20120502 on June 29, 2016.

Ross, S. (2015a, March 19). *Archaeology* [Video file]. Accessed at https://animoto.com/play/0ZcXqyo3qSEHuw0wKumtyg on June 29, 2016.

Ross, S. (stephanie ross). (2015b, September 5). *Archaeology assignment* [Video file]. Accessed at www.youtube.com/watch?v=noVNwJkI7bs&feature=youtu.be on June 29, 2016.

Ross, S. (stephanie ross). (2015c, November 13). *Kabil* [Video file]. Accessed at www.youtube.com/watch?v=Woo55Wp6vEI&feature=youtu.be on June 29, 2016.

Ross, S. (stephanie ross). (2016, March 4). *Ross MovieMaker TutorialRevised* [Video file]. Accessed at www.youtube.com/watch?v=LYU2UjnVPV8&feature=youtu.be on June 29, 2016.

Schamel, D., & Ayres, M. P. (1992). The minds-on approach: Student creativity and personal involvement in the undergraduate science laboratory. *Journal of College Science Teaching, 21*(4), 226–229.

Schools We Need Project. (n.d.). *An engaging program of real world learning*. Accessed at http://schoolsweneed.wikispaces.com/Real+World+Learning on January 26, 2015.

Schreiber, A. (2009). *Penguins!* Washington, DC: National Geographic.

Schwartzbeck, T. D., & Wolf, M. A. (2012). *The digital learning imperative: How technology and teaching meet today's education challenges*. Washington, DC: Alliance for Excellent Education.

SeaWorld Parks and Entertainment. (n.d.a). *Penguin: Behavior*. Accessed at https://seaworld.org/en/animal-info/animal-infobooks/penguin/behavior on June 29, 2016.

SeaWorld Parks and Entertainment. (n.d.b). *Penguin: Physical characteristics*. Accessed at https://seaworld.org/en/animal-info/animal-infobooks/penguin/physical-characteristics on June 29, 2016.

Sharer, R. J., & Ashmore, W. (1993). *Archaeology: Discovering our past*. Mountain View, CA: Mayfield.

Simpson, R. (2008, June 25). *Visualizing technology integration: A model for meeting ISTE educational-technology standards*. Accessed at www.edutopia.org/ferryway-school-saugus-ironworks on June 11, 2015.

Skinner, E. A., & Belmont, M. J. (1993). Motivation in the classroom: Reciprocal effects of teacher behavior and student engagement across the school year. *Journal of Educational Psychology, 85*(4), 571–581.

Sousa, D. A. (2006). *How the brain learns* (3rd ed.). Thousand Oaks, CA: Corwin Press.

Stewart, A., & Rivera, Y. (2010, July 22). *Inquiry-based learning* [PowerPoint slides]. Accessed at www.slideshare.net/teeneeweenee/inquiry-based-learning1 on May 29, 2015.

Stobaugh, R. (2013). *Assessing critical thinking in middle and high schools: Meeting the Common Core*. Larchmont, NY: Eye on Education.

Sulla, N. (2011). *Students taking charge: Inside the learner-active, technology-infused classroom*. New York: Routledge.

Swartz, R. J., & Parks, S. (1994). *Infusing critical and creative thinking into content instruction: A lesson design handbook for the elementary grades*. Pacific Grove, CA: Critical Thinking Press.

Tassell, J. L., Maxwell, M., & Stobaugh, R. (2013). CReaTE excellence: Using a teacher framework to maximize STEM learning with your child. *Parenting for High Potential, 3*(2), 10–13.

techn0teach. (2011). *A day in the life of a penguin: A digital storytelling example* [Slide show]. Accessed at www.slideshare.net/techn0teach/a-day-in-the-life-of-a-penguin-10126853 on June 29, 2016.

Tucker, M. S. (Ed.). (2011). *Surpassing Shanghai: An agenda for American education built on the world's leading systems*. Cambridge, MA: Harvard Education Press.

The United Nations Educational, Scientific and Cultural Organization. (2004). *Integrating ICTs into education: Lessons learned—A collective case study of six Asian countries*. Bangkok, Thailand: Author. Accessed at www.unescobkk.org /fileadmin/user_upload/ict/e-books/ICTLessonsLearned/ICT_integrating_education.pdf on January 26, 2015.

U.S. 21st Century Workforce Commission. (2000). *A nation of opportunity: Building America's 21st century workforce*. Washington, DC: Author. Accessed at http://digitalcommons.ilr.cornell.edu/cgi/viewcontent.cgi?article=1003 &context=key_workplace on January 27, 2015.

VanCappellen, G. (2014, November 24). *VEX pull-toy for IDP project LME 535* [Video file]. Accessed at www.youtube.com /watch?v=2rAxQRMAXpU on June 29, 2016.

van Opstal, D. (2008). *Compete 2.0: Thrive—The skills imperative*. Washington, DC: Council on Competitiveness.

Virginia Board of Bar Examiners. (2014, September). *Law reader memorandum: A memorandum on the concept of reading law under an attorney's supervision*. Accessed at www.vbbe.state.va.us/reader/readermemo.html on January 26, 2015.

Willingham, D. T. (2009). *Why don't students like school?: A cognitive scientist answers questions about how the mind works and what it means for the classroom*. San Francisco: Jossey-Bass.

Wolf, M. A. (2012, May). *Culture shift: Teaching in a learner-centered environment powered by digital learning*. Washington, DC: Alliance for Excellent Education.

Wood, D. F. (2003). ABC of learning and teaching in medicine: Problem based learning. *British Medical Journal, 326*(7384), 328–330.

Wood, R. (n.d.). *ES1405: Observe an animation of cave formation* [Animation]. Accessed at www.classzone.com/books/earth _science/terc/content/visualizations/es1405/es1405page01.cfm on June 29, 2016.

Yazzie-Mintz, E. (2010). *Charting the path from engagement to achievement: A report on the 2009 High School Survey of Student Engagement*. Bloomington: Indiana University Center for Evaluation and Education Policy.

Zhao, Y. (2012). *World class learners: Educating creative and entrepreneurial students*. Thousand Oaks, CA: Corwin Press.

Zigmond, M. (Meghan Zigmond). (2013, September 2). *Aurasma: Channel set up and create auras* [Video file]. Accessed at http://tinyurl.com/zh492vs on June 29, 2016.

Index

Real-World Learning Framework for Secondary Schools
Marge Maxwell, Rebecca Stobaugh, and Janet Lynne Tassell
Using the Create framework, educators can help students find greater fulfillment in learning, while also meeting the guidelines of curriculum standards. Explore the framework's main components, and understand how to use the framework for classroom, school, and district pursuits.
BKF656

Implementing Project-Based Learning
Suzie Boss
Explore how project-based learning (PBL) has the potential to fully engage students of the digital age. Discover user-friendly strategies for implementing PBL to equip students with essential 21st century skills, strengthen their problem-solving abilities, and prepare them for college and careers.
BKF681

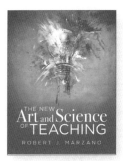

The New Art and Science of Teaching
Robert J. Marzano
This title is a greatly expanded volume of the original *The Art and Science of Teaching*, offering a framework for substantive change based on Robert J. Marzano's fifty years of education research. While the previous model focused on teacher outcomes, the new version places focus on student outcomes.
BKF776

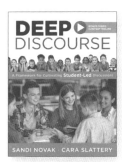

Deep Discourse
Sandi Novak and Cara Slattery
When educators actively support student-led classroom discussions, students develop essential critical-thinking, problem-solving, and self-directed learning skills. This book details a framework for implementing student-led classroom discussions that improve student learning, motivation, and engagement across all levels and subject areas.
BKF725

Connecting the Dots
Edited by James A. Bellanca
Confront the issues that profoundly affect student success. Discover the shift in day-to-day practice that must occur to prepare students for college and careers, and look forward to what exemplary professional practices will be crucial in deepening student learning as the 21st century progresses.
BKF659

Solution Tree | Press

a division of
Solution Tree

Visit solution-tree.com or call 800.733.6786 to order.

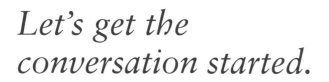